WILLIAM BLAKE
VS
THE WORLD

Also by John Higgs

I Have America Surrounded

The KLF

Stranger Than We Can Imagine

Watling Street

The Future Starts Here

William Blake Now

WILLIAM BLAKE
VS
THE WORLD

JOHN HIGGS

WEIDENFELD & NICOLSON

First published in Great Britain in 2021 by Weidenfeld & Nicolson
an imprint of The Orion Publishing Group Ltd
Carmelite House, 50 Victoria Embankment
London EC4Y 0DZ

An Hachette UK Company

1 3 5 7 9 10 8 6 4 2

A CIP catalogue record for this book is
available from the British Library.

ISBN (Hardback) 978 1 4746 1435 1
ISBN (eBook) 978 1 4746 1437 5
ISBN (Audio) 978 1 4746 1438 2

Typeset at The Spartan Press Ltd,
Lymington, Hants

Printed and bound in Great Britain by Clays Ltd,
Elcograf S.p.A.

www.weidenfeldandnicolson.co.uk
www.orionbooks.co.uk

'There is certainly another world, but it is in this one'
Paul Éluard

CONTENTS

A NOTE ON QUOTATIONS

William Blake did not attend school as a child and the home-learnt nature of his writing is often apparent. Historically, this has bugged academics a great deal. Blake scholars have typically had a rigorous formal education and been taught to attach high importance to grammar, punctuation and spelling. For them, the urge to tidy up Blake's text and to fix mistakes here and there, to make things easier for the reader, has been almost irresistible.

The problem with this was knowing when to stop. Scholars began by just adding a few harmless missing commas. Yet the temptation to keep polishing remained strong, and before long they added their own rhythms to the text. Different academics made different fixes, and in time Blake's work began to vary from source to source.

The current academic attitude is that it's best to leave the whole thing alone, and that we should learn to live with Blake's punctuation and grammar. This is the approach I also use. The majority of quotations from his works are taken from the 1988 revised edition of *The Complete Poetry & Prose of William Blake*, rather than earlier, politely amended sources.

This choice was not made just for reasons of academic purity. It was also done out of a love of the writing quirks displayed. What type of person doesn't love stray capitals, random punctuation and a giddy abundance of ampersands? Like the fingerprints visible in the clay of early Aardman animations, or the warts-and-all one-take rawness of early rock 'n' roll recordings, a writer's idiosyncrasies and mistakes humanise their work. They reveal their writing to be the painstakingly built creation of an imperfect soul trying to construct something extraordinary. Blake's works were so visionary that the presence of the fingerprints of a flawed human creator in the text itself can only add to them.

This rule only applies to the words of Blake, of course. The reader is entirely within their rights to view any typos by the author as unforgivable and unprofessional, and as a source of eternal shame.

1.

THE END OF A GOLDEN STRING

On 10 December 1825, the fifty-year-old English lawyer Henry Crabb Robinson attended a dinner at the home of his friend, the London businessman Charles Aders. Eliza, Aders's wife, was a painter and printmaker, and she had invited a few artist and engraver friends to the party. Over the course of the evening Robinson became increasingly fascinated by one of the guests – an elderly, relatively unknown poet and painter by the name of William Blake, whose conversation casually roamed from the polite and mundane to the beatific and fantastic.

Blake was short, pale and a little overweight, with the accent of a lifelong Londoner. He was dressed in old-fashioned, threadbare clothes and his grey trousers were shiny at the front through wear. His large, strong eyes didn't seem to fit with his soft, round face. Robinson noted in his diary that he had 'an expression of great sweetness, but bordering on weakness – except when his features are animated by expression, and then he has an air of inspiration about him'.

For all his wild notions and heretical statements, Blake was pleasant company and easy to like. The aggressive and hectoring voice of his writings was not the Blake those who met him recall. Many years later, another guest at that party, Maria Denman, remarked that, 'One remembers even in age the kindness of such a man.'

What made Blake so fascinating was the casual way in which he talked about his relationship with the spirit world. Blake, Robinson wrote, 'spoke of his paintings as being what he had seen in his visions – And when he said "my visions" it was in the ordinary unemphatic tone in which we speak of trivial matters that everyone understands and cares nothing about.' Blake peppered his conversation with remarks about his relationship with various angels, the nature of the devil, and his visionary meetings with historical figures such as Socrates, Milton and Jesus Christ. Somehow, he did this in a way that people found endearing rather than disturbing. As Robinson wrote, 'There is a natural sweetness and gentility about Blake which are delightful. And when he is not referring to his Visions he talks sensibly and acutely.'

Robinson walked home with Blake that night and was so struck by the conversation that he spent the evening transcribing as much of it as he could remember. The two men became friends, and Robinson's diary an invaluable record of how Blake acted and thought during the last two years of his life. 'Shall I call him Artist or Genius – or Mystic – or Madman?' Robinson mused that first night. He spent the rest of their relationship attempting to come up with a definite answer. 'Probably he is all', was the best he could find. It is a question that has puzzled many who have encountered Blake's work over the following two centuries.

Through his attempts to understand his new friend, Robinson only became more confused. Some of Blake's declarations appeared to be foolish nonsense. When they first met, Blake told him that he did not believe that the world was round, and that he believed it to be quite flat. Robinson attempted to get Blake to justify this outrageous claim, but the group were called to dinner at that moment and the thread of the conversation was lost. While some of Blake's opinions appeared obviously wrong, others were simply baffling. When Robinson asked him about the divinity of Jesus, Blake replied that, 'He is the only God. And so am I and so are you.' How could Robinson even begin to interpret an answer like that? If there was any sense to be found, it was quite outside mainstream nineteenth-century theology.

Yet Robinson couldn't bring himself to dismiss Blake as a simple madman, nor could he shake the suspicion that there was something important and vital about his worldview, even if it was frustratingly obscure. As he later wrote, 'It is strange that I, who have no imagination, nor any power beyond that of a logical understanding, should yet have great respect for the mystics.'

A week after the party, Robinson made his first visit to Blake's home at Fountain Court in the Strand, where he lived with his wife, Catherine. The building itself has long since gone, but it was roughly where the Savoy hotel now stands. Robinson was unprepared for the level of poverty in which the couple were living. 'I found him in a small room, which seems to be both a working room and a bed room,' he wrote. 'Nothing could exceed the squalid air both of the apartment & his dress, but in spite of dirt – I might say filth – an air of natural gentility is diffused over him.'

This was the second of the two rooms that the Blakes rented on the first floor of the building. The first was a wood-panelled reception room, which doubled as an unofficial gallery for Blake's drawings and paintings. The second, at the rear, was reserved for everything else. In one corner was the bed, and in the other was the fire on which Catherine Blake cooked. There was one table for meals, and another on which Blake worked. From here he looked out of the southern-facing window, where a glimpse of the Thames

3

could be seen between the buildings and streets that ran down to the river. This sliver of water would often catch the sun and appear golden. Behind it, the Surrey Hills stretched into the distance. For all the evident poverty, visitors spoke of the rooms as enchanted. As one later recalled, 'There was a strange expansion and sensation of Freedom in those two rooms very seldom felt elsewhere.'

Blake, Robinson remembered, was 'quite unembarrassed when he begged me to sit down, as if he were in a palace. There was but one chair in the room besides that on which he sat. On my putting my hand to it, I found that it would have fallen to pieces if I had lifted it, so, as if I had been a Sybarite, I said with a smile, "Will you let me indulge myself?" and I sat on the bed, and near him, and during my short stay there was nothing in him that betrayed that he was aware of what to other persons might have been even offensive, not in his person, but in all about him.'

'I live in a hole here, but God has a beautiful mansion for me elsewhere,' Blake once said. He knew that he was pitied by the occasional prosperous artist who visited, but he thought that it was he who should be pitying them. 'I possess my visions and peace,' he argued. 'They have bartered their birthright for a mess of pottage.' Robinson was struck on that first visit by how at ease the Blakes seemed with their poverty. 'I should be sorry if I had any earthly fame, for whatever natural glory a man has is so much detracted from his spiritual glory,' Blake told him. Despite how the world had treated him he was quite happy, he insisted, because he wanted nothing other than to live for art and had no desire to do anything for profit. But as Robinson also noted, 'Though he spoke of his happiness, he spoke of past sufferings, and of sufferings as necessary. "There is suffering in heaven, for where there is the capacity of enjoyment, there is the capacity of pain." '

During later visits, Blake's failing health was clear. In December 1826, Robinson visited Blake to tell him about the death of their

4

mutual friend, the celebrated sculptor John Flaxman. Blake's first reaction was a smile. 'I thought I should have gone first,' he said, then remarked that, 'I cannot consider death as anything but a removing from one room to another.'

Blake died in that room the following August. The painter George Richmond reported that he died 'in a most glorious manner. He said He was going to that Country he had all His life wished to see & expressed Himself Happy [...] Just before he died His Countenance became fair. His eyes Brighten'd and he burst out Singing of the things he saw in Heaven.'

With Blake gone, Robinson could no longer hope to find the answers to the riddle of his strange but fascinating friend. Turning to the work he left behind usually caused more confusion. Perhaps there hadn't ever been a coherent vision to be decoded in his work? The simplest explanation was that there was only madness there all along.

Five days after Blake died, he was given a pauper's burial in an unmarked grave at the Bunhill Fields dissenters' burial ground, beyond the northern boundary of the City of London. The name 'Bunhill' derives from 'bone hill' – the place had long been used to dispose of the unwanted dead.

With his bones under the ground and his spirit departed, that should have been the end of his story. Blake's friend John Flaxman, in contrast, was one of the most influential and famous artists of his day, and those who mourned him assumed posterity would keep his name alive for centuries. There had been no such earthly fame for William Blake and precious few had been prepared to part with money for his work. He would remain in the memories of those who knew him as a fond curiosity – history, surely, would not remember him.

On the face of it, the story of the clash between the world and William Blake seems a straightforward one. Blake had lacked the

5

ability to respond to the pressures and challenges of contemporary life and society. As a result, he spent his life impoverished and misunderstood, alternately mocked and ignored. He was thought of as a madman first and an artist second. This clash had not been a fair fight, and Blake had lost. For those who knew him, it had at times been painful to watch. It was perhaps some comfort, then, that when his bones were under the soil, the struggle that was the world versus William Blake finally came to an end.

Some 191 years later, in the early afternoon of 12 August 2018, people began making their way to Bunhill Fields. London has expanded massively since William Blake's death, and the graveyard has gone from being on its outskirts to near its centre. People kept arriving, some walking by themselves, others in small groups. They congregated on the north lawn and, standing together, they looked an unlikely bunch. They varied so widely in age, wealth, ethnicity and class that it was as if representatives had been dispatched from every corner of British society.

By 3 p.m., close to a thousand people were gathered to witness the unveiling of a grave marker above Blake's remains and to pay their respects to his memory. The Blake Society had raised money for a flat piece of Portland stone, carved by the stonecutter Lida Cardozo Kindersley, which was set into the grass. The event was unticketed and barely advertised, except for a tweet which gave details of the time and place along with the words, 'All are welcome!' Who could predict, in this modern age, how many people would assemble to witness the unveiling of a grave marker for a long-dead Georgian poet?

The Blake Society certainly hadn't expected a turnout of this size. There were no microphones or PA systems for speakers to address the crowds; no one had realised that they would be needed. Instead, speakers stood on a bench, or spoke as loudly as they could.

Just over a year later, a retrospective of Blake's work was held at Tate Britain, three and a half miles to the southeast. The exhibition contained an almost overwhelming collection of more than 300 original works, including paintings, prints and illuminated texts. It was extraordinarily popular, selling close to a quarter of a million tickets over its four-and-a-half-month run. The crowds at the exhibition led to an article in the *Guardian* entitled 'Caught in the crush: are our galleries now hopelessly overcrowded?'

The huge demand for tickets for the Blake exhibition was perhaps unsurprising, given the ecstatic nature of the reviews. The exhibition, according to the *Evening Standard*'s five-star review, was 'weird, dark and magnetic'. 'The artist's reputation has waxed and waned, but this Tate show blows away all our preconceptions,' said the *Sunday Times*, adding that 'viewing it is like being drunk'. The five-star review in the *Guardian* thrilled at how Blake's genius as an artist was not overshadowed by his reputation as a poet, claiming that: 'He blows away Constable and Turner – and that's with his writing hand tied behind his back.' Even the *Daily Mail* was wowed, although they took a slightly more sensational angle: 'Naked genius! He was a nudist obsessed by sex who talked to angels for inspiration, but for all his madness, William Blake was one of our greatest artists – as a new exhibition reveals.'

Among the rapturous reviews, it was difficult to find anyone not convinced of Blake's genius. A review by the BBC's Will Gompertz appeared, at first glance, to be one such exception, awarding the exhibition only three stars. Yet Gompertz had nothing but praise for Blake and his work. Instead, he took issue with how the large-scale exhibition was produced and offered ideas for how it could have been done differently. 'Covering the entrance foyer leading to the exhibition in a hideous bright red was a mistake,' he tells us. 'A block of vulgar, shouty colour setting completely the wrong tone for this most sensitive and ethereal of artists.' Despite his opinions on the colour scheme of the foyer, Gompertz still recommended that his readers attend the exhibition: 'To have so much of William Blake's psychedelic imaginary world laid out before you is a once-in-a-generation occasion and not to be missed.'

The almost total lack of negative criticism aimed at Blake and his work was striking, especially in the current media ecosystem. When everyone comes together in universal praise of a popular subject, it presents a golden opportunity for a professional con-trarian to step forward. An opposing view will almost certainly result in that most valuable of modern currencies, a great deal of attention.

There are many valid lines of criticism that could be used to take such a stance. The generally recognised incomprehensibility of Blake's later writings, for example, is an obvious place to start, as is the argument that many of his biblical and eighteenth-century references are irrelevant to a modern audience. Blake's lack of skill at drawing from life, rather than his imagination, has often been noted, and his illustration of 'The Tyger' from one of his best-known poems has frequently been mocked. Then there is always the option of dismissing him as a madman, as his contemporaries did, and denying that there is any coherence, truth or wisdom in his philosophy. It is not difficult to make the argument that Blake's work is gibberish.

Yet no one was prepared to do this. In the attention economy, it is rare indeed for such low-hanging fruit to remain unpicked. This was certainly not because everyone understood his work and approved of what he was trying to do. For the majority of the 233,000 who attended this exhibition, his art remained as strange, enigmatic and incomprehensible after the exhibition as it did before.

Yet there was something about Blake's work that these great crowds recognised as important and valuable, even if they couldn't verbalise exactly what it was. It was as if they knew that denying this mysterious something was wrong and that doing so might damage them on a deep and little understood level. Whatever it is about his art that we connect to, we somehow know that to deny it is taboo. These are secular times. We are largely secular people. We have difficulty in admitting that we have recognised something which feels sacred.

It is not unusual to feel a little fear when you first encounter Blake. His understanding of how the world works is so far removed from the modern consensus that we can be wary of trying to see the world through his eyes. Perhaps his madness is contagious? Perhaps exposure to his work will change you permanently, in a way that marks you out as different in your current social circles? Robinson asked whether Blake was 'Artist or Genius – or Mystic – or Madman?' We approach his work hoping that we'll discover which of those apply to Blake, but our fear is that we'll also discover which apply to ourselves.

Despite all this wariness and uncertainty, the undeniable attraction that pulls us in has taken Blake from an obscure, mocked failure to a position so central to British culture that he is now beyond criticism. The specific spark of attraction varies from person to person – it might be a line of poetry that moves us in a way we can't understand or an unexpected glimpse of one of his paintings that takes us unawares, like passing a window into another world. Whatever it is, we somehow know when we feel that pull that understanding Blake is a risk worth taking.

For all his arcane references and reputation for incomprehensibility, Blake was trying to communicate with us. The engraving on the grave marker at Bunhill Fields concludes with a quote from his epic illustrated book *Jerusalem*:

9

I give you the end of a golden string
Only wind it into a ball
It will lead you in at Heaven's gate
Built in Jerusalem's wall.

Those lines make explicit the promise Blake made to those who approach his work. He has found a way to a numinous place, and he beckons us to accompany him. Deep down, we all suspect that there is something missing, some part of our basic humanity that has become invisible to us. Blake was claiming that he had found it. His work is a trail he has left. He wants us to follow. It's not surprising that we're tempted. After all, what have we got to lose?

For all his seeming incomprehensibility, his current fame and the size of his audience suggest that understanding Blake is not something that we have given up on yet. On the contrary, our efforts seem to be increasing with every passing year. We have many advantages now that Robinson lacked. Our understanding of both the mind and the nature of reality are far in advance of the world two centuries ago. We also have easy access to the huge amount of research and analysis into his work that occurred in the twentieth century. Once his art was extremely rare and every page found was precious; now his entire body of work is just a few mouse-clicks away.

Blake's art contains rare gold, but to mine it is not always easy. It forces you to grapple with abstract philosophical ideas and arcane mythologies, of the type it is much easier to ignore. It is powerful and strange, and it may indeed change us for good. But what sort of life would it be if we shunned opportunities like this, which might just transform both ourselves and the world around us?

Many thought that the world had beaten William Blake, but there was a reason why that fight seemed like such a one-sided battle. Blake never agreed to a material struggle, and he made no effort to defend himself on that level. Instead, his time, energy and work were dedicated to an entirely different set of objectives, and he fought for those on a battlefield of his own choosing. The way in which the world attempted to shape Blake was very different to the way Blake attempted to shape the world.

Blake's attention was focused somewhere that is not easy for us to define or label. We do intuitively feel, however, that it exists. Our desire to understand it better is the reason why we are so drawn to Blake, and part of the reason why he has received such immense posthumous fame and praise.

William Blake versus the world, we will discover, turns out to be a far more interesting story than that of the world versus William Blake.

2.
TWOFOLD ALWAYS

The Blake family house stood on the corner of Marshall Street and Broad Street (now Broadwick Street), in central London. It was tall and narrow, with the family haberdashery shop on the ground floor and a further three floors above for the growing family. William Blake was born in this building on 28 November 1757, the third of seven children (two of whom died in infancy). The house had been built on top of an old burial ground; above the stench of the dirty, noisy city, it was said that the smell of the dead could still be overpowering.

Blake's home was in an area which then represented – as it still does – a mixture of poverty, commerce and genteel excess. A workhouse and an abattoir stood nearby, but so did the elegant lawns and gravel walks of Golden Square. It was a short walk along Oxford Street to the Tyburn gallows, which still drew large crowds for its regular hangings. The streets were muddy hollows, the city a maze of dark twisting alleyways, and violence and drunkenness were commonplace. It was in this house when, at the age of four, young William looked at the window and saw the face of God pressing in. He screamed.

The first decade of Blake's childhood was carefree. His parents recognised that he was a sensitive child and made the decision not to send him to school with other children. Instead he was home-schooled by his mother, on the recommendation of the Moravian Church she had previously belonged to. Young Blake learnt to read and write, although his punctuation and spelling would always be eccentric. The principal object of study in those early years was the Bible, and this text remained the foundation of his work and imagination for the rest of his life.

Blake's lack of formal education afforded him time and freedom to wander, and as a boy he loved to explore. London was then still small enough that he could leave the hectic streets of Soho behind and walk out into the lanes and footpaths of the countryside. A typical walk, described nearly a century later in 1863 by his first biographer, Alexander Gilchrist, took him south over Westminster Bridge, past St George's Fields to the 'large and pleasant' village of Camberwell and the fields and hedgerows beyond. He would continue for a few more miles, perhaps to Blackheath or the 'antique rustic town of Croydon'. The landscape Blake explored has now been almost entirely overlaid with concrete and construction, but it survives in idealised form in his work.

Blake enjoyed a level of freedom that modern-day children would find incomprehensible. From the evidence of his later recollections and work, it can appear that, to his innocent child's eyes, unburdened by responsibility, he was free to explore paradise. Britain was at peace between Blake's fifth and seventeenth years, so he grew up believing this was the natural condition of the world.

On one summer's morning, around the age of eight or ten, he went out to Peckham Rye. As Gilchrist famously described this incident, 'Sauntering along, the boy looks up and sees a tree filled with angels, bright angelic wings bespangling every bough like stars.' On returning home, Blake innocently related the incident to his parents. His father's initial reaction to what he assumed was a lie was to hit him. It was only his mother's intervention that saved him from a severe beating.

Gilchrist described the tree full of angels as Blake's 'first vision'. This may seem like an error, given that we have heard how he saw the face of God in the window at the age of four. But on one level, the reaction of his father does justify the description of the tree of angels as his first vision, because this was the moment when Blake learnt that his visions were not considered normal. Other people, he discovered, didn't share them. As his dad's reaction showed, regular people not only didn't believe in them, but they could react to them with great anger.

Children accept the world they grow up in unquestioningly, regardless of poverty or privilege. Before this incident, Blake could have believed that the things he saw were a common part of the world. If you were being raised on the Bible, you might expect to occasionally see angels in much the same way that you occasionally saw cows, or stables, or palaces. It was only after his father reacted violently that Blake discovered this wasn't the case. Blake's Peckham Rye 'first vision' was the moment he realised that he was different – the first crack in his innocence.

The Middle English word 'vision' originally referred to a supernatural apparition, but its meaning has since been downgraded to describe regular, everyday sight. Nowadays, visions – in the original sense of the word – are almost entirely absent from the world we read about in the media or see reflected on our TV screens. Most people live their lives without once glimpsing an angel, let alone the face of God.

Because Blake's visions continued throughout his entire life and inspired his painting and poetry, it's not possible to tell his story without tackling them. His visions are central to his modern fame and more fundamental to our idea of the man than even his genius for painting and poetry. History is full of great artists, and there is no shortage of mystics who report strange and baffling visions. But people who experience visions, and who are also great enough artists to give others a convincing glimpse of what they have seen, are few and far between.

Most accounts of Blake's life and work explain his visions away as a form of 'eidetic imagery' – a vivid mental image which a person can see either in their mind's eye or externally, as if the mental image was part of the observer's environment. The term 'eidetic imagery' may be an appropriate label for what Blake experienced, but a label is very different to an explanation. If we want to really understand William Blake, we need a deeper understanding of what it means when someone sees 'a vision'.

There are many ways to interpret accounts of visions of angels or spiritual entities. One, which is common in the modern era, is to assume that people are simply lying – angels don't exist, therefore anyone claiming to see them must not be telling the truth.

Few find this explanation satisfying in the case of William Blake. Given the artistic obscurity in which he lived his life and his reputation as a madman that these visions engendered, it is difficult to find a plausible reason why he would lie about them. It is not just that he reported such visions over his entire life, from childhood to old age, that makes him believable, but the eerie qualities of the work he produced inspired by them. After seeing the startling originality of many of his paintings, it can be harder to believe that he didn't experience visions than it is to believe that he did.

Another explanation is that the spiritual beings do in fact exist, external to their observers, and that reports of them are straight-forward accounts of actual encounters. This was the approach favoured in biblical and classical texts. When we read about how God spoke to Moses from the burning bush, or how Helen encountered Aphrodite in the *Iliad*, it was understood that these were regular accounts of things that happened. It is hard not to be sceptical of an explanation like this in the materially minded twenty-first century. Even in Blake's time, there were few who would have accepted a literal interpretation of his visions. Blake himself recognised that the entities he saw weren't 'really there' in the everyday sense. He knew that the people he was with did not see the things that he saw.

So if he wasn't lying and if his visions weren't objectively real, how should we interpret what was going on?

The first academic to really tackle this question was the American philosopher William James, who published *The Varieties of Religious Experience* in 1901. James was uninterested in theology or the structure and history of religions. Instead, he was concerned with religious experience itself. He wanted to know what was happening to people in the moments when they felt they were in touch with something larger and more important than the physical world. These experiences, he recognised, were universal. They occurred to people in different cultures, religions and historical periods. Those people interpreted the incidents through different cultural frameworks, of course, but the actual experiences they described were fundamentally similar. If experiences such as these occurred regularly throughout history to people of widely different cultures, James reasoned, then the scientific worldview needed to recognise and study them. Science is an enquiry into the whole universe, after all. It is not an enquiry into only the parts of the universe that scientists are comfortable with.

As James realised, there were several qualities that reports of religious experiences had in common. The most obvious, and the most frustrating, was the quality of ineffability – the impossibility of communicating exactly what the experience was like. As he described a spiritual experience, 'no adequate report of its contents can be given in words [...] mystical states are more like states of feeling than like states of intellect. No one can make clear to another who has never had a certain feeling, in what the quality or worth of it consists.' Just as you couldn't explain to a person who had never tasted mustard exactly what the experience of eating mustard was like, people who had experienced a mystical state were equally unable to adequately describe it to others.

The American neurosurgeon Eben Alexander III experienced a visionary state in 2008. He spent seven days in a meningitis-induced coma, during which time he entered what he later described as 'a world of consciousness that existed completely free of the limitations of my physical brain'. After he had returned to a normal mental state, he struggled with the difficulty in expressing exactly what he had experienced. It was, he wrote, 'rather like being a chimpanzee, becoming human for a single day to experience all of the wonders of human knowledge, and then returning to one's chimp friends and trying to tell them what it was like knowing several different Romance languages, the calculus, and the immense scale of the universe'.

The second quality that James identified was that the experience was noetic – meaning that it was imbued with information: 'Although so similar to states of feeling, mystical states seem to those who experience them to be also states of knowledge [...] They are illuminations, revelations, full of significance and importance, all inarticulate though they remain; and as a rule they carry with them a curious sense of authority.' It is this noetic quality, and the sense that during the experience you were granted profound, new knowledge, that gives a religious experience a sense of revelation. It is a glimpse of a larger state of mind that shows the poverty of our everyday awareness. Without this, an ineffable experience could be dismissed as little more than a period of feeling strange.

James also identified two subsidiary qualities, namely transiency and passivity – the experiences do not last for long, and they involve a lack of agency. As he wrote, 'the mystic feels as if his own will were in abeyance, and indeed sometimes as if he were grasped and held by a superior power.' Despite their transient nature, these experiences can produce lasting changes in people.

The author Philip Pullman, who is a prominent critic of religion, has had similar experiences. 'The sense that the whole universe is alive – not just inanimate, but alive and conscious of meaning – is one that I've felt on two or three occasions, and they made such a deep impression on me that I shall never forget them,' he said in a 2002 talk at the Oxford University Department for Continuing Education.

> I'd never taken any drugs stronger than alcohol or cannabis, and not much of that, so I can't compare it to a drug-induced trance, and there was nothing trancelike about it. I was intensely and ecstatically awake, if anything. I just saw connections between things – similarities, parallels. It was like rhyme, but instead of sounds rhyming it was meanings that rhymed, and there were endless series of them, and they went on forever in every direction. The whole universe was connected by lines and chains and fields of meaning, and I was part of it. It lasted about half an hour in each case, and then faded. I've hardly ever talked about it because it seems like something whose significance is private.

Pullman has a great dislike of the words 'spiritual' and 'mystical' and he avoids using them to describe what happened to him, but the ineffable, noetic and transient nature of his experiences suggests that they were of the same type as those that James was trying to understand a century earlier. It seems likely that these experiences have been an influence in Pullman's move away from a strict atheistic worldview. As he told the comedian Adam Buxton in 2019, 'I'm believing more and more firmly in this thing called panpsychism, the idea that consciousness is actually everywhere. Consciousness is a normal property of matter just like mass or electric charge, and it's not something that is restricted to human beings.'

Although James was able to move our understanding of visionary experience on from being considered as either lies or literal truth, the shared qualities he identified were still frustratingly slippery things to get to grips with. There wasn't much that objective study could do with reports of transient, passive reception of ineffable knowledge that had little impact on anything other than the recipient's quality of life.

This is what makes the ineffable nature of these mystical moments so frustrating. To give others a glimpse of what these experiences were like was beyond most visionaries. Attempts to explain the impact of the visionary state can come across as trite, sentimental or embarrassingly obvious. The experience of a mystical state in which you understand that all is love can be life-changing, but to be simply told that all is love can have about as much emotional impact as reading a greetings card.

Perhaps more than any visionary before or since, Blake had the creative skill to express what he experienced. Not completely, of course, and not always clearly. But for those who have never had even a whiff of a vision themselves, the work of William Blake can do more than anything to convince them that such experiences are real. One poem in particular gives a revealing look at the form his visions took.

In 1801, when Blake was living on the Sussex coast, he went for a long walk across open countryside and got into an argument with a thistle. His description of this incident survives in a poem he sent with a letter to his friend and patron Thomas Butts.

2. TWOFOLD ALWAYS

Blake starts by describing an idyllic scene of natural beauty, but very quickly he begins to populate this scene with supernatural beings:

> With happiness stretchd across the hills
> In a cloud that dewy sweetness distills
> With a blue sky spread over with wings
> And a mild sun that mounts & sings
> With trees & fields full of Fairy elves
> And little devils who fight for themselves

As the poem continues, the otherworldly contingent escalates. Blake talks about the presence of God, along with silver angels and golden demons, but there is nothing to suggest that this is anything more than poetical metaphor. He then mentions the spirit of his father 'hovering upon the wind', along with his brothers Robert and John. 'Tho dead, they appear upon my path', he states, and describes how they beg and entreat him to make an unspecified change in his life. It takes effort to drive these spirits away, suggesting that they are more real to him than the fairy elves and golden demons previously mentioned. Those were ideas he could easily move on from. His dead family, in contrast, were stubborn.

It is then that he encounters the 'frowning Thistle', who he sees as an angry old man. It picks up where his family had left off, imploring him to make the unspecified change in his life that he was stubbornly refusing. The thistle warns him that going ahead as planned will lead to poverty, envy, old age, fear and the death of his wife. It is the voice of all his worry, anxiety and guilt. Blake is not for turning, however, and angrily kicks the thistle to pieces with his boot.

Fortunately for us, Blake describes what he means when he talks about arguing with the thistle:

What to others a trifle appears
Fills me full of smiles or tears
For double the vision my Eyes do see
And a double vision is always with me
With my inward Eye 'tis an old Man grey
With my outward a Thistle across my way

He is aware that other people would not see anything more than a normal thistle. He himself also sees the normal thistle, with his 'outward' eye. This is not a regular hallucination, in which something not present is seen and believed to be real. Instead, it is a case of 'double vision', in which Blake is seeing two contradictory realities at once. He is entirely aware that the thistle is just a regular thistle while at the same time seeing it as an 'old Man grey'. The imagined aspect of this seems to have its origins in the physical, because a spiky thistle does seem to be, out of all the plants and wildlife you'd encounter in the Sussex countryside, the one most apt to portray a hectoring old man.

This 'double vision', Blake tells us, is normal for him. It is 'always with me'. To see the real world with his 'outward' eye and also an imagined counterpoint with his 'inward' or mind's eye is, for Blake, his regular mode of perception. Remaining aware of the dual nature of his visions was therefore important, as it kept him on the right side of sanity. Most of us would experience a similar phenomenon if we were kept in isolation for long enough, away from other people. It is normal for people to start talking to themselves when they are alone for any length of time, and if isolation continues they may start projecting their inner monologues out into the world and argue with people who are not present. To a passing observer, this is how Blake would have looked, out in the fields shouting at the thistle.

Events then move up a gear. Out of the sun comes a character from Blake's own personal mythology. This is Los, who represents creative fire, and who we will talk more about later:

Then Los appeard in all his power
In the Sun he appeard descending before
My face in fierce flames in my double sight
Twas outward a Sun: inward Los in his might.

Again, Blake remains aware of the dual nature of what he describes: to the regular, 'outward' eye it was the sun; to the inner eye it was Los. The content of the vision may have escalated, for a burning mythological figure stepping out of the sun is considerably grander than an abusive thistle, but the nature of his vision was the same.

Blake stands his ground and argues his case against this terrifying flaming figure. Even now that the argument is taking place on a mythological scale, the subject is still Blake justifying his life choices to himself. A relatively minor personal matter has become, when projected out into the world, a great cosmic struggle. Blake goes into battle with Los 'With the bows of my Mind & the Arrows of Thought', and eventually defeats him.

Then something extraordinary happens, and the nature of his vision changes. Blake tries to describe what happens clearly, but his description can appear bewildering to those new to his work:

Now I a fourfold vision see
And a fourfold vision is given to me
Tis fourfold in my supreme delight
And three fold in soft Beulahs night
And twofold Always. May God us keep
From Single vision & Newtons sleep

These are strange statements that need some unpacking.

What Blake is trying to do here is to describe four different modes of perception, or states of awareness. The 'twofold' vision we have already encountered. This is a dual mix of physical reality and mental imagination, and again Blake stresses that he has this mode of perception 'always'. The implication is that it is far superior to 'single vision', by which Blake means the material world objectively observed, without any contribution from the mind or the imagination. This is 'Newton's sleep', the scientific perspective that Blake views with horror.

This scientific mode of perceiving the world had been largely unknown in Britain before the seventeenth century, but it had been growing ever since, especially after the founding of the Royal Society in 1660. A good example of the objective observation that the Royal Society promoted is an article entitled 'Effects of Lightning in Northamptonshire 1725' in the Royal Society journal, *Philosophical Transactions,* written by a J. Wasse. This was a lengthy, dispassionate description of the corpse of a shepherd, who was killed when struck by lightning out in the fields. Wasse describes the effect of the lightning strike on the shepherd's body and on the objects he had around him with a level of forensic detail that would make Sherlock Holmes proud. What was new here was the absence of any reference to the mythological associations of thunder and lightning, which any earlier account of a similar scene would have contained. There was no sense of awe about the 'wrath of God'. Nor was there any trace of human feeling for the victim.

In Blake's writings there are confusing references to the importance of seeing 'through' rather than 'with' the eye. This was another way to state his belief in the superiority of double rather than single vision. To see the world with single vision was, for Blake, to be robbed of everything that mattered in life – one of the many ways in which he was in opposition to the spirit of his times.

2. TWOFOLD ALWAYS

Nowadays, we have a greater understanding of the role that the mind plays in supposedly objective, passive observation. We suffer from many psychological biases which affect how we see the world, and as a result we often see what we expect to see. As Blake wrote, 'A fool sees not the same tree that a wise man sees.' As the role of the mind in perception becomes increasingly understood, we are learning that we too tend to see the world in twofold vision, rather than the single vision of Newton's sleep. The difference is that, unlike Blake, we are largely unaware of it.

If single vision is detached, objective observation and twofold vision is a merging of what we see and what we think, then what is the 'threefold vision' he talks about? Blake's description of it as being 'in soft Beulahs night' is not, for most readers, immediately helpful. Beulah is, like Los, another aspect of his personal mythology. It is a sweet moonlit place, associated with dreams, love and divine inspiration. Blake probably got the name from John Bunyan's *The Pilgrim's Progress*, in which the land of Beulah is an earthly paradise on the borders of heaven. To experience the state of Beulah is to experience a blissful, post-coital embrace from the whole universe.

The paradise of Beulah is how many would imagine heaven, but Beulah as Blake understood it is just a temporary state. It is too passive to be a true heaven. For Blake, the idea that the afterlife consisted of angels sitting around on clouds playing the harp was not something he found remotely appealing or plausible. Instead, the heaven of Beulah is a temporary kindness that acted as a respite from the constant work of the universe. It was something we could enjoy for as long as it lasted, but it was a holiday from existence, not our ultimate goal. Beulah was also a necessary buffer between the world of men and the higher realm above.

By calling this state a 'threefold vision', Blake is saying that the world of Beulah is an addition to, not a replacement for, the twofold vision previously described. It was as if a state of grace descended upon him after exercising his imagination and experiencing twofold vision. It did not change the content of what he was experiencing, but instead altered what it felt like. There he was, in angry dispute with a thistle out in the gentle rolling fields of Sussex, when from nowhere a blissful spiritual balm found and embraced him.

After threefold vision comes fourfold vision – a glimpse of the higher realm that Blake refers to as Eternity. This, he tells us, is the 'supreme delight'. It is also noetic, as William James explained, and profoundly ineffable. Here is the full-blown mystical state that James analysed and studied. It is a much rarer state of mind than Blake's 'twofold vision', and not something he experienced every day. Blake himself struggled with how to describe fourfold vision. As he wrote in his epic poem *Milton*:

O how can I with my gross tongue that cleaveth to the dust,
Tell of the Four-fold Man, in starry numbers fitly orderd

For now, we will have to leave this strange state of awareness, although we will return to this subject later. Blake was not able to describe or explain this ineffable visionary state in the poem he sent to Thomas Butts. He did, however, manage to describe the route by which he achieved his glimpse of Eternity.

It began with his imagination, or 'twofold' vision. By exercising his imagination, he was able to visualise his personal concerns and difficulties in mythological terms. With his problems brought out into the light and projected onto the world in this way, their contrasting positions were compelled to struggle until a conclusion was reached. Blake had made a psychological breakthrough. It is at this point that Blake's vision went from twofold, to threefold, to the fourfold of Eternity. This 'supreme delight' was not something he created himself, but something he said was 'given to me'. It was a side effect of Blake's imaginative struggles. In many ways, it was a reward for achieving a psychological breakthrough.

Blake was always clear that his route to Eternity came through the exercising of his imagination. On one occasion he was at a party, and he described a walk he had recently taken. 'I came to a meadow, and at the farther corner of it I saw a fold of lambs,' he said. 'Coming nearer, the ground blushed with flowers; and the wattled cote and its woolly tenants were of an exquisite pastoral beauty. But I looked again, and it proved to be no living flock, but beautiful sculpture.' We can now recognise this statement as another example of his twofold vision, in which living lambs were also perceived as timeless art. A lady at the party, however, pressed him for more details. 'I beg pardon, Mr Blake,' she said, 'but may I ask where you saw this?' Blake touched his forehead and said, 'Here, madam.'

Blake's visions, then, were neither lies nor objective truth. They were a state of mind he could achieve by exercising his imagination. 'Imagination' is a word we all feel we understand, yet it proves to be a tricky concept to define, as we shall see later. For now, however, it's worth noting that Blake's claims that his vision was 'twofold always' suggests an unusually powerful imagination at work.

But how can a strong imagination lead to the experience of a vision state? As we will see, a clue can be found in another aspect of the mind – the sense of self. Or, more accurately, in the sense of self being dissolved.

3.

I COME TO SELF ANNIHILATION

Blake had a very different childhood to modern English children. The carefree innocence of his first ten years and the freedom to wander unhindered in the idyllic English countryside never left him. He returned to this garden of Albion repeatedly in his adult work. For Blake, paradise was part of the world that we should be able to walk to at any time, rather than a far-distant spiritual realm which we hope to one day be allowed to access. For all that Blake is known as a working-class London artist, it is the Eden-like countryside he explored as a child in which much of his work was set.

High-functioning athletes and highly skilled musicians sometimes talk about becoming so focused that they lose all sense of time, space and ego. They become so fully immersed in what they are doing that it is as if they do not exist, except in their actions. This state is called 'flow' by psychologists, or more casually 'being in the zone'. In a similar way, Blake's work suggests that there were moments when his sense of self dissolved as he wandered the countryside as a child. This state of mind is a profound one, and mystics go to great lengths to experience it. At such a moment, all is truly one and no division exists, because when there is no sense of 'you', there is no way that 'you' can be separate from the rest of the universe. This is perhaps why the countryside, in Blake's work, has all the qualities of a prelapsarian paradise.

Blake certainly valued the experience of the loss of sense of self and viewed it as a spiritual goal. In his epic poem *Jerusalem*, he writes:

> O Saviour pour upon me thy spirit of meekness & love:
> Annihilate the Selfhood in me, be thou all my life!

In his poem *Milton*, he dismisses earthly laws in favour of the 'Laws of Eternity', in which the loss of the sense of self is paramount:

> ... know thou: I come to Self Annihilation
> Such are the Laws of Eternity that each shall mutually
> Annihilate himself for others good, as I for thee

'Self Annihilation' is something other than death; during the horrors that unfurl in *Jerusalem*, a character seeking freedom from his struggles desperately cries out, 'O that Death & Annihilation were the same!' Blake understood the self as a mental creation separate and distinct from physical life, which can be annihilated without our bodies coming to harm.

This loss of a sense of self, it should be noted, is different to the psychological experience known as dissociation, a state in which the mind becomes detached and disconnected, often as a way of avoiding dealing with trauma. Unlike the loss of a sense of self, it is a fundamentally passive experience. In contrast, the flow state is intensely active – the mind is so absorbed in an experience or activity that it forgets to conceive of itself as being in some way separate.

In the twenty-first century, science has made great advances in understanding how the brain generates its sense of self. In 2001, the American neurologist Marcus Raichle started recording the mind 'at rest' when he was studying the brain with fMRI scanners at Washington University. His aim was to help calibrate the machine and to understand the differences in brain activity caused by performing mental tasks. To his surprise, he discovered that patients' brains didn't just go quiet when they were lying back and doing nothing. Instead, several specific brain sections lit up and started communicating with each other. What that mental activity was about was not immediately obvious, but those brain regions were clearly communicating about something.

The functions of the brain areas in question related to autobiographical information, such as remembering the past and predicting the future, or thinking about other people and predicting how they might behave. These are all brain functions needed for daydreaming, so it makes sense that they would be active when people were lying back and letting their mind wander. This network of brain areas has now been given the somewhat dull name of the 'default mode network' – the network which becomes active by default when we didn't seem to be doing anything specific.

What Raichle had discovered was the structure of the brain's high-level, top-down organising network. Some researchers refer to the default mode network as a 'task-negative network' because it goes quiet when the brain has a specific task that it needs to pay attention to, and only starts up again when the job is done. It is when the brain is intensely focused on a task that the default network becomes sufficiently quiet for the selfless 'flow' state to be experienced. There is an exception to this general rule, which is that the default mode network also becomes active during tasks that require access to our autobiographical memories or social understanding. This makes sense, because the combined actions of the areas of the default mode network are our current best neurological model for how the brain constructs that most elusive of things: our sense of self.

The sense of self has long been a tricky problem for philosophers, psychiatrists and neuroscientists alike. We all think we have a sense of self and intuitively believe that it therefore must exist, but it has proven frustratingly difficult to find, or even define. As children, we might assume that our eyes operate like windows, letting light into our heads and allowing our 'self' to see the world outside. But how exactly would this work? Is 'the self' like a little person who watches this information, as if on a TV screen, with eyes of their own? If that was the case, would that little person also have another person inside their head, in order to watch what was going on in front of their eyes? That person would then need an even smaller person inside them, and so on to absurdity.

Neurologists have diced and sliced the brain pretty finely and there is no little person to be found, nor indeed any singular part of the brain which seems to act like one. Our sense of self is not a discrete thing, it turns out. It is perhaps better thought of as a story. It is the story of who we are, what we are like and where we are going, and as such it grows out of our history, our relationships with others and our goals for the future. All this is an emergent quality that arises from the interplay of many different areas of the brain, of which the most prominent are the same that make up our default mode network. It is when these areas are communicating that the story of ourselves can be told and our sense of self can be said to exist.

If it is the case that a profound spiritual feeling of unity is the result of a reduction in the brain's sense of self, then this has significant implications for another hallmark of the visionary experience. Those who have had visions frequently claim that the experience was in some way *more real* than normal life. They often view the immaterial spiritual realm that they have encountered as a more fundamental state of reality than our everyday world of matter. This was very much Blake's opinion, and it was also the conclusion of countless mystical seekers going back centuries, from the mystery schools of the ancient world onwards. Outside the West, however, this is not always the case. In Buddhism, for example, visions are valued, but it is accepted that they may be delusions and the product of the imagination.

Is this sense of things being 'more real' simply a side effect of the absence of a self? When you are present and self-aware you are able to question what is going on around you, and apply doubts and criticisms where necessary. But when the self is absent there is no 'you' to question anything, so all that there is can only be accepted as unarguable and true. The voice that questions whether this is nothing more than a dream is no longer present.

Given our current understanding of consciousness – or rather, our lack of it – a suggestion like this remains speculative. It may, in fact, be that the reason why visionary states feel more real than the everyday world is because that is exactly what they are, and mystics and visionaries are genuinely gaining access to the unfiltered experience of a more fundamental reality. However, for those sceptical of such a position, the suggestion that it is the absence of a sense of self which causes this belief can be a helpful one. The idea that Blake's visions convinced him that there was a greater reality than the material world can then be accepted, without having to also accept that this was true. With this intellectual hang-up neatly sidestepped, we are free to examine Blake's visions and explore what it is about them that is of value.

*

The default mode network helps us to understand how the physical world works, allowing us to make reliable predictions about what is likely to happen next. It is a stubbornly practical and rational system, and as such it is not interested in populating our material environment with characters from the imagination. The default mode network cuts out a lot of unstructured chatter between different parts of the brain and is therefore a highly efficient way for a brain to function. As a result, our imagination can be constrained by the default mode network. It can become subservient to what we know about the world.

If you imagine that the connections between different brain regions are a map of the road network, then the default mode network is like the motorway network – the busiest, strongest and most used connections, and the fastest and most efficient way to go from A to B. Deliberately using the motorways to travel is more efficient than heading down country lanes at random, with no clear destination in mind, just to see what we might find.

We are not born with a default mode network. Babies' brains are like blank slates, and they are ready to learn and adapt to whatever time and place they find themselves in. This explains why people have no memory of their first years, because autobiographical information requires the default mode network to develop. Gradually, as babies grow, their default mode networks start to emerge and strengthen, and they begin to understand the world around them and their place within it. Our first long-term memories form between the age of two and four. Once we have a memory, we can begin to understand ourselves as a story that is acting out in time.

While the child brain is developing, and the emerging default mode network is still weak, it is less rational and structured than an adult brain. As a result, the imagination is less constrained. We see this in the phenomenon of imaginary friends, in which a non-existent companion is conjured so strongly that the child perceives them as real. It is tempting to see a similarity here with Blake's 'twofold vision', in which intense imagination leads to a weakened sense of self that results in imagined entities being perceived as externally present. It is rare for an adult to get into an argument with a thistle, but it would be less surprising for a child.

In child development terms, imaginary childhood friends are believed to be a positive phenomenon that can lead to improved social, linguistic and creative skills. There is evidence from surveys in UK nurseries, however, that imaginary childhood friends have become rarer in recent years. Children now have far less opportunity to be bored, and with less time in their busy schedules for unstructured play and daydreaming they are less likely to invent characters so rich and interesting that they pass as real. Blame for this is sometimes placed on the use of tablets by pre-school children. It is possible that the use of screens is helping children learn about the world and causing their default mode networks to strengthen earlier, while at the same time reducing their need to flex their imaginations.

The adult mind is, in a sense, in a rut. Once it knows what is likely to happen in the world, it does not usually bother itself imagining scenarios that do not fall into this pattern. A child who has yet to develop a fully formed default mode network may spend time imagining what their life would be like if they had a pet dinosaur they could ride to school and impress their friends with. An adult, in contrast, will think about what they need from the shops and what to watch on Netflix that evening. On one level, this is a much more practical and energy-efficient use of the brain, but it may not be the way to a richer, more fulfilling life.

In a 2014 paper called 'The Entropic Brain', a team of researchers led by Robin Carhart-Harris from Imperial College London looked at the consequences of what they called 'entropy'. In this context, the word 'entropy' referred to how chaotic or ordered the activity in the brain was, with chaotic, unexpected brain activity being classed as high entropy and calm, predictable brain patterns being classed as low entropy. Carhart-Harris's argument is that the brain has evolved to limit entropy as much as possible, in order to run efficiently. As he explained in his paper, the brain tries 'to promote realism, foresight, careful reflection and an ability to recognize and overcome wishful and paranoid fantasies'. It does this through several top-down brain networks, with the default mode network being a prominent example. These try to keep the brain running in a predictable and monotonous way with as little wild or unnecessary activity as possible.

As sensible as this may sound, the brain can take its quest for efficiency too far. Addiction, obsessive compulsive disorder, eating disorders, depression and rigid or fundamentalist thinking are all the result of a brain that is too efficient, and which has too little entropy. Where these problems arise, a sprinkling of chaos is needed. In Carhart-Harris's terminology, what is required is more entropy, not less. To achieve this, it is necessary to quieten rigid structures such as the default mode network. One way to achieve this is to practise certain forms of meditation. Another is to take psychedelic drugs.

The link between a quiet default mode network and psychedelic drugs was something of a surprise to Robin Carhart-Harris. When his team of researchers from Imperial College London conducted fMRI scans of subjects under the influence of psilocybin, the psychedelic ingredient found in magic mushrooms, they found that blood flow in certain parts of the brain decreased. This result was further corroborated by measurements of oxygen consumption in the brain. This was a shock – the team had been working on the assumption that taking compounds like LSD or psilocybin would cause the brain to become more active, not less. The falloff in activity, they realised, was concentrated in the default mode network. The influence of psychedelics was weakening these rigid structures.

The idea that William Blake took psychedelic drugs, and that this was an explanation for his work, was a common belief in the psychedelic counterculture of the 1960s and 1970s. Reading accounts of Blake's visions, it is easy to see how such a belief could take hold. A good illustration of this was an incident in which Blake was in his home in Lambeth reading an edition of Edward Young's *Night Thoughts*, which he had agreed to illustrate. As he read, he was struck by a question Young asked: 'Who can paint an angel?' Blake later recounted what happened next to the portrait painter Thomas Phillips.

According to Phillips, Blake closed the book and cried, 'Aye! Who can paint an angel?' At that point he heard a voice in the room reply: 'Michelangelo could.' Blake looked around, but he saw nothing except a brighter light than usual. 'And how do *you* know?' he asked suspiciously. 'I know,' said the voice, 'for I sat to him: I am the archangel Gabriel.' 'Oho!' Blake responded, 'you are, are you: I must have better assurance than that of a wandering voice; you may be an evil spirit – there are such in the land.' 'You shall have good assurance,' said the voice. 'Can an evil spirit do this?'

'I looked whence the voice came,' Blake told Phillips, 'and was then aware of a shining shape, with bright wings, who diffused much light. As I looked, the shape dilated more and more: he waved his hands; the roof of my study opened; he ascended into heaven; he stood in the sun, and beckoning to me, moved the universe. An angel of evil could not have *done that!*'

There's a lot to unpick here. It is telling that when Blake heard a voice claiming to be the archangel Gabriel, he didn't fall to his knees in worship. Instead, he cried 'Oho!' and tried to catch him out. Blake is frequently contemptuous of doubt; in 'Auguries of

Innocence' he writes: 'If the Sun & Moon should doubt / Theyd immediately Go out'. But this incident shows us that while he didn't doubt the reality of his visions, he did not blindly accept their contents.

Blake's story, and in particular the sudden rush upwards from the normal world to an expansive cosmic vision as the roof of his study opened, has all the hallmarks of a high-dose psychedelic experience. Yet the idea that Blake can be 'explained' as a drug user is not convincing, not least because he experienced the same visions from early childhood to the end of his days. Psychedelic mushrooms do grow in southern England, a fact that some have used to explain Blake's visions. But there was no tradition of ingesting them deliberately, and the idea that British people in the eighteenth century voluntarily used mushrooms for consciousness expansion is ahistorical. As the author Andy Letcher notes in his study *Shroom*, 'while [European] people appear to have been eating hallucinogenic mushrooms for as long as there have been records, until the twentieth century they always did so accidentally and unintentionally'.

The few accounts we have of people in Blake's period unwittingly eating psychedelic mushrooms resulted in experiences of horror, during which the mushroom eater was convinced that they had gone mad or been possessed by demons. There was no cultural frame to understand the experience in any way other than madness or religious horror. There was not a shamanic religious tradition, for example, within which the experience could be placed in context. It would be many years before twentieth-century authors such as Aldous Huxley and Timothy Leary were able to frame the experience as a positive one in Western culture.

This is not to say that physical factors had no part to play in Blake's visions. The mind and body are complicated and interconnected. It is possible that something like the paucity of a poverty

3. I COME TO SELF ANNIHILATION

diet, for example, may have had an influence on his mind. But while a physical cause is unlikely to be anything more than a contributing factor to Blake's visions, what he was experiencing neurologically does seem to be a state similar to that which can be triggered by psychedelic compounds. This idea is further supported by the models created by the psychedelic counterculture of the 1960s, which have distinct similarities with Blake's view of the cosmos, as we shall see later.

It is a lovely detail that after Gabriel stood in the sun, he beckoned to Blake before he moved the universe – as if the archangel were excited or proud of what he was going to do. But what does Blake mean by saying that Gabriel 'moved the universe'? Perhaps he is referring to the constant dance of movement and evolution within the universe, and, if so, the reason this proves Gabriel's identity is that only angels, and not demons, are responsible for this movement. Regardless of the truth or otherwise of such metaphysical speculation, we do at least have some idea of the rapt expression on Blake's face as he recounted this incident. Phillips was painting Blake's portrait as he told this tale, and the result has become the best-loved and most known image of Blake.

Because Blake was not initially sent to school as a child, he was untrained in the normal academic way of dividing the world into categories and learning lists of facts. This may be a factor in why his default mode network does not seem to have been as well defined as those of other children. By itself, of course, this is not sufficient to explain the unique individual that was William Blake. Many children are not sent to school and do not grow up to become visionaries. But a background like this could still have been an important factor. For most people, the strengthening of the default mode network and the emergence of a strong sense of self is what casts us out of Eden, making us separate from the natural world. Growing up, in other words, is the equivalent of the biblical Fall.

As adults, we forget what it was like to be a child. There is a sense that the world was different then, and that something important has been lost, but we are unable to recall what this is, or exactly what it felt like. Very few adults can sincerely and unquestioningly believe in an imaginary friend. Those who can have their own subcultures and safe spaces online – they are aware that if they talk about these things in regular society, they are assumed to be suffering from some form of mental illness.

Blake recognised the link between the innocence of childhood and his visions, and the importance to his imagination of maintaining a youthful mind. In his 1794 poem 'The Angel', he fears that he will one day become too old to still see the divine figures of his visions:

> Soon my Angel came again;
> I was arm'd, he came in vain:
> For the time of youth was fled
> And grey hairs were on my head.

In this, Blake did not need to fear. His imagination and capacity for visions never dimmed as he grew older. Accounts of Blake in the last decade of his life frequently focus on the childlike qualities of sweetness and kindness that he possessed, as we have seen. He was described as that rare thing, 'a man without a mask' who had no interest in wealth or possessions but who could joyfully lose himself in music or watching children at play. It is striking that all these qualities indicate a lack of focus on the self.

Of course, Blake's ego could rear up ferociously when circumstances required. He could be stubborn and self-focused, and this side of him is amply demonstrated in his writing. But at other times his ego would be placed back in its box and his sense of self would be quiet, so that his imagination was free to roam undisturbed.

By 1767, when Blake turned ten years old, it was clear to his parents that their child had an artistic disposition – and the necessary inclination and talent to apply himself. It was also evident that, given their status as shopkeepers, there was little hope that young William could become an apprentice to a famous portrait painter. This was the established route into one of the few areas of art where success and wealth could then be found. Instead, Blake was sent to Mr Par's drawing school on the Strand – a preparatory art school, which would prepare students to enter the St Martin's Lane Academy or, after it was established in 1768, the Royal Academy of Arts. Here Blake had access to plaster casts of classical statues. By copying these, he learnt to draw.

After four years of training, the decision was made to apprentice Blake to an engraver – a logical compromise between Blake's clear inclination to the world of art and his merchant family's desire for him to learn a trade to support himself in later life. The first candidate for Blake's new master must have initially seemed promising. William Wynne Ryland had been appointed engraver to King George III, a position that secured him a pension of £200 per year. He was an accomplished and well-liked artisan with good contacts, and being apprenticed to him would have been an ideal start in life. Blake, however, did not take to him. When he and his father were returning home from a visit to Ryland's studio, Blake confessed his unease. 'Father,' he said, 'I do not like the man's face. It looks as if he will live to be hanged.'

This was quite an accusation at a time when gentlemen were thought to be honourable and respectable, and a different breed to the 'criminal classes'. Twelve years later, however, Ryland was accused of forgery and went on the run. He was traced to a small house in Stepney, where he attempted to cut his own throat rather than be apprehended. The suicide attempt failed, which meant that after being found guilty at the Old Bailey he was indeed hanged at Tyburn.

This is an unusual story about Blake, as it is the only one in which he makes a prediction about the future. For all that he would refer to later works as 'prophecies', they were prophetic in the sense that they were told with the force of revelation, not that they made claims about events yet to happen. It is possible, of course, that Blake felt an intuitive dislike of the man when they met, and that the story became enhanced in further telling after Ryland's downfall. Regardless of the truth, Blake was instead apprenticed to a very different engraver, James Basire of Great Queen Street, Lincoln's Inn Fields. It was a decision that would shape the rest of Blake's life.

Basire was reliable and respected, and known for his work with the Society of Antiquaries. As Blake's first biographer Gilchrist describes Basire, 'He was an engraver well grounded in drawing, of dry, hard, monotonous, but painstaking, conscientious style; the lingering representative of a school already getting old-fashioned, but not without staunch admirers, for its "firm and correct out-line," among antiquaries.' These were attitudes that Blake readily admired and absorbed. He too held the past in great esteem, developed a style that focused on the importance of outline, and took for granted the need for long hours of detailed work. In time, this would put a wedge between him and the fashionable society of the late eighteenth century, which favoured a lighter, more florid style. After being apprenticed to Basire for seven years, Blake's natural inclination to be on the side of the timeless, rather than the contemporary, was fixed.

After a couple of years of Blake's apprenticeship, Basire was commissioned to produce engravings for the book *Sepulchral Monuments in Great Britain* by Richard Gough. Pressed for time, but also respectful of his apprentice's abilities, Basire sent Blake to Westminster Abbey to prepare drawings of the royal tombs that line the eastern end of the Abbey. Here Blake found life-sized, carved stone likenesses of the monarchs of antiquity, lying atop their tombs as if sleeping, with their hands pressed together above their chests in prayer and the cares of the world gone from their shoulders. Blake found Elizabeth I, with her expansive Tudor ruff intricately carved in marble and her feet raised on sleeping lions, lying peacefully on the opposite side of the chapel from Mary, Queen of Scots, whose death warrant Elizabeth had signed. Here he found the frozen likenesses of the endless Richards and Edwards who dominated the medieval monarchy, their fierce anger now dissipated into peace without end. In the cloisters and chapels of the Abbey, Blake found, in the words of his biographer Peter Ackroyd, 'the legendary history of Britain revealed. For him it was as much a spiritual as a national or an antiquarian revelation; he entered into a communion with the dead, with the passage of the generations, and thereby was granted a vision of the world that never left him.'

The architecture of Westminster Abbey was a physical expression of the spiritual vision Blake knew well. While the floor plan of the Abbey's passages and transepts is built on a relatively human scale, in terms of length and breadth, the height of the building is astonishing. It is as if some higher being has wrenched the sky away. The Gothic columns and arches flow up towards the heavens, pulling the eye with them and leaving the ground-based observer feeling insignificant and awestruck. In later life, the archangel Gabriel pulled away the roof of Blake's study and ascended with him into the spiritual sun. Here was a representation of that experience manifested out of stone and craftsmanship in the material world.

At times, Blake was left alone in the Abbey to work in solitude and occasionally he had visions there, seeing grand processions of ghostly monks and priests and hearing their choral chant and song. He was present when the tomb of Edward I was opened and the corpse inspected, bringing the young boy face to face with the darkened, leathered skin of an English king who had been dead for over four centuries.

On at least one occasion Blake was bullied by public schoolboys from Westminster, who frequently used the Abbey as a playground. Westminster schoolboys have historically shown little respect for the building. The Coronation Chair, for example, which was made in 1301 and which has been used in the coronation of every English monarch since, is covered with their graffiti, some of which is as recent as the twentieth century.

In order to draw the tombs properly, Blake often had to climb on top of them so that he could see the sculptured effigies clearly. Some of the tombs were up to three metres from the ground. One Westminster schoolboy climbed up to Blake's level, in order to continue his taunts. Blake later told his friend Frederick Tatham how, 'in the Impetuosity of his anger, worn out with Interruption', he knocked the boy off his perch and 'precipitated him to the ground, upon which he fell with terrific Violence'. Basire had sent Blake to the Abbey in part because of tensions between Blake and Basire's other apprentice, a boy named James Parker. It is tempting to see a pattern in which Blake was singled out by his peers as in some way different or overly serious, and that this was used as an excuse for bullying. Blake's willingness to strike back at his tormentors, however – in this case by sending the schoolboy falling to the stone floor beneath – is certainly in keeping with his adult personality.

3. I COME TO SELF ANNIHILATION

The sense that Blake was different to other boys of his age is confirmed by his early poetry, some of which was privately published in 1783 under the title *Poetical Sketches*. Blake was twenty-six when this small volume appeared, but it included work that he wrote when he was as young as twelve. One example is the poem 'How sweet I roam'd from field to field', which was written when he was fourteen, and which is the product of a boy who was remarkably sensitive for his age. It recounts an encounter with Phoebus, which is another name for the Greek sun god Apollo, the most beautiful of all the male Greek gods. He is introduced here as the 'prince of love':

How sweet I roam'd from field to field,
    And tasted all the summer's pride,
'Till I the prince of love beheld,
    Who in the sunny beams did glide!

He shew'd me lilies for my hair,
    And blushing roses for my brow;
He led me through his gardens fair,
    Where all his golden pleasures grow.

With sweet May dews my wings were wet,
    And Phoebus fir'd my vocal rage;
He caught me in his silken net,
    And shut me in his golden cage.

He loves to sit and hear me sing,
    Then, laughing, sports and plays with me;
Then stretches out my golden wing,
    And mocks my loss of liberty.

The poem is often assumed to be written in the voice of a female narrator, due to the lilies in the hair, the roses on a brow, and the encounter with a prince of love. If this is the case, it is a remarkably empathetic and unexpected perspective for a fourteen-year-old boy. Blake's later work, however, frequently portrays the spiritual aspects of people as largely androgynous, and in many of his paintings and engravings male and female spirits look remarkably similar. Blake appears to have been cisgendered and heterosexual, but there may have been a transgender aspect to his sense of self when it was let free in his imagination. That the poem starts with carefree wandering through the fields in a landscape that becomes a garden of the gods does make it sound as if Blake himself is the subject of the poem. In the third stanza, the narrator has wings and sings, and is caught and placed in a cage. Our narrator now appears to be a songbird, which is at odds with the previous reference to their hair and brow. The poem's narrator is a shifting, metaphorical thing, more spirit than living being. That spirit is an aspect of Blake's imagination, even if it is not simply Blake himself.

The idea that love is something that restricts liberty, trapping the soul in a god's golden cage, is an emotionally advanced idea for a fourteen-year-old. You might expect a boy of that age to be dazzled by new-found feelings of attraction to others, and to focus on the chase rather than the more subtle qualities of love. It is possible that a relationship with an early childhood girlfriend earned him this insight, or that he borrowed the idea from an older poet – an artist's early work is often an attempt to copy those who inspire them, after all. It is also possible that this idea was self-generated, and an insight into the way that his visionary mind worked. Regardless of how he came to it, it seems a safe bet that the Westminster schoolboys who bullied him would not have produced poetical ideas as refined as this.

Those schoolboys would have then been perceived as his social betters. It is likely that they would have gone on to successful and well-paid careers in government, the military or commerce. Blake's later work shows clear scorn for the delusion of superiority that permeates the English social hierarchy, and he was frequently contemptuous of the minds produced by the public school and university system. It is tempting to assume he had already reached this conclusion by the time that he, 'with terrific Violence', knocked his tormentor to the cold stone floor of Westminster Abbey.

While he was showing potential as a teenage writer, his early artwork was also extremely promising. One example is an engraving entitled *Joseph of Arimathea among The Rocks of Albion*, which he produced at the age of sixteen while apprenticed to Basire. Inspired by a Michelangelo print, it showed a muscular, bearded and hooded figure standing on a rock next to the sea. Blake's skill is such that it is clear that this man is cold, and the look on his face is somewhere between ambivalence and regret. Joseph of Arimathea was a figure from the New Testament who took responsibility for the burial of Jesus, and later mythology claimed that he travelled to Britain, bringing with him the Holy Grail. From Blake's engraving, he appears to have stepped ashore and found the land of Albion to be cold and disappointing. It is a perfectly British expression of our mythic history.

Blake thought sufficiently well of this image to revisit it in 1820 when he was sixty-three years old. He added the title and, underneath:

Engraved by W Blake 1773 from an old Italian Drawing
This is One of the Gothic Artists who Built the Cathedrals in
what we call the Dark Ages
Wandering about in sheep skins & goat skins of whom the
World was not worthy such were the Christians
in all Ages

Joseph was a great-uncle of Jesus who, in later legends, was said to have taken Jesus on a journey to Britain as a child. It is this legend that some of Blake's most famous lines are often thought to refer to:

> And did those feet in ancient time,
> Walk upon Englands mountains green:
> And was the holy Lamb of God,
> On Englands pleasant pastures seen!

Blake's understanding of what Jesus represented was sophisticated and heretical, and the meaning of those lines proves to be more interesting than their popular interpretation, as we will discuss later. What is important here is how the themes and characters of his later, most celebrated lines appeared fully formed in his developing teenage experiments. There is little sense of an artist attempting to find their voice in the way that David Bowie, for example, experimented with different styles and forms of expression before becoming the artist we recognise today. William Blake was simply William Blake from the start. His childhood visions showed him a greater world than the material one, and from the beginning he expressed that visionary world in the form of art. This was as clear and straightforward a mission statement as you can find. Blake did not have to search for his path or wait to hear the call. He just had to begin.

4.
WITHOUT CONTRARIES IS NO PROGRESSION

In 1789 Blake wrote, illustrated, printed and self-published *Songs of Innocence*. A small volume of songs for children, they were simple and clear, with no hint of the complex personal mythology that dominates his later work. As a result of their simplicity, they are among the most read and best-known examples of his work. They are also fairly unrepresentative. To judge Blake by *Songs of Innocence* is like judging the Beatles by the song 'Yellow Submarine'. Both examples are sufficiently shaped by their creator's personality that they could not have been written by anyone else, but neither hints at the depth of their creator's wider body of work.

Songs of Innocence is well named. Many of the nineteen poems are written from the perspective of children and capture a sense of wide-eyed, open-hearted wonder, as yet undamaged by the realities of the world. This in itself was unusual. Children's books at the time tended to be moralistic. They took the form of an adult voice instructing children on correct behaviour. In contrast, Blake described a world of play and delight, infused with the message that spiritual beings were watching over all children, so they had nothing to fear. It was a perfect example of Blake's understanding of, and sympathy for, the mind of a child.

The repeated lines and simple rhymes were clearly intended to be sung rather than read. The melodies that Blake had in mind are, unfortunately, lost to us, although countless musicians over the past century have written replacement tunes. Blake was musically untrained but he had a good singing voice, and the tradition of a singsong when Londoners socialised was something he enjoyed. It is interesting that he chose to write a collection of songs for children, however, rather than for adult gatherings. Blake had been married for seven years when this volume was first published, and it was becoming apparent that he and his wife, Catherine, were not going to have children of their own.

Most of the songs have a pastoral setting and seem influenced by memories of Blake's childhood wanderings through the English countryside. Blake was thirty-one at the time, so it serves as evidence that his prepubescent consciousness remained alive and unsullied in part of his adult mind. A typical example is 'The Lamb', which Blake illustrated with a naked child, a flock of sheep and a country cottage surrounded by delicate saplings and oak trees. In the song, the child speaks to a lamb about their creator:

> Little Lamb who made thee
> Dost thou know who made thee
> Gave thee life & bid thee feed.
> By the stream & o'er the mead;
> Gave thee clothing of delight,
> Softest clothing wooly bright;
> Gave thee such a tender voice,
> Making all the vales rejoice!

Little Lamb who made thee
Dost thou know who made thee

Little Lamb I'll tell thee,
Little Lamb I'll tell thee!
He is called by thy name,
For he calls himself a Lamb:
He is meek & he is mild,
He became a little child:
I a child & thou a lamb,
We are called by his name.
   Little Lamb God bless thee.
   Little Lamb God bless thee.

This is now one of the most read English verses from the 1780s, a fact that might initially seem strange given its simplicity and the nursery age of its intended audience. That the *Songs of Innocence* are held in such wide regard is partly because of something Blake did five years later – in 1794, he wrote and illustrated a companion volume of twenty-six *Songs of Experience*, which looked at the world from a more adult perspective. Perhaps owing to their darker tone, the pieces are more like poems than songs.

Songs of Experience was not intended to be a replacement or a sequel to his earlier work. Instead, Blake combined the two into one volume: *Songs of Innocence and of Experience* or, to give it its full title, *Songs of Innocence and of Experience Shewing the Two Contrary States of the Human Soul*. These new *Songs of Experience* were frequently a mirror image of the earlier *Songs of Innocence*, most obviously in poems such as 'Infant Sorrow', which was a reaction to the earlier 'Infant Joy'. The counterpart to 'The Lamb' has become perhaps Blake's most famous verse, 'The Tyger':

Tyger Tyger, burning bright,
In the forests of the night;
What immortal hand or eye,
Could frame thy fearful symmetry?

In what distant deeps or skies.
Burnt the fire of thine eyes?
On what wings dare he aspire?
What the hand, dare seize the fire?

And what shoulder, & what art,
Could twist the sinews of thy heart?
And when thy heart began to beat,
What dread hand? & what dread feet?

What the hammer? what the chain,
In what furnace was thy brain?
What the anvil? what dread grasp,
Dare its deadly terrors clasp!

When the stars threw down their spears
And water'd heaven with their tears:
Did he smile his work to see?
Did he who made the Lamb make thee?

Tyger Tyger burning bright,
In the forests of the night:
What immortal hand or eye,
Dare frame thy fearful symmetry?

It is something of a jolt to go from the simplicity of 'Little Lamb
who made thee' to the foreboding question, 'Did he who made
the Lamb make thee?' The original message 'don't worry, for

God has made a just world' has morphed into the question of whether that same God was responsible for making the monsters that also prowl this earth. The imagery, meanwhile, has moved from wholesome countryside to the noise and fire of industrial manufacture. The rhythm and pacing of the words has become faster and more insistent, and the new poems have moved from simple statements to troubled questions. Crucially, Blake is content to ask those questions and leave the answers to the reader. It is, clearly, no longer a work intended for children.

Some paired poems are more pointed and less open to interpretation. In *Songs of Innocence*, 'The Chimney Sweeper' tells of the plight of small boys sold by their family to be indentured to a master sweep until they became adults. Their childhood was one of hard, suffocating work in cramped, inhumane conditions, and many died on the job. Those who survived often showed signs of stunted growth and deformity of the legs, arms or spine, due to being stuck in unnatural positions while their bones were still supple and growing. Blindness and cancers were also common. In this verse, one young sweep called Tom has a vision of being in a dark coffin when an angel appears to unlock the coffin and release him into the light of the sun:

> And the Angel told Tom if he'd be a good boy,
> He'd have God for his father & never want joy.
>
> And so Tom awoke and we rose in the dark
> And got with our bags & our brushes to work.
> Tho' the morning was cold, Tom was happy & warm,
> So if all do their duty, they need not fear harm.

This last line was in keeping with a general theme in *Songs of Innocence*, the idea that a loving paternal God would protect all who were good. This was both naive and untrue, as the reality of child sweeps' lives demonstrated. When Blake came to write a companion verse for *Songs of Experience* five years later, he had clearly realised his mistake. This new poem, also called 'The Chimney Sweeper', introduces us to the child as:

> A little black thing among the snow:
> Crying weep, weep, in notes of woe!
> Where are thy father & mother? say?
> They are both gone up to the church to pray.

For Blake, it was pious hypocrisy for parents to consider themselves Christian after condemning their own child to such a hellish life. By the end of the short poem he has extended his contempt to all pillars of society who turn a blind eye to the suffering of children. The parents:

> [...] are gone to praise God & his Priest & King
> Who make up a heaven of our misery.

This second version of 'The Chimney Sweeper', with its wider focus, is a later corrective to the naivety of the original. Yet the original simple children's songs are retained as part of the work – they have not been abandoned or superseded. In Blake's eyes, the innocence they display remains relevant.

In some of the newer poems, Blake was able to include the contrasting perspectives alongside each other. One such poem was 'The Clod & the Pebble':

> Love seeketh not Itself to please,
> Nor for itself hath any care;
> But for another gives its ease,
> And builds a Heaven in Hells despair.

4. WITHOUT CONTRARIES IS NO PROGRESSION

So sang a little Clod of Clay,
Trodden with the cattles feet:
But a Pebble of the brook,
Warbled out these metres meet.

Love seeketh only Self to please,
To bind another to Its delight:
Joys in anothers loss of ease,
And builds a Hell in Heavens despite.

The clod of clay is soft and humble, and trampled on by cattle, but through its humility and willingness to put others first it understands love as something that transforms even the darkest world into a heaven. The pebble, by contrast, is hard and unyielding, and does not give way to the waters around it. For the pebble, love is something that controls and binds. It is a cause of darkness in this otherwise heavenly world. There is no real judgement here, and Blake is not explicitly favouring the perspective of the clod or the pebble. Different readers can consider either to have the correct perspective, depending on their dispositions, and Blake is not interested in which position is right. He is interested in the contrasting dynamic between the two.

In the early 1790s, between writing *Songs of Innocence* and *Songs of Experience*, Blake composed *The Marriage of Heaven and Hell*. An important theme of this illustrated work is the necessity of contrary positions. As he writes, 'Without Contraries is no progression. Attraction and Repulsion, Reason and Energy, Love and Hate are necessary to Human existence.' So important to Blake is this dynamic that he makes a startling claim: 'Opposition is true Friendship.'

The contrasting positions he called reason and energy are, Blake explained, the root of good and evil. Passively obeying reason is good, which creates heaven, while activity springing from energy is evil, which creates hell. This sounds at first to be a simple dualist position, in which the world is divided into positive and negative things. But Blake also claims that: 'Energy is Eternal Delight.' The energy he had just defined as the source of evil is also portrayed as a lovely thing.

Blake was uninterested in campaigning for one side or the other. Instead, he argued for the necessity of both. Even today, most writers position themselves on one side of a divide and argue passionately that their perspective is the correct or most valid one. A writer like Richard Dawkins is firmly in favour of a materialist view of the world, for example; while a writer like Deepak Chopra champions a spiritual perspective. The works of Ayn Rand campaign for isolated, individualistic libertarianism, while an author and scientist such as James Lovelock argues for a holistic, systemic communal perspective. Single-focused studies like these are a hallmark of Western thought. They are predicated on the belief that, in order to understand something, you need to focus on it, isolate it from external factors, and then take it apart to see what it is made of.

Blake eschews this singular approach. His thinking often has more in common with Chinese thought, which examines how things interact as part of a larger system. As Lao Tzu wrote in the *Tao Te Ching* in the sixth century BC:

> When people see some things as beautiful,
> other things become ugly.
> When people see some things as good,
> other things become bad.

Being and non-being create each other.
Difficult and easy support each other.
Long and short define each other.
High and low depend on each other.
Before and after follow each other.

For Blake, as for Lao Tzu, things are defined by their context. A military historian may study war for their entire life, but he will never truly understand its horror unless he also understands peace. The value of good health is only really apparent to those who have been seriously ill. If you are blind to the greater context when you try to understand something, then you can never truly appreciate why things behave as they do.

Note that Blake is not trying to remain neutral. His position is not a proto-postmodern belief that all perspectives are equally valid. He is quite prepared to call out one side as good, and the other evil. Instead, his position is that both sides of the clash are necessary, because there is no such thing as light without dark or hot without cold. For Blake, the conflict between these divides is the fuel that moves the universe. Any view of the world must include them, because a universe without these dynamics simply couldn't exist. To try to solve problems by favouring one side and dismissing the other is to fail to understand how the world works.

One of the reasons why Blake's work proves to be so multi-faceted is because of the way he accepts all sides. If you dig into his work looking for something in particular, you are very likely to find it. It doesn't matter whether your primary interest is political, spiritual, occult, sexual, social, historical or radical, when you explore Blake's mind you find that he has thought about what you are preoccupied by. He saw all aspects of the world as a fit subject for his work, in a way that suggests he had somehow transcended and escaped the perspective of a single person. It was as if he could see the world from the outside, rather than attempting to describe it from within. This is, perhaps, why Blake speaks to all people, regardless of where in society they stand. The most used word in the body of Blake's writing, bar common conjunctives like 'and' and the definite article 'the', is 'all'.

Arguments, division and tribalism are, of course, a source of hurt and confusion. It is unsurprising that most people choose a side and want to see that side triumph. They long to enjoy the outbreak of peace that would – supposedly – arrive after their chosen enemies had been wiped away. But from Blake's perspective, a scenario like this would result in a static, unchanging world devoid of joy or surprise. Without the energy of clashing perspectives, the universe would ground to a halt and die. Blake did not think, however, that we were always trapped in a state of perpetual conflict. It was possible to find respite from these squabbles. This was the state he called Beulah, the 'threefold vision' we encountered earlier.

Blake introduces the state of Beulah in both of his major works, *Milton* and *Jerusalem*, with the line: 'There is a place where Contrarieties are equally True'. A contrariety is defined as opposition or inconsistency between two things. This place, he explains, is 'a pleasant lovely Shadow / Where no dispute can come'. The inability for dispute to exist in the state of Beulah is not because one contrary position has been wiped away, but because in the state of Grace that typifies Beulah there is no antagonism felt towards either extreme. They both exist, are recognised, and are simply accepted.

Rationally, we struggle with the notion that two contrary positions can both be true. Logic tells us that this is an either/or situation. The idea that the earth is flat, for example, and the idea that the earth is round, are contradictory statements that can't both be true. It must be one or the other, and we are usually pretty sure we know which. There are, however, at least two possible ways for contradictory statements to both be true.

The first of these is only possible at very small scales, at the level of reality from which our everyday world emerges, in the strange world of quantum mechanics. In the quantum realm, subatomic particles can be in two different places at the same time and exhibit other logic-defying behaviour. This intensely odd quality of the small-scale world is usually illustrated with the 'Schrödinger's cat' thought experiment, which features a cat in a box that is said to be both alive and dead at the same time. According to quantum mechanics, these 'Contrarieties are equally True'. It is only when the box is opened, and the cat is observed, that normal logic returns. At this point the cat can be said to be either alive or dead, but certainly not both.

In many interpretations of quantum theory, it is the presence of a conscious observer that turns reality into something fixed, comprehensible and useful. Before that, all that exists is a cloud of probability, an indistinct sea of potential that obeys its own laws despite not physically existing as we would understand it. The way in which this ineffable cosmos is transformed into a fixed, logical world can be said to be an act of creation, in which the definite appears out of the indefinite. A process such as this is central to Blake's own personal philosophy. It is the work of one of the key characters in his mythology. His name is Urizen.

Urizen is the personification of reason. He is the intellect that creates law, he is controlling and associated with language, and it is he who constructs the human-scale world of rationality and logic in which contrary positions cannot both be physically true. Urizen is the conscious observer that forces Schrödinger's cat to become either alive or dead. In *The Book of Urizen* (1794), Blake has Urizen describe his creation of the solid world while he was being buffeted by the storms that shake the realm of pure potential:

Inwards, into a deep world within:
A void immense, wild dark & deep,
Where nothing was: Natures wide womb

And self balanc'd stretch'd o'er the void
I alone, even I! the winds merciless
Bound; but condensing, in torrents
They fall & fall: strong I repell'd
The vast waves, & arose on the waters
A wide world of solid obstruction

From this new-built material world, Urizen calls for a tent to cover the definite world from the great seething void from which everything came:

"Spread a Tent, with strong curtains around them
"Let cords & stakes bind in the Void
That Eternals may no more behold them"

They began to weave curtains of darkness
They erected large pillars around the Void
With golden hooks fastend in the pillars
With infinite labour the Eternals
A woof wove, and called it Science

This 'woof', or woven cover called Science, was the creation of Urizen's reason. It hid the primordial void from the objective world he had created, just as the quantum realm of indefinite potential remains hidden from us now. Urizen then wrote his laws down in a great brass book.

Urizen is sometimes described as casting nets of religion, which he used to ensnare people in his reasoning and laws. His laws demand obedience, and their restricting, controlling nature filled Blake with horror. They reduce infinite possibility down to a single fixed certainty, and offer only:

> One command, one joy, one desire,
> One curse, one weight, one measure,
> One King, one God, one Law.

The Ancient of Days, one of Blake's most famous images, shows Urizen in this act of creation. He is leaning out of a golden orb with his long white beard buffeted by the storm winds of the dark, cloudy unformed void, and he reaches down with an outstretched compass to measure the solid world he is building. Here, Blake's use of the compass owes a debt to the freemasonry movement. Freemasons call God the 'Great Architect' of the universe and use a compass as his symbol. The primary art practised by Urizen is architecture.

The scientist Isaac Newton takes the place of Urizen in another of Blake's most famous paintings. He is shown intently focused on measuring a circle on a scroll of paper with a similar pair of outstretched compasses. The primal void that Newton inhabits makes it look as if he is under the ocean, sat on a coral rock, yet both Newton and the paper are dry. The environment is indistinct, dark and strangely primal, due in part to the experimental printing technique that Blake used for this work. It stands in sharp contrast to the clean, clear lines on the paper that Newton is so deeply focused on. If any modern artist were to attempt to visualise the shift from the probabilistic clouds of the quantum world to the objective certainty of the world as we perceive it, they would be hard pressed to improve on this.

Newton's intense focus on the mathematical shapes he is drawing is intended as an attack on the Newtonian worldview – his narrow focus makes him unaware of the larger, organic, mysterious environment in which he works. Blake recognised that Urizen's reason could create, but only by abstracting and dividing, and only then by becoming blind to what he was creating from. The circle he draws is finite, a limitation suggested by both explanations for the etymology of the name Urizen. The name implies both 'Your Reason' and 'horizon' – 'horizon' being a word derived from the Greek 'to limit'.

Blake has a long history of attacks on Newton's single focus, as we have already seen in his description of single vision as 'Newton's sleep'. Yet it is worth noting that he painted the naked figure of the scientist with the idealised physique and golden curls of a Greek hero. Although Blake disliked how Newton's rational mind shrank and limited the universe, he still recognised the importance of his work, and Blake had no argument with Newton's elevated position in our history. In his spiritual form, Blake believed, a great man like Newton should be pictured as a vision of strength, health and beauty – another example of Blake's love of contrary positions and the dynamic that they create. It produced a much richer and deeper work than just ridiculing Newton outright.

Blake's Urizen resembles an entity from Gnostic thought called the Demiurge. According to the Gnostics, the Demiurge is the creator of the material universe and, because he is the creator, he assumes that he is God. In this, however, the Demiurge is mistaken. There is something much greater and more fundamental behind this figure, which in *The Ancient of Days* is depicted as the golden orb that Urizen leans out of. Because the Demiurge is focused on the physical universe he is creating, he has his back to this greater power and is unable to see it. For those of us who are inside the physical world of creation, the Demiurge can block this pure light, making this creator a negative and harmful figure.

The idea of the Demiurge first appears in Plato's dialogue

Timaeus, and it became increasingly influential in Gnostic sects before the early Christian Church declared it a heresy. Different Gnostic texts disagreed about why the Demiurge mistakenly believed himself to be God. Some said he was misguided, ignorant or malevolent. Others argued that he was quite mad. As heresies go, 'God exists but he is mad' is pretty extreme.

Blake describes Urizen as being, like the Gnostic Demiurge, the 'Creator of men, mistaken Demon of heaven'. He equates him with the 'jealous god' of the Old Testament. Because this figure is only the creator of the material world, the status of 'god' that the Bible grants him is a delusion of grandeur. His association with matter rather than soul in part explains Blake's claim about his true status: 'Urizen is Satan', he wrote in his epic poem *Milton*. The idea that Blake equated both the God of the Old Testament and Satan himself with the same character sounds at first like the worst of heresies, if not straight up blasphemy. Once we understand more fully the nature of Urizen, however, it may not seem quite so strange.

Many mystics and religions over the centuries have talked about a fundamental void similar to the one described by Blake. It has been given various different names, such as Brahman or the Tao. Blake gave this ocean of formless potential the name Udan-Adan. He repeatedly refers to it as being found at a scale too small for normal human perception, which further supports the association with the quantum realm. In *Milton*, for example, he claims that all spaces larger than a globule of blood exist as creations of our mind – a strange notion that we will return to later. The nature of spaces on a smaller scale than this, however, is very different:

> And every Space smaller than a Globule of Mans blood. opens
> Into Eternity of which this vegetable Earth is but a shadow:

The idea that the delights of Eternity are found at extremely small scales is one he keeps returning to:

> Thou percievest the Flowers put forth their precious Odours!
> And none can tell how from so small a center comes such
> sweets
> Forgetting that within that Center Eternity expands

This is another of Blake's ideas that can also be found in Taoism. In a modern translation of the *Tao Te Ching*, Lao Tzu says that:

> The Tao can't be perceived.
> Smaller than an electron,
> it contains uncountable galaxies.

In the scientifically minded twenty-first century, the idea that there is a strange world entirely unlike our normal reality at scales too small for us to see has been readily accepted. The microchips our society runs on, for example, rely on our understanding of quantum mechanics to function. This was not the case in the eighteenth century, when such ideas belonged to mysticism and philosophical speculation. We may be unable to perceive this realm, but Blake's description of Beulah suggests that there is solace to be gained from thinking in its terms.

If we are looking for a modern, scientific concept we can equate with the unformed void beyond our material universe, out of which Urizen creates our world through an act of intellectual reason, then the quantum realm is an obvious candidate. As we've noted this is, like Beulah, 'a place where Contrarieties are equally True'. Because Beulah is a respite from the limited, rational world created by Urizen, it makes sense that it has qualities that Urizen's world lacks. Blake's claim that we can experience Beulah, then, suggests that we are not totally ensnared in the rational world of Urizen's making, and that it is possible to move our awareness outside of its nets and snares.

Because Urizen's sense of himself as a creator god is built on the denial that there is anything outside of him, he finds this idea extremely threatening and he uses all the logic at his disposal to ridicule it. Urizen, it's important to remember, is a personification of the rational aspects of our minds. Biologically, he is closely related to the default mode network, the top-down efficient network that cauterises chaotic imagination. It is Urizen who has built our ego in his own image. What he likes above all other things is the idea that he is right, because this takes far less mental effort than understanding error.

All this brings us to another 'place where Contrarieties are equally True', which can give us insights into the nature of Beulah. Happily, this is away from the strange, inhuman quantum worlds and a place which we are all familiar with from everyday life: the immaterial world of the mind.

Here we need to recognise that the contrarieties that Blake talks about are nothing more solid than ideas. The idea that the world is flat and the idea that the world is round are both real ideas, regardless of how accurately they correlate with the actual shape of the world. These ideas are not reality itself. Instead, they are models of reality that we have constructed in our minds. They are what we believe reality to be.

A mental model of the real world can be extremely useful. It allows us to make predictions and helps us decide how to act. But a model is, by definition, a smaller, simplified version of the thing that it was built to represent. It will not always match what it models exactly. The chances are that we won't notice this, however, because our ideas are so convincing. When we are presented with the contrasting ideas that the world is flat and the world is round, for example, we feel certain that we are correct when we think that one of these is true. In reality, both are crude approximations. To the best of our understanding, the world has a complex topology in four-dimensional spacetime, which is warped by the gravity of the sun. Visualising its true shape is an extraordinarily complicated problem. It is not surprising, in these circumstances, that we build simplified models in our mind and mistake these models for reality. But as the Zen philosopher Alan Watts explained, the map is not the territory and the menu is not the meal.

For most of our day-to-day needs, the simple idea that the world is flat is all we need to get by, because this model works well enough for us to find our way around. If we are planning long-distance travel or arranging a call with someone in a different continent, then the flat world model will prove to be insufficient and we need to use the slightly more complex idea that the world is round. If we wanted to send a satellite on a never-ending circuit orbiting both the earth and the sun, neither model would be sufficient, and we'd have to think in terms of four-dimensional spacetime.

Living inside our mental models is so seductively convincing that it can be a shock to realise that they are not the real world. A good example of this is sound. Reality is silent, as we understand the term. The collision of objects causes waves to ripple through the air, but this is not the same as 'sound' as we subjectively experience it. The qualities of birdsong, guitar chords or laughter that so delight us are created by our minds, based on air ripples detected by our ears, and they exist only there. Another example is colour, which also does not exist in external reality. Different wavelengths of light are reflected off different surfaces, and these different wavelengths are registered by our eyes, which send this information to our brains. This is not the same, however, as a colour such as red objectively existing in the external world. Before there was life on earth that had evolved eyes to look, there was no sense in which the sky was blue or that grass was green. This only happened after living things invented green and blue in their minds.

We state this now with some confidence thanks to the work of generations of scientists, but students of Zen Buddhism came to the same realisation through detailed study of their own minds. Zen students were asked, 'Who is the master who makes the grass green?' and left to observe their own minds until they were able to answer this question and understand that, in the words of the American neurobiologist Dean Buonomano, 'The brain is an illusion factory.' Or, in the words of Nietzsche, 'we are much more the artist than we realise'.

The idea that we live in a mental model of reality, rather than reality itself, is fundamental to the philosophy of William Blake. As he explained in *Jerusalem*, 'In your Bosom you bear your Heaven and Earth & all you behold; tho' it appears Without, it is Within, in your imagination.' Like many of Blake's statements, this can seem bewildering and mystical at first glance, but when we reread it we see that Blake was being clear and concise: although the world appears to be outside of you, what you experience as the world is created in your mind.

When we recognise this, we see that our ideas are just that – ideas. Once we accept this, we stop confusing ideas with reality and we find ourselves in 'a place where Contrarieties are equally True'. Both 'the world is flat' and 'the world is round' are true in the sense that they are real ideas. There is no conflict regarding validity here, because one is not more of an idea than the other. In Blake's words, 'Everything possible to be believ'd is an image of truth.' Here, then, is an aspect of Beulah, the peace that descends when we realise the extent to which the hectic world outside is a world inside, which we ourselves have created in our own image.

*

Imagine that your mind was wiped clean, so that it was as blank and fresh as that of a newborn baby. Then imagine you are on the top of a hill in an unexplored wilderness. Your brain has no immediate access to this world because it is locked away inside the dark, silent cavern of your skull. The only way it can make sense of your environment is by interpreting the messages being received by your senses.

You slowly turn around through 360 degrees, and your eyes receive information about the world you find yourself in, which they forward to your brain. As you turn, you see as far as the horizon in all directions. A circular model of the outside world has been created inside your head, with you at the centre. As far as you know, the horizon is the limit of this creation, the literal ends of the earth. If you watched the world change and evolve over time, you would start to develop beliefs about cause and effect and how things work. The mental model you are creating is the basis of your rational understanding of the world.

Blake describes this situation in *Milton*. In his reference to the 'Sons of Los', Blake is referring to the work of the imagination. The space that we perceive, he believes, becomes a model of our world built in the mind:

The Sky is an immortal Tent built by the Sons of Los
And every Space that a Man views around his dwelling-place:
Standing on his own roof, or in his garden on a mount
Of twenty-five cubits in height, such space is his Universe;

Because you are constructing that 'Universe' yourself in your mind, you are effectively its creator. This explains the strange quote of Blake's mentioned earlier, when he said that all spaces larger than a globule of blood exist as creations in our mind. The aspect of our mind that falls for this internal world and believes it to be real is

Urizen, who believed that the construction of this mental model of a small part of the universe made him a creator god. Urizen's delusion was caused by his limited awareness: being blind to what was beyond himself, he couldn't imagine anything greater than he was.

Urizen is not the typical personification of reason that you might expect to find in the Age of Enlightenment. Reason was then being lauded as a golden key with which to escape from the prison of faith, but Blake emphasised how small and limited it was and how deluded we become when we fail to recognise this. Urizen, as we've noted, is a personification of the default mode network in the brain. It is this which constructs the world in which we live, the story of our self or ego, and our rational beliefs and expectations about the world. This is a small, approximate model of the world, for reasons of mental efficiency, but it does at least try to be useful. It is flawed, but its intentions are not necessarily evil or cruel. Problems arise not through intent, but because it is unaware of the world beyond its limitations. Like our minds, Urizen has no knowledge of what he doesn't know and deep down this terrifies him, because it threatens his very sense of identity. He will attempt to belittle, mock, or otherwise deny evidence that there is more than he knows, and that he is not the powerful creator he thinks he is. Deeply insecure, Urizen is the aspect of our minds that needs not just to be right, but to be thought of as right. You will recognise him immediately if you use social media.

As much as we like to think we live in the real world, our brains inside our skulls are isolated from that world and instead create a simulacrum of this exterior based on information from the senses. This simulation is seductively convincing, as we've noted, and we remain blind to the ways it differs from external reality. Aspects of the world that our senses are not capable of perceiving, such as infrared light, microwave radiation or the magnetic field that some migratory birds use for navigation, are absent in our mental models. Some qualities that we do perceive, such as colour, sound and pain, seem entirely real to us even though what we are experiencing is a wild abstraction of the information our nerve impulses report. Our eyes detect which wavelengths of light bounce off objects and the mind uses this information to create the illusion that we are looking at a verdant green, cherry red or International Klein Blue. A collision of objects creates shockwaves in the air, but that is not the same as the experience of hearing a cymbal crash or a mournful clarinet. Pain can be so overwhelming that the idea it isn't a quality of the physical world seems like a tasteless joke, but the electrical impulses carried through our nervous system are simply electrical impulses. They are not the experience of agony.

Newton's 'single vision' sees only the materialistic aspect of the world, devoid of any mental qualities. From this perspective, it is logical to argue that colour, sound and pain are not physical qualities of the universe. Yet for anyone interested in what it is like to be human, those experiences need to be treated as real. Things that are 'only in our minds' are important, and that is true of ideas, regardless of the extent to which they correlate with objective reality. Blake recognised that what we think of as the external world is a product of the mind and, as we've already seen, he was aware that his visions were also the product of his imagination. It seemed logical, therefore, to treat both with equal validity. It also seems likely that his experience of visions helped him understand the extent to which the exterior world is actually interior.

The implications of the mind-created nature of the visionary world are profound, but Blake saw them clearly. He stated boldly in *The Marriage of Heaven and Hell* that 'men forgot that All Deities reside in the Human breast'. Gods, demons and angels were all ideas, he is saying, created in the white-hot forge of the human imagination. The jealous, controlling creator God of the Old Testament, he believed, was none other than Urizen, a part of our minds projected out into the exterior world.

Blake was not the first to view God as the creation of the human mind, but there were not many who stated this as clearly as he did. Much can be implied from Michelangelo's painting of the Sistine Chapel, for example, in which God is depicted emerging from or lying upon a strange pink cloud which is an exact, anatomically correct cross section of a human brain. Michelangelo may have been prepared to hint at this idea, but he was wise enough not to state it outright. Established religions viewed the idea that we made the gods, and not vice versa, as blasphemy. Blake was much more comfortable with the idea, but then he did not see it as a reason to think any less of divine entities.

Ideas like this coloured Blake's view of the God of the Old Testament, with whom he had a complicated relationship. As has often been noted, the Old Testament deity was a difficult, contradictory character. The classical historian Tom Holland describes him as: 'Wise, he was also wilful; all-powerful, he was also readily hurt; consistent, he was also alarmingly unpredictable [...] the God of Israel was hailed in the Jewish holy books as all these things, and more.' To Blake, this showed all the hallmarks of a God born in the minds of man. He called this God 'Nobodaddy', a rather contemporary sounding neologism, whom he frequently criticised in the pages of his notebook:

Then old Nobodaddy aloft
Farted & belchd & coughd
And said I love hanging & drawing & quartering
Every bit as well as war & slaughtering

73

These criticisms were extended to religions that falsely worshipped this mankind-created God, and even at times to the religious texts that supported these religious interpretations.

> The Hebrew Nation did not write it
> Avarice and Chastity did shite it

Satirical lines such as these should be interpreted as an attack on how the Bible was used and interpreted, rather than an attack on the book itself. Blake considered the Bible to be the product of what he called 'Poetic Genius', and therefore divinely inspired. To Blake, the book itself was more precious and heavenly than the deluded creator God it glorified. He saw poetic inspiration like this as evidence of a greater power, beyond the delusion of Nobodaddy, which could only be glimpsed by looking outside the limits of Urizen. It was probably this ultimate God to whom he addressed the following lines. They show an understanding of our limited perspective, but also sympathy for those trapped inside it:

> To God
> If you have formed a Circle to go into
> Go into it yourself & see how you would do

Blake's almost Taoist recognition of the importance of opposites, along with his understanding of the mental nature of the world we experience, had profound consequences. As we can see, they have already taken him far beyond ideas that were acceptable in contemporary theology. His position was so deeply heretical that, without deep study of his work, it could sometimes be difficult to recognise just how extreme it was. The importance of angels in his writings, for example, could distract readers from his belief that the God worshipped by religion was a product of the human mind.

4. WITHOUT CONTRARIES IS NO PROGRESSION

Blake's worldview did not only affect his views on religion and spiritual matters. The dividing line between the external and internal was extremely vague in his mind, as we have seen, and as a result, events in the external world were often seen as being interchangeable with internal states. This had a profoundly human impact on his political ideas.

5.

THE TYGERS OF WRATH

In the eyes of political historians, the eighteenth century is about as wild and exciting as it gets. An explosion of new, radical political ideas caused unprecedented upheavals in global power and still affect our lives today. Such epoch-changing ideas often emerged in strange and unlikely ways.

In 1749, for example, the Genevan philosopher and musician Jean-Jacques Rousseau visited his friend Denis Diderot, who was then held captive in the fortress of Vincennes in Paris. Idly thumbing through a book as he walked, Rousseau was overwhelmed by a wave of inspiration. 'Suddenly I feel my spirit dazzled by a thousand brilliant insights,' he later wrote. 'A host of ideas crowd in upon me all at once, troubling my mind with a force and confusion impossible to express. I feel my head spinning with a giddiness like intoxication. A violent palpitation oppresses and expands my breast.'

Unable to stand, he collapsed under a tree, powerless to avoid 'a flood of great truths which for the space of a quarter of an hour engulfed me in light'. This was a visionary experience with noetic qualities, as William James would have recognised. When he was finally able to get up and leave the safety of the tree, he found that his shirt was wet with tears that he had no memory of shedding. The key insight in his vision was that man was born good, and that it was the abuses of our society and institutions which turned him bad. This was a denial of the teaching of the Church, which claimed that we were born in a state of original sin. If it was true that there was no such thing as original sin and that people were born good, it logically followed that the world could be turned into paradise, if we just fixed or replaced our corrupting institutions.

This was revolutionary talk. The institutions of Church and State claimed divine authority. The king was on the throne because that was the will of God. In 1710, the German polymath Gottfried Leibniz had wrestled with the question of evil and concluded that we must be living in the 'best of all possible worlds', because an all-powerful God would permit nothing less. This position would be much mocked, not least by Voltaire in his 1759 novel *Candide*. If it was not true that this was the best of all possible worlds, then this meant that the world could be improved. And if Rousseau's vision was correct and the problem lay with society's institutions rather than the nature of man himself, then the route ahead became clear: institutions needed to be replaced. The first steps on the trail of logic that would lead to the French Revolution had been taken.

After his vision under the tree in Paris, Rousseau wrote a series of books in which he attempted to express what he had understood in those moments of inspiration. He later lamented that he had only managed to convey a quarter of that revelation, but it was still enough to cause huge upheavals in European politics. 'Man is born free and everywhere he is in chains,' began his book *On the Social Contract* (1762). 'One thinks himself the master of others, and still remains a greater slave than they.'

Those ideas were also explored in his novel *Julie, or the New Heloise* (1761), which went on to become one of the best-selling books of the century. Demand was so great that publishers could not print enough, and copies were made available to rent by the day or even by the hour. The Vatican put the novel on its *Index Librorum Prohibitorum*, its list of banned books, but this was no deterrent to the pre-revolutionary French. Readers were frequently overwhelmed by emotion and Rousseau became one of the first celebrity authors.

As the idea of man's innate goodness spread through culture, the old established class systems began to appear flawed, and people found themselves entertaining the spectre of revolution. Rousseau's ideas could not help but impact on Blake, although it should be no surprise by now to learn he would view them from a very different perspective to his contemporaries.

Rousseau died in 1778, over a decade before the French Revolution. He was honoured as one of the great thinkers of the Age of Enlightenment and an architect of the Revolution, and his remains were disinterred and placed in the Panthéon. But for all that he became seen as a great rationalist, and would be mocked by Blake for this reason, his arguments came to him in a single, blinding vision. As he wrote in *Emile* (1762), 'The world of reality has its limits; the world of imagination is boundless.'

In the summer of 1780, at the age of twenty-two, Blake encountered King Mob.

He was walking in the vicinity of Basire's house in Lincoln's Inn Fields when he found himself engulfed by an angry, violent crowd. This was made up, in Gilchrist's telling, of 'boys, pickpockets and "roughs" ', who were 'flushed with gin and victory' after destroying a number of Catholic chapels. Swept along by the mass of rioters, Blake found himself at the front of the mob as they surged towards the imposing prison at Newgate. The rioters attacked the gates with sledgehammers and pickaxes. The building was set on fire and the prisoners inside screamed in terror, fearing that they would be burnt alive. Fortunately, the mob swarming the building managed to rip open the roof and drag the prisoners out of their smoking cages. Three hundred convicts were set free, many shuffling off to liberty with their legs still bound in heavy chains. As the historian Christopher Hibbert described the chaos: 'Showers of sparks and pieces of red-hot metal shot up into the sky as iron bars and flaming beams and great hunks of elaborate masonry tumbled with a "deafening clangor... on to the pavement below." While all the time the screaming, wild, triumphant figures of the "demoniac assailants" added the final touch of horror to the inferno-like scene.'

On 2 June, around 50,000 Protestants had descended on the Houses of Parliament, to protest at a Catholic relief bill that allowed Catholics to serve in the armed forces. Events quickly turned ugly as protestors abused and beat members of the House of Lords and attacked their carriages. This was the start of a week-long period of the most destructive rioting in London's history. Catholic churches and the houses of establishment figures were methodically looted, burnt and destroyed, while the prisons and breweries were opened and Irish communities attacked. Each night the flames around the capital 'got to such a height that the sky was like blood with the reflection of them', as Lady Anne Erskine wrote in a contemporary letter. By the end of the week, hundreds of bodies had washed up in the Thames and the army were attempting to calm the protests by methodically shooting into crowds.

The Gordon Riots, as they became known, were named after Lord George Gordon, the President of the Protestant Association who arranged the original protest. George Gordon was the sixth and youngest son of the Duke of Gordon, a family of which Prime Minister Robert Walpole had said, 'They were, and are, all mad.' George Gordon was sent away as a child and bullied at Eton, then entered the Navy where he was considered 'a damned nuisance wholly unsuitable for promotion'. A seat in parliament was subsequently bought for him, where he was considered something of a joke. Privileged, narcissistic and generally mediocre, personalities like Gordon are sadly familiar in the history of populist violence. He had not intended for things to get so out of hand, of course, but he had stoked popular anti-Catholic prejudices with no concern for the consequences. By the time the Gordon Riots burnt themselves out, at least 850 people were dead.

Newgate was the first prison to be targeted, although all London jails would be attacked before the week was out. It was chosen as the first to be liberated because four protestors who had been arrested were incarcerated there. The liberation of the Newgate prisoners was both a rescue mission and a rejection of the establishment's legal authority. On the walls of the burning prison was painted a declaration: these prisoners had been freed, it said, by the authority of 'His Majesty, King Mob'. In times of revolution the people were sovereign, in all their fire and noise and anarchy.

London was a dangerous place that week. Dozens of burning buildings lit up the evenings. The nights echoed with the screams and clatter of pitched battles between the mob and whatever inadequate militia could be raised to face them. Householders chalked 'No Popery' on their doors, in the hope that this anti-Catholic slogan would please the mob and spare their homes from the fire. As the week progressed, however, the logic and aims of Gordon's original protest were forgotten. Violence and chaos spread with little reason or intent.

For an anxious and sensitive young man like Blake, the experience must have been traumatic. His life had been in danger both during the storming of Newgate and afterwards. Had he been recognised by a soldier, he might have been hanged with other protestors at Tyburn. Of the twenty or thirty people who were tried and executed, many were boys under the age of fourteen. 'I never saw boys cry so!' recalled one witness of their hanging.

The Gordon Riots took place in the explosive years between the American Declaration of Independence and the French Revolution, when old structures of power were being attacked by new ways of thinking and the establishment was prepared to be ruthless to defend itself. That Blake's times were unstable is evident in his work, and he is usually portrayed as a political radical and revolutionary. His presence at the burning of Newgate is often cited as evidence. But being caught up in revolutionary times is not in itself evidence of political activism. The Gordon Riots were the product of populist anti-Catholic prejudice, and their modern-day equivalents would be far-right anti-Muslim protests. There is no evidence that Blake himself shared those views, and they hardly fit with his belief that 'every thing that lives is Holy'. He appears to have been drawn into the Gordon Riots by chance, and remained for reasons of curiosity or horror rather than sympathy for the cause.

For Blake, what was significant about the Newgate burning was not the politics that drove it, but the terrifying adrenaline rush of the experience. He knew that the fire of revolution burns to some extent within all of us. It is the will to overthrow, to destroy, and to wipe the current situation from the face of history. King Mob usually sleeps, but he still dwells within our psyches.

Blake's response was to personify this aspect of us. He gave this spirit the name Orc. Orc plays a prominent role in the work Blake produced during the revolutionary 1790s, from his illustrated manuscripts to watercolours such as *Los and Orc* (*c*.1792–3).

Orc's arrival coincided with an important development in Blake's art. Like other artists and writers of the time, his early work relied heavily on established mythology and characters taken from classical or biblical sources. From around 1790 onwards, however, a new mythology of his own devising starts to emerge. Although he is not specifically named, the 'new born terror howling' born in the last section of *The Marriage of Heaven and Hell* (1790) is usually interpreted as Orc. It is not hard to imagine that Blake's experience at Newgate had a profound influence on how he was depicted. He describes how a king was confronted by the newly born spirit of revolution and:

> [...] hurl'd the new born wonder thro' the stary night.
> The fire, the fire, is falling!
> Look up! look up! O citizen of London [...]
> The fiery limbs, the flaming hair, shot like the sinking sun into
>   the western sea.
> Wak'd from his eternal sleep, the hoary element roaring fled
>   away:
> Down rushd beating his wings in vain the jealous king: his grey
>   brow'd councellors, thunderous warriors, curl'd veterans,
>   among helms, and shields, and chariots horses, elephants:
>   banners, castles, slings and rocks,
> Falling, rushing, ruining! buried in the ruins [...]
>   crying
> Empire is no more! and now the lion & wolf shall cease.

Orc is fire, violence and destruction, because that is what is needed to overthrow the 'lion & wolf', or the king and his armies. In a few short years the French ruling dynasty would find this out for themselves.

Orc appears in several of Blake's works written or begun in the 1790s, including *America, Europe, The Book of Urizen* and *The Four Zoas*. Like the rest of Blake's mythology, the story of this character must be pieced together from multiple different works which can often be contradictory. It is not the case that Blake conceived of his immense mythology as a complete, perfect thing, and then spent decades recording it. Rather, he was constantly trying to understand the energies that these characters represented. He did this by placing them in differing combinations, to observe and record their conflicts.

Orc was frequently explored as the contrary of Urizen, because the engine of progress was often powered by the dynamic struggle between ordered convention and the fire of revolution. Orc was also the serpent in the Garden of Eden, tempting Eve by recognising her repressed desire for power and knowledge. Orc is deeply anti-authoritarian. He justifies his furious destruction on the grounds that it is the only way we can overthrow what keeps us down and prevents us from reaching our true potential.

In *The Four Zoas* (1797–1807), Orc was bound by his parents on top of a mountain with a 'Chain of Jealousy'. His limbs, the rock, the chain and the vegetation all knotted together, permanently trapping him physically, but leaving his fiery imagination free to spread throughout the world. The binding of an energy was, for Blake, always a tragedy, but he recognised and understood the necessity of suppressing Orc's revolutionary fire. He also knew that an energy like Orc would always burn itself out in time.

Blake's examination of Orc in his writing was an attempt to discover where the desire for revolt came from. Orc was the child of Los, who represents the imagination, and Enitharmon, who represents spiritual beauty. In theory, Orc should be the creation of something new and wonderful. But Orc, having been bound by those 'chains of Jealousy', was repressed or in shadow. As a result, he is the process by which love turns to war. In one account, the children of Los and Enitharmon are said to be characters representing wrath, pity, frustrated desire and logic. These, Blake suggests, are the constituent elements of Orc, the fiery spirit of revolution.

It wasn't that Blake was against revolution; he was delighted to see the people of France take power from King Louis XVI and Marie Antoinette. On one occasion he wore a red bonnet to show support for the republican cause, a risky act in those paranoid times. As he wrote, 'The tygers of wrath are wiser than the horses of instruction.' But for all that revolutions can sweep away the unjust and the tyrannical and can be necessary and unavoidable, they also have a dark aftermath. In practice, revolutions typically lead to a power vacuum which results in bloodshed and the rise of a powerful military leader, such as Napoleon or Cromwell. From Blake's accounts of Orc, we see that he understood this process clearly.

Blake had a far more profound and nuanced understanding of revolution than most of his contemporaries. The young Wordsworth visited Paris and famously eulogised the French Revolution: 'Bliss was it in that dawn to be alive / But to be young was very Heaven!' Enraptured, Wordsworth looked at the political upheaval with only hope and excitement. As a result, he was entirely unprepared for the Reign of Terror that followed. He responded by rejecting his earlier politics and came to value tradition and stability over calls for social justice that might lead to revolution.

Blake's understanding was different. He was not as concerned with the immediate political results of revolution, seeing it, like everything else, as the expression of mental energies. His primary interest was in the root causes of this part of our minds. Having a deeper understanding of its cause, he was more prepared for the darkness of its fallout.

When we think of Britain in the late eighteenth and early nineteenth centuries, what usually comes to mind is high society. Thanks to the novels of Jane Austen and others, and the popularity of TV adaptations, we imagine the era as a time of balls, bonnets and grand houses. We are aware that the Industrial Revolution was occurring at the time, of course, but few find this as fascinating as Austen's world of fashion and labyrinthine social politics. The wider politics of the era, from the clashes of the Whig and Tory parties to the Napoleonic Wars, the growth of colonialism and events such as the Peterloo Massacre, all tend to be secondary in the popular imagination.

. Because there is much more recorded information about those at the top of society, historians invariably spend more time analysing them. They are aware, of course, that the lack of sources detailing the lives of the poor majority gives a skewed picture of the age. One problem is that many of the surviving descriptions of the 'common' people come from those who described themselves as their 'betters'. This often painted a picture of forelock-tugging, happy subservience. This is one reason why the work of Blake can appear so at odds with its times. The politics he displayed in his work are notably different to those depicted in contemporary high society and establishment sources. They were not, however, entirely unprecedented, or unique to him.

There was a brief historical time when the political views of wider sections of society had been recorded. This was a period of a few decades before the English Civil Wars, when censorship broke down and the thoughts and ideas of the poor made it onto the printed record. Although this was over a century before Blake was born, it is striking how many of his ideas are identical to, and seem to originate with, seventeenth-century radicals. In order to understand Blake's political ideas, then, it is more productive to look further back in time and explore this English radical tradition than it is to examine the battles between the Whigs and the Tories in Blake's own time.

As the historian Christopher Hill has noted, the poor were not stupid, and resentment about the unequal structure of society had existed for centuries. In the seventeenth century, he writes, 'there was a greater background of class hostility in England before 1640 than historians have normally recognized'. Hill's work paints a picture of a recognisably British discontent, never far from the surface, which emerged from a population who saw themselves from a very different perspective to how they were imagined by the gentry. He portrays a people marked by a lack of deference, who were quick to display a distrustful or mocking attitude to the clergy and nobility.

One factor in this was the rise of what were called 'masterless men'. In the hierarchical medieval feudal system, it was assumed that men and women were loyal to the lord who owned the land they lived on. But large parts of the population were becoming increasingly mobile, moving around the country as opportunities for work dictated, and hence had no 'lord' to speak of. Masterless people were not just the traditional vagabonds or gypsies, but included itinerant craftsmen, labourers, actors and performers, traders, pedlars, foresters, the unemployed and demobbed soldiers. The American political theorist Michael Walzer has argued that the experience of being masterless was at the root of many religious and political changes, such as Puritan attitudes to self-reliance and inner discipline.

Once freed from rigid social hierarchy, masterless men and women could only look to themselves for guidance. In effect, they were forced to see themselves as their own masters. Many made their way to London, where they had more options to make a living. As early as 1602, it was estimated that there were 30,000 masterless men and women in London alone. This was a significant demographic, and their anti-hierarchical worldview would have made an impression on the wider London population. In a population that already had a healthy scepticism of the nobility, such views would not have been overly controversial.

As the country moved towards the English Civil Wars of the

mid-seventeenth century, these attitudes became increasingly wide-spread. As one account of the life and death of Charles I from 1651 noted: 'The present hatred of the citizens was such unto gentlemen, especially courtiers, that few durst come into the City, or if they did, they were sure to receive affronts and be abused.'

These anti-authoritarian attitudes were in part a reflection of the great religious changes that had taken place in the country. Before the dissolution of the monasteries, when England was a Catholic country, the Church was accepted as the source of spiritual authority. When the Protestant reformation arrived, it argued that it was the Bible itself, and not the Church, which we needed to look to for authority. Reformers pointed out that many aspects of Catholic worship and Church behaviour had no precedence in the Bible, most notably the buying and selling of pardons and indulgences to offset an amount of earthly sin. In this way, Protestants used the authority of the Bible to undermine and dismiss the Catholic Church's claims of authority. The Bible was understood to be a divinely inspired fixed text, so the assumption was that using it as a source of authority would produce clarity and harmony. It didn't work out like that.

After the Bible was translated into Early Modern English and became widely available and studied, it was soon apparent that it contradicted itself in numerous places. It was also a book that was frequently open to interpretation. At first, it was felt that the ensuing debates were a good thing, because people were thinking deeply about the Word of God and what it meant. It was hoped this would lead to a more enlightened and spiritual population. In practice, these arguments led to splits, disagreements and bitter repercussions.

Take a relatively simple issue such as baptism. Was baptism necessary in order to be saved? Did it require the willing par-ticipant of an adult, or could it be done to a baby? Did it require whole body immersion, as had been originally practised, or was a splash of water enough? There were many perspectives you could take, all of which were the sincere product of deep Bible study by committed Christians. These arguments can sound trivial from the perspective of the twenty-first century, but at the time the potential eternal damnation of the soul was considered to be at stake. With the stakes so high, people clung to their preferred interpretation and were often unwilling to compromise. And baptism is just one issue in the huge arena of ideas that constitutes Christian belief.

The result of looking to the Bible as the source of authority turned out to be the creation of countless different sects. Amid this confusion, some radical thinkers started to argue that the Bible itself shouldn't be thought of as the ultimate authority. Instead, we needed to look to the divine light within us for guidance. Because we needed to be free to listen to our hearts if we were to hear the Word of God, liberty of conscience became an issue of fundamental importance. For some groups, such as the Quakers or the Family of Love, this meant that the scriptures could only be properly understood by believers for whom the spirit of God lives within. Others went further and argued that, so long as you were moved by the divine spirit, the scriptures were not necessary and neither were priests and bishops. The visionary preacher Theaurau John Tany burnt the Bible at St George's Fields in the winter of 1654, arguing that 'the people say it is the Word of God, and it is not'. It is here, in the arguments of seventeenth-century theology, that the spark of individualism took hold.

To believe in individual conscience and to experience the light within was to realise that you were free. For the first time, people no longer had to worry about priests, magic, hell or even sin. A person who experiences the nature of Christ, this argument claimed, was incapable of sin. They were no longer bound by the 'Moral Law' of the Ten Commandments. Before Christ, people needed this Law in order to understand how to behave because they did not know any better – or so the thinking went. The Moral Law may have been a blunt tool, but it was a necessary part of Old Testament society. But once Jesus had entered the hearts of men, they knew what was good and how to behave without being told. At this point, the Moral Law became irrelevant. Some argued that for a true believer all law was irrelevant, both religious and secular. This position was called antinomianism, which means 'against law'. There is a strong antinomian streak in the work of William Blake.

Once theologians set off down this road, it led to some radical conclusions. Some denied the existence of sin altogether and claimed that it had been invented by priests and kings in order to keep men subjugated. Others practised what they preached and took the antinomian argument to the logical extreme. Being free from law and incapable of sin, they were free to indulge in as much drinking, sex, feasting, smoking and sport as possible, and made a point of doing so publicly. In this tradition, religious gatherings were frequently held in taverns. 'To be called a libertine is the most glorious title under heaven,' wrote the London-born antinomian clergyman Tobias Crisp. 'If you be freemen of Christ, you may esteem all the curses of the law as no more concerning you than the laws of England concern Spain.' As Crisp saw things, 'sin is finished'. A similar attitude is found in the introduction to Blake's epic poem *Jerusalem*. Here he writes, 'The Spirit of Jesus is continual forgiveness of Sin: he who waits to be righteous before he enters into the Saviours kingdom, the Divine Body, will never enter there. I am perhaps the most sinful of men! I pretend not to holiness! yet I pretend to love, to see, to converse.'

In the words of the Lancashire preacher Lawrence Clarkson, 'There is no such act as drunkenness, adultery and theft in God [...] What act so ever is done by thee in light and love, is light and lovely, though it be that act called adultery [...] No matter what Scripture, saints or churches say, if that within thee do not condemn thee, thou shalt not be condemned.' It is possible that there were some who made this argument who did not genuinely feel the light of Christ within themselves.

Although the name is very loosely defined in theological terms, those who favoured these extreme views were referred to as Ranters – usually by their enemies. They were frequently held up as a warning against heretical thought, even if a grudging admiration can sometimes be detected among the criticism. 'They are the merriest of devils for extempore lascivious songs [...] for healths, music, downright bawdry and dancing', explained one Puritan with perhaps a hint of jealousy. Blasphemy and swearing were great favourites of the Ranters, for they were a symbolic expression of freedom from social constraints and the liberty of conscience. The Ranter and writer Abiezer Coppe is said to have sworn for a solid hour in the pulpit. In 1652, a lady stripped naked during a service in the chapel at Whitehall while shouting, 'Welcome the resurrection!' In the heady atmosphere of the times, pigs and horses were heretically baptised. The Wiltshire rector Thomas Webbe, who had long shaggy hair and enjoyed music and mixed dancing, is said to have declared that 'there's no heaven but women, nor no hell save marriage'. He made this claim in his defence during his trial for adultery, for which he faced the death sentence.

It is in the ideas of the Ranters and their ilk that we find a tradition for the political views of Blake. Many historians have been confused to find those concepts still in circulation well over a century after their time. Much of our knowledge about these radical beliefs comes from a period between 1640 and 1660, when censorship broke down and subversive ideas were able to be published as cheap, popular pamphlets. After the monarchy was restored in 1660 and Charles II took the throne, extreme ideas like these seem to drop away from the historical record.

There are many reasons for this change, most obviously the desire for calm after the bloodshed of the civil wars. In the late seventeenth century, those listening to their inner light were unsurprised to find that it began to counsel pacifism. Unlike other religious heretics, the Ranters and radicals who were arrested and tried proved to be quite willing to recant their beliefs, if it meant they would not be put to death. Theirs was not a philosophy that pushed people towards martyrdom.

Some groups, such as the Quakers, moved away from their radical roots and gradually became respectable. Most Ranters were anarchistic individuals only loosely tied to established organisations, so it was easy for them to disappear. Society moved on from the austere Puritan years, for example by reopening the theatres, and Britain became more liberal and less judgemental. In this atmosphere, it was easy for ex-radicals to rejoin the established Church of England, which did not concern itself too deeply with the actual beliefs of its members. The Toleration Act, which became law in May 1689, granted a whole range of nonconformists the freedom to worship as their conscience dictated, just so long as they weren't atheists or Catholics. English Protestantism concluded that it would be better to be a broad church than a shattered and divided one. After the Restoration, the English radical tradition, at least as far as the establishment was concerned, simply faded away.

And yet, we find those ideas alive and well in the work of Blake over a century later. For example, the Family of Love, who were founded by the sixteenth-century mystic Henry Nicholas, preached that heaven and hell were to be found in this world, not the next. A group called the Family of the Mount rejected prayer and also thought that heaven and hell only existed in life. As far as they were concerned, heaven was when people laughed, and hell was sorrow, pain and grief. Groups such as the Anabaptists and the Diggers believed that all men were alike and that any differences between masters and servants were essentially manmade delusions with no religious support. The fourteenth-century English preacher John Ball was enthusiastically quoted during this time. In a sermon during the Peasants' Revolt, Ball had asked, 'When Adam delved and Eve span, who was then the gentleman?' The Digger Gerrard Winstanley equated heaven with mankind. As he wrote: 'There is no man or woman who needs to go to Rome nor to hell below ground, as some talk, to find the Pope, Devil, Beast or power of darkness; neither to go up into heaven above the skies to find Christ the word of life. For both these powers are to be felt within a man, fighting against each other.' These are all profoundly Blakean ideas.

There have been several attempts made to link Blake to surviving radical groups, such as the Muggletonians, in order to account for these similarities. Blake, however, was not one for joining groups and he resisted organised movements, either political or spiritual. Blake's knowledge of these ideas suggests that, although they disappeared from the historical record and were shunned by the universities and publishers of the eighteenth century, they did not vanish from the streets of London. His working-class nature and his lack of interest in fashion may have made him more drawn to old ideas than his wealthier and better educated peers, but those ideas were still in the air, being discussed, mocked or celebrated, whether the establishment was looking or not.

There are recorded incidents that give credibility to this idea. When Washington defeated Cornwallis in 1781 at Yorktown in the last major land battle of the American Revolutionary War, the British band are said to have played the old radical ballad 'The World Turn'd Upside Down' as they surrendered. The leading Methodist John Wesley recorded conversations with people in Birmingham during a tour of the Midlands in 1746 who held views identical to those of the Ranters, and who claimed that they were not bound by the law as they possessed the light of faith. Although the views seemed shocking to Wesley, they did appear considered and sincerely held. 'Have you also a right to all the women in the world?' Wesley asked, perhaps trying to catch the person out with an extreme position. 'Yes, if they consent,' came the reasonable reply.

The English radical tradition itself makes a good analogy to this situation. Many British people who were educated about history at school, and consume stories of British history through books and television, have never heard of the English radical tradition. It sits in the blind spot of establishment media, which is far more enthused about Tudors, Victorians and the Second World War. Yet it continues to this day, and can be found wherever politics and spirituality intersect, especially regarding issues of land ownership and popular authority. The writer C. J. Stone has traced the English radical tradition from the Diggers and Levellers of the seventeenth century, through Blake, and onwards through individuals like the socialist druid George Watson MacGregor Reid in the early twentieth century to the counterculture festivals founded in the 1970s.

Ultimately, there is no need to seek evidence of Blake's secret membership to arcane political groups in order to explain his use of these ideas. Instead, we simply need to recognise that his background differed to other writers and thinkers of his age. As a result, the ideas he was exposed to differed also. What matters is not how he knew about these ideas, but that he agreed with them.

In 1784, after Blake had gone into business with his fellow apprentice James Parker, he received commissions for engravings from the radical publisher and bookseller Joseph Johnson. Raised in a Baptist household in Liverpool, Johnson went on to become a

Unitarian who published and promoted many Unitarian and other religious works, as well as books on topics including medicine, poetry and children's literature. Unitarianism is the belief that God was not the trinity of the Father, Son and Holy Ghost, but instead just one being, which meant that Jesus could not have been a god incarnate. Johnson was steeped in the English radical tradition from his earliest years and he encouraged heretical thought for the rest of his life.

Johnson was famed for the regular weekly dinners he threw for open-minded or radical thinkers and writers. The food he served was simple and plain, but the guests were drawn to the events for the stimulating conversation and invigorating ideas they encountered. The 'Johnson circle' forged many friendships and helped shape the growth of religious toleration and humanitarian thinking. Those who are known to have attended included Tom Paine, Mary Wollstonecraft, Henry Fuseli and Joseph Priestley.

Given Blake's reputation as a political radical, together with his connection to Johnson, it is easy to imagine he would have been drawn to the Johnson circle. But Blake is thought to have attended only one of these dinners, and his personality was not ideally suited to polite society. He attended a different literary salon in the mid-1780s led by a patron of the arts called Mrs Matthews, who was initially supportive of Blake's writing. A fellow attendee, the writer John Thomas Smith, recalled that 'in consequence of his unbending deportment, or what his adherents are pleased to call his manly firmness of opinion, which certainly was not at all times considered pleasing by every one, his visits were not so frequent'.

The spirit of open-minded exploration and freedom of thought that Johnson's circle promoted was not of great interest to Blake. He did not need debate and conversation to help form his opinions. He already knew exactly what his position was. Socially he could be blunt or stubborn. He believed wholeheartedly in his own truth and did not see the need to discuss, test or refine his ideas. As he later explained, 'When I tell the truth, it is not for the sake of convincing those who do not know it, but for the sake of defending those that do.'

Although there is a story that Blake knew Tom Paine sufficiently well to warn him to leave the country in the 1790s, he did not generally mix with politically active people. Nor did he debate or campaign about specific issues. He was not known for his affiliations with political parties or support for particular candidates. Blake certainly had political and religious views which are easy to locate in his work, and he clearly deserves his place in the story of the English radical tradition. But politics was secondary for him; it informed his work, but was not the driving force behind it.

As far as Blake was concerned, the external world was an echo of the internal world. If you wanted to understand the politics of the material world, it was necessary to understand the energies of the mind. His works that appeared at first to analyse global history, such as *America a Prophecy* (1793) or *Europe a Prophecy* (1794), were as much concerned with his own mythological personifications of mental states as they were with actual history.

Blake was focused on his own reactions to global politics, rather than the details of the events themselves. To an extent, this is true of all political commentators, whether they recognise it or not. There are, however, degrees to which people focus on the outer and inner worlds. When Mary Wollstonecraft decided to write about the French Revolution, she travelled to Paris and risked her own life to observe events as they were happening. When Blake wrote about the French Revolution, he stayed home and looked inside himself. It may be tempting to mock his approach, but it produced some remarkable insights. His analysis of the impulses behind revolution, in the form of his character Orc, is a good example.

Instead of campaigning, Blake created. He spent long hours as a working engraver, fulfilling whatever commercial jobs came his way, as well as producing his own work. The act of engraving was laborious. It involved scratching intricate patterns of lines, dots, stippling or cross-hatching into a flat sheet of copper, a practice quite different to drawing with a pencil or brush. These scratches held ink after the copper plate had been wiped clean, so that when it was pressed against paper a black and white picture was reliably printed. Another technique was etching, in which a layer of wax was applied to the copper and the design drawn into it with a needle. A weak solution of nitric acid was then applied to the plate, which would burn into the copper where it had been revealed by the needle. Etching could be a less time-intensive, and therefore cheaper, technique to engraving.

Blake practised both, but he also developed an original technique of his own. This, he claimed, was given to him by the spirit of his beloved dead brother Robert. It involved painting directly onto a copper plate with a quill or brush dipped into acid-resistant varnish. The plate was then bathed with acid, and the parts of the surface which were not covered by varnish were eaten away. This allowed Blake to include both text and illustration on the same plate, perhaps entwined and part of the same design – something which could not be done through engraving and etching, which left space for a separate pass of type-set print. The difficulty with this technique was that the printed image would be the mirror-image of what was painted onto the plate, meaning Blake had to write all his text backwards. For the creative freedom that this technique allowed, Blake was quite prepared to learn the art of mirror writing. As his friend Cumberland noted, 'he alone excels in that art'.

Blake toiled away with his metal plates, acid and printing presses. He alludes to this practice in *The Marriage of Heaven and Hell*, explaining his vision 'by printing in the infernal method, by corrosives, which in Hell are salutary and medicinal, melting apparent surfaces away, and displaying the infinite which was hid. If the doors of perception were cleansed everything would appear to man as it is, infinite.'

As Blake saw it, his printing technique was a way to bring text from the eternal realm into the world of man. By dissolving the metal, he was revealing the infinity hidden within. In the same work he describes a 'mighty Devil', who we can easily interpret as Blake himself, using this technique to give infernal wisdom to humanity:

> I saw a mighty Devil, folded in black clouds, hovering on the sides of the rock: with corroding fires he wrote the following sentence now perceived by the minds of men, & read by them on earth.
>
> How do you know but ev'ry Bird that cuts the airy way,
> Is an immense world of delight, clos'd by your senses five?

Eighteenth-century printing was a complex job which involved many specialist tradesmen. One person wrote the book, another was responsible for editing it, and a third typeset the text. An artist designed illustrations for an engraver to produce, and a printer put each page through the press, once for text and a second time for the images. On occasions, these would be hand-coloured by another specialist, and finally a bookseller would sell the finished book. Thanks to Blake's new technique, he had the ability to do all these tasks himself. He was a one-person publishing industry, writing, designing, printing and colouring illustrated works of his own devising. Although he was still in the Georgian era, Blake was practising the 'do it yourself' ethos of punk rock.

Steeped in the antinomian tradition, Blake had escaped from the belief that other people had authority over him. He referred to such societal constrictions as the 'mind forg'd manacles' which keep so many of us down. Those who recognise no masters or leaders must lead themselves and take responsibility for their own life. By taking control of every aspect of the creation, production and publication of his works, Blake was free from compromise. He could express himself freely, constrained only by his own abilities.

Because the exercising of his creative abilities was so important to Blake, it is not surprising that a personified form of it has such a prominent role in his personal mythology. In his work, the character who represents the expression of the imagination in this world is known as Los. Typically portrayed as a blacksmith, Los is said to be endlessly labouring with his hammer at the furnace, constructing a city of art known as Golgonooza. This sense of creative effort as hard physical labour without end, forged by sweat, fire and determination, stands in contrast to images of refined aristocratic poets being visited by the graceful muses. It is, however, an apt description of Blake spending his entire life working with metal and acids.

The creation of art, as Los represents it, is not a pleasing pastime or mild entertainment. It is hard and necessary; it is the only way in which our world can be redeemed. In *Jerusalem*, Blake describes both himself and Los when he writes:

Trembling I sit day and night, my friends are astonish'd at me.
Yet they forgive my wanderings, I rest not from my great task!
To open the Eternal Worlds, to open the immortal Eyes
Of Man inwards into the Worlds of Thought: into Eternity
Ever expanding in the Bosom of God. the Human Imagination

Los can be seen as the hero of many of Blake's works, and his selfless labours are ultimately the cause of mankind's redemption, as we shall see. Los is smart and insightful, and he understands the nature of all, including himself. He knows, for example, that he exists in the human mind. In *The Four Zoas*, Los states that:

> Tho in the Brain of Man we live, & in his circling Nerves.
> Tho' this bright world of all our joy is in the Human Brain.
> Where Urizen & all his Hosts hang their immortal lamps

Blake's politics were encapsulated by Los. They existed in what he created. He may have had great empathy with the poor, but he did not spend his days working to better their situation. Instead, he believed that the imagination was the tool needed to improve society, and that the labours of Los would do more to liberate people than canvassing or protesting. To do this would take integrity, self-belief, and effort.

It is here that we find the strongest expression of Blake's politics. True politics are not ideologies to discuss, but an attitude to your relationship with the world which is enacted in your daily life. Your politics are not what you tell yourself you believe. They are not the set of ideas that you identify with, or look to for personal validation of your goodness as a human being. Your politics are expressed in the choices that you make, the way you treat other people, and the actions you perform. It is here that hypocrisy and vanity fall away, as the reality of your politics is revealed in the countless decisions that you make every day. Who you work for, whether you volunteer for charity work, if you become a landlord, whether you eat meat, the extent to which you pursue money and consumer goods – these are the types of decisions in which our true politics are expressed.

On a practical level, Blake needed commercial engraving work to keep a roof over his head. But he also needed to be free of compromise when it came to his own work. He produced his art as an individualist antinomian, asking no permission, answering to nobody – a position that we have come to understand better over the past couple of centuries. In Blake's time, however, these were radical politics indeed.

6.

CONVERSED NOT WITH DEVILS

One name that appeared frequently on the self-produced pages that rolled off Blake's printing press was Emanuel Swedenborg. For many, Swedenborg is an obscure figure, whose importance and fame have faded over the past two and a half centuries. In his own lifetime, he was respected as an engineer and proto-scientist who worked on designs for machines including a submarine, a form of machine gun and an aeroplane. Because of this, he is often described as the Scandinavian Leonardo da Vinci. In later life he underwent a profound spiritual change and claimed to have visited heaven, hell and alien worlds – perhaps the reason he is not better remembered for his many scientific achievements.

It is easy to see why Blake was drawn to the works of Swedenborg when he discovered them in the 1780s. Swedenborg had produced a body of philosophy and theology that seemed to support the reality of Blake's visions, and Blake studied his books seriously, making many notes and arguments in the margins. Swedenborg claimed that spirits left the body after death in order to enter the spirit world, where they become physically incarnate once more. This matched Blake's view on the post-death survival of spirits. Blake claimed to have seen his brother Robert's soul floating upwards as he left his body, for example, clapping his hands with joy.

The two men never met – Swedenborg died in 1772 at the age of eighty-four – although there is always the possibility that as a young boy Blake may have passed the ageing Swedenborg in the crowded streets of London. As we have noted, Blake was not one for joining societies, but we do know that he and his wife, Catherine, who we will meet more fully later, attended a five-day general meeting of the Theosophical Society in April 1789. This was a different organisation to the occult body of the same name that was formed in the Victorian era, and the purpose of the meeting was to establish 'the truths contained in the Theological Writings of the honourable Emanuel Swedenborg'.

To enter the assembly, the Blakes had to pass through a door marked with a quote that Swedenborg had seen in a vision: 'Now it is allowable.' The assembly produced a manifesto, which both William and Catherine signed and approved. It consisted of a list of thirty-two resolutions, including:

Swedenborg had a Divine Revelation.
The Old Church, which means all other churches, is dead.
The Old Church faith should be abolished.
The establishment of the New Church is good.
Miracles do not occur.
True conjugal married love is good.

This manifesto led to the establishment of the New Church, which was devoted to Swedenborg and his works. Despite their initial enthusiasm, however, the Blakes did not join the Church. Although Blake was at first attracted to Swedenborg's teachings, the more he studied them, the more he found fault, for reasons we will examine soon. Some of his most important works, most notably *The Marriage of Heaven and Hell*, were intended as criticisms of Swedenborg and his beliefs. For anyone attempting to understand those works and what they reveal about the mind of William Blake, an introduction to the ideas of Emanuel Swedenborg is extremely helpful.

Swedenborg was born Emanuel Swedberg, into a privileged family in Stockholm, Sweden, in 1688. His mother, Sarah, was the daughter of a wealthy mine owner, and his father, Jasper, was a theologian who would rise to the rank of bishop and be ennobled by the Swedish queen – hence the reason the family name changed in 1719, from Swedberg to Swedenborg.

Young Emanuel enjoyed the benefits of his fortunate position. He studied at Uppsala University and took a 'grand tour' through France, Germany, the Netherlands and England. His interest was in science and engineering, and the first half of his life was one of material productivity and success. He spent a few years publishing a scientific periodical entitled *Daedalus Hyperboreus* (*Northern Inventor*), which detailed new inventions. Swedenborg then worked as an assistant to Christopher Polhem, Sweden's most celebrated inventor, which led to him becoming friendly with King Charles XII. He wrote several books, particularly on subjects such as chemistry and mineralogy, and attained the lucrative position of Assessor of Mines for the Swedish government. He was probably the first person to recognise the existence and importance of neurons, cerebrospinal fluid, and the idea that stars circle the galaxy in a spiral motion. He became a member of parliament and travelled widely, meeting and conversing with the great minds of the time. It is often assumed that he also acted as a spy for the Swedish government.

In all outward appearances, Swedenborg was a sane, rational, productive citizen up until 1745, when he was fifty-seven years old. The spiritual side of his life, however, had been severely neglected. As he wrote in his journal: 'I, in spiritual things, am a stinking corpse.' This unbalanced self tipped him into a profound psychological crisis. Swedenborg began seeing spiritual entities, had visions of heaven and hell, and held long conversations with the dead. As Swedenborg's biographer Gary Lachman explains, 'the experiences Swedenborg went through during his crisis were harrowing, and ran the gauntlet from extreme psychological dread to almost painful ecstasy'.

The Swiss psychologist Carl Jung described experiences like this as *enantiodromial*. He defines enantiodromia as 'the emergence of the unconscious opposite in the course of time. This characteristic phenomenon practically always occurs when an extreme, one-sided tendency dominates conscious life; in time an equally powerful counterposition is built up which first inhibits the conscious performance and subsequently breaks through the conscious control.' In this way, Swedenborg flipped from being a rational, establishment figure into a full-blown visionary mystic, dedicated to expressing the truth of the spiritual realm.

It began with strange dreams. Swedenborg had been keeping an otherwise unremarkable journal to record his travels, but this suddenly changed after August 1743. Then we find blank pages, evidence of entries being torn out, and undated accounts of the dreams and trance-like states he experienced. He notes that he had almost entirely lost interest in both sex and science, which was unexpected, because these had been his two great enthusiasms in life. When Swedenborg resumes regular entries again, in March 1744, the book has become a dream diary – a record of his nocturnal travels rather than those taken during the day.

When these diaries were published in the mid-nineteenth century, with the title *Journal of Dreams*, the casual reports of several sexual dreams were considered profoundly shocking. They included, for example, two accounts of vaginas filled with teeth. With hindsight, this material is now taken as evidence that Swedenborg's detached, scientific mind was still at play, making an objective recording of the actuality of his dream life rather than prettying it up later.

After his interest in dreams, the visions began. It was as if by paying close attention to the inner workings of his mind, he had in some way woken it up. His inner world effortlessly transcended and overpowered the objective, detached worldview he believed he could maintain. Swedenborg found himself unable to reverse this change and return to what had previously been understood as normal. His great ambition had been to produce a scientific account of the soul, but, as Lachman notes, it became clear that 'he would never find the soul in the manner he had hoped he would, at the point of a scalpel or the end of a syllogism. It was a mistake even to think he would find it at all. Rather, it seemed that it had come looking for him.'

Swedenborg classified his visions into four distinct types of 'sight'. These differed in how vivid and overwhelming they were, rather than in terms of their actual content. The first type was 'the sight during sleep, as vivid as that of daytime, so that in sleep itself I would say that if this were sleep, wakefulness would also be sleep'. An unusually vivid dream, in other words, of the type that many people are familiar with.

The second type was 'with closed eye, which is as vivid as when the eyes are open, and like objects, even more beautiful and lovely, are offered to the sight'. One example of this second type of sight is hypnagogia, which is a transitional state between waking and sleeping, during which phenomena such as liminal dreaming and hallucinations can occur. Swedenborg himself was very fond of hypnagogia, and apparently had the ability to stay in that state for hours. He wrote that: 'Another vision is that between the time of sleep and the time of wakefulness, when the man is waking up, and has not yet shaken off sleep from his eyes. This is the sweetest of all, for heaven then operates into his rational mind in the utmost tranquillity.' He notes that similar visions can occur with the eyes open, which suggests the 'eidetic imagery' frequently associated with Blake mentioned earlier.

Swedenborg describes the third kind of sight as being 'when the eyes are open, and the things in heaven, both spirits and other things, are represented', adding that this type of sight 'differs entirely from the ordinary imagination'. This was a kind of sight that Blake knew well.

By the fourth kind of sight, it is no longer the angels that are appearing in the earthly realm, but Swedenborg himself who is being transported into the spiritual worlds. He stresses that he doesn't mean this as a dream, metaphor or a poetic description; the experience was one of physically being in heaven or hell. He 'enjoys all his senses, as that of touch, hearing and sight, and I have no doubt the other senses as well'. The sense of smell was certainly vivid in Swedenborg's descriptions of divine heaven and damned hell: 'It is a fuller sight than that of wakefulness, because more exquisite; and in that state one does not apperceive otherwise than that he is awake.'

It's worth noting here that Swedenborg was not immediately thrust into the spirit world, nor did he wake one day able to see angels. From his *Journal of Dreams* onwards, there had been a gradual strengthening of his imaginative faculties. Swedenborg's encounters with spirits occurred first in dreams, and then in the hypnagogic state between waking and sleeping. These meetings became increasingly vivid, and the boundary between the spiritual world and the material one increasingly permeable, until he started to see and talk with angels while awake. Finally, the visions became fully immersive, and he left the real world behind and entered the immaterial realm. His four types of visionary state, then, can also be described as an increase in the power of his imagination, as the contents of his inner world gradually leaked into, and then took over, his perception of the material world.

Swedenborg understood that all this was the product of the imagination, just as Blake did. He saw the imagination as something that could, with practice, be strengthened. If you desired an encounter with the numinous, therefore, it was advisable to work on improving your imagination.

The graduated scale of imagination that Swedenborg describes in these four kinds of vision sights recalls Blake's descriptions of single vision, twofold, threefold and fourfold sight. Although the similarities are striking, there are some differences between the two models. Blake is less interested in the world of dreams than Swedenborg, and he treats the visual appearances of spiritual beings as a normal, everyday occurrence. Here we might detect a difference in perspective between a man who experienced visions throughout his lifetime, compared to one who first gained them in his late fifties. Blake also views the blissful grace experienced in Beulah, his 'threefold sight', as being a distinct stage in itself, whereas Swedenborg, who was still enamoured by the visual aspect of his visions, categorises it as just a side effect of the hypnagogic state. These differences aside, the similarities between Blake's and Swedenborg's visions are hard to ignore.

To these similarities we can add the importance both men placed on the imagination of childhood. Although Swedenborg's life was largely rational, his parents recalled him playing with imaginary friends as a child, the existence of whom he seemed entirely convinced by. As we shall see, both men also connected the sexual imagination with the development of visionary sight.

The story of the unexpected visionary turn in Emanuel Swedenborg's life is a reminder that whatever strange chemistry was bubbling away in Blake's brain was not unique to him. It was something that other people could experience too – including rational, pragmatic people for whom the first fifty-seven years of their life were largely neurologically unremarkable. It can, in theory, happen to anyone, no matter how unremarkable they feel, when they are least expecting it.

According to Swedenborg, after the spirit leaves the body upon death, it finds itself physically incarnated in the world of the spirits. Claiming that something is 'physically' incarnated in the 'world of the spirits' sounds like a contradiction, but Swedenborg insists that this is exactly what happens. 'When we enter the spiritual world or our life after death, we are in a body as we were in this world. There seems to be no difference, since we do not feel or see any difference,' he wrote. 'We see the way we used to, we hear and talk the way we used to; we smell and taste and feel things when we touch them the way we used to; we want, wish, crave, think, ponder, are moved, love, and intend the way we used to.' Blake, of course, would remind us that what we experience of the exterior world is a model created in our minds. It is perhaps not so surprising, given this, that the spiritual realm could feel so similar.

After we arrive in the spiritual world after death, Swedenborg tells us, we 'can talk to anyone when we want to, to friends and acquaintances from our physical life, especially husbands and wives, and also brothers and sisters. I have seen a father talking with his six sons and recognising them. I have seen many other people with their relatives and friends.'

This social mingling and human-like existence does not last. The world of the spirits is a place in which earthly self-delusion falls away and the spirit truthfully faces up to its real nature. It is not possible to deceive anyone in the spirit world, least of all yourself. As a result, the recently deceased realise whether they belong in any of the three heavens above or the multiple hells below. The dead are not 'sent' or otherwise forced into these places. Instead they come to understand where they should be, and where they will be happiest.

While we can grow and evolve during our time on earth, in heaven our soul is fixed in the state it was in when we died. As Swedenborg puts it, 'after death we can no longer be reformed'. After souls climb the staircase to their chosen level of heaven or enter the caves that lead to the various hells, they no longer have the ability to mix with people whose souls belong on different levels.

Those who were selfish and caused pain and suffering to others make their way to their preferred hell, becoming demons in the process. Swedenborg describes the various hells as filthy, foul, stinking slums, riddled with violence and crime, yet this is where many people feel at home. Those in hell find it far more agreeable and pleasing than heaven. 'Just as we find delight in our own evil in this world we find delight after death in the stench that corresponds to our evil,' Swedenborg wrote in *Heaven and Hell* (1758), his best-known work. 'I heard one man who screamed aloud in utter torment at a breath of air from heaven, but was calm and happy when a breath from hell reached him.'

Our natural inclination towards heaven or hell is dependent on one factor: the extent to which we are focused on ourselves. Those whose thoughts and attention are predominantly turned inwards, onto what they want and what they can get, will find themselves more at home in hell than heaven. This was one of the reasons why Swedenborg found his spiritual awakening so traumatic, because he realised the extent to which 'self love' had been his guiding principle.

To gravitate to the various layers of heaven requires looking upwards and outwards, away from self-centredness and self-obsession, and focusing on the larger world that we are part of.

This causes a loss of the sense of self, because simple individuation falls away once we look at the bigger picture and focus on the unity we find there. This is an idea that fits well with Blake's belief that 'Self Annihilation' is necessary to encounter the divine. Our choice of hell or heaven, in other words, is a question of whether we prefer looking in the mirror or looking at the wider world. Regardless of which heaven or hell we choose, we always convince ourselves that our choice was the right one. A person who becomes more cynical and pessimistic as they age will tell themselves that they are becoming wiser, for example, even though in the eyes of others they are becoming bitter.

This voluntary self-selection described by Swedenborg has been, for many, difficult to accept. Surely, if we had free choice, we would all take the option of heavenly bliss rather than hellish suffering? Regardless of whether our understanding of how heaven and hell work comes from the teachings of the Church or from a sitcom like *The Good Place*, the idea that we might voluntarily choose to be damned can seem strange to us. In the online modern world, however, there is evidence that this is exactly how we behave, when we are left to our own devices. We see this in the choices people make about which forums and websites they choose to frequent; no one is forced to spend hours looking at lifestyle posts on Instagram, or to visit Mumsnet, 4chan, the *Mail Online* or indeed any of the countless niche interest discussion groups and comment boards available. We naturally gravitate to areas where we feel comfortable. Our choices may strike others as awful, just as the thought of spending hours in other people's chosen online arenas might fill us with horror. The internet, in this aspect, is Swedenborg's spiritual self-selection in action.

What is surprising about Swedenborg's descriptions of heaven is how similar it is to life on earth. No one in heaven is idle, and there is no lying around on clouds strumming harps for eternity. 'Such a life would not be active', he wrote, and, 'there is no happiness in life apart from activity'. This is an idea that Blake would approve of. Angels live in houses, eat food, hold down jobs and live together as married couples. In some circumstances the angelic husband and wife were the same people who were together on earth, but more commonly angels find that their true heavenly partner is someone they never met, or someone they failed to connect with, during their earthly lives. Swedenborg had seen his own future, heavenly wife in the spirit world – this was the Countess Elisabeth Stierncrona Gyllenborg, who was already married to another in this life. Perhaps this was why Swedenborg never married, despite having a string of mistresses throughout his life.

Our sex lives, Swedenborg insisted, did not end at death. They continued in the afterlife, where they improved wonderfully. Angelic congress was blissful and gloriously fulfilling and, Swedenborg insisted, 'mutually satisfying'. It left the post-coital angels feeling energised and renewed, and never frustrated or ashamed. Sex was so important in heaven that it was also, in some way that is hard to explain, continuous. Angels, Swedenborg tells us, are always engaged in the sexual act, a detail that certainly casts a few sections of the Bible in a new light.

Swedenborg's account of heaven has a perplexing relationship with time and space, which we will look at in more detail later. On one level, his heaven sounds exactly like earth, yet it is clear that things do not work in quite the same way. Whichever way an angel faces, it always faces God, he tells us, and it is impossible to stand behind an angel. Things are separated not by distance, but by association. In Britain, Land's End and John O'Groats are about as far apart as it's possible for British places to be, but because they are often linked together in people's minds they would be understood as being next to each other under the logic of heaven.

It is striking how many of the ideas in Swedenborg's books

appear in later works by artists and writers known for their engagement with the depths of consciousness. Swedenborg described the speech of angels, for example, as being quite unlike earthly language. 'Angels', he tells us, 'can say more in a minute than many can say in half an hour. They can also set down in a few words the contents of many written pages.' Anyone struggling to imagine how such language would work should read the epic Blakean novel *Jerusalem* (2016) by the English writer Alan Moore, who successfully manages to write exactly this type of angelic dialogue. He does this by using the same modernist techniques James Joyce applied in *Finnegans Wake*. Moore, incidentally, was unaware of Swedenborg's description of angel language at the time. A second example can be found in David Lynch's TV miniseries *Twin Peaks: The Return* (2017). It includes sequences in which the character of Dougie Jones, played by Kyle MacLachlan, keeps seeing a small floating flame, invisible to everyone else, which by its position indicates to him the correct course of action. Swedenborg also saw a stable, contained image of a flame, which he believed was a sign showing him he was on the correct path.

Once Swedenborg had moved into the spiritual period of his life, stories and rumours began to circulate claiming that he possessed paranormal abilities. Their accuracy is now impossible to judge, but such stories do give an insight into how he was seen at the time. He does not appear to have been overly mocked or rejected by society, as Blake was. If you are going to start talking about visions of heaven and hell, it helps if you are rich and well connected.

One story about Swedenborg's abilities took place after a meeting with Queen Louisa Ulrika of Sweden in 1758, during which she asked him to make contact with her deceased brother, Prince Augustus William of Prussia. The following day, Swedenborg approached the Queen and reported that he had done as she had asked. He passed on her brother's regards and also his apology for not answering her last letter. Swedenborg explained that her brother had asked him to pass on his reply. He then whispered something in the Queen's ear, which none of the court could hear. They could, however, clearly see the Queen's reaction. She went pale and was visibly shaken, and was reported to have exclaimed, 'No one but God knows this secret.'

On another occasion he was approached by the widow of a Dutch ambassador. The widow had received demands for payment for a silver tea service, which she was sure her husband had paid for before he died. Her problem was that she could not find the receipt and hoped that Swedenborg might be able to make enquiries in the spirit world. He returned a few days later and told her that the receipt was in a bureau that the widow had already searched. He explained that the bureau contained a secret drawer and passed on her late husband's instructions on how to find this hidden compartment. The receipt proved to be where Swedenborg had claimed. What particularly amazed the ambassador's widow was that, she believed, no living person had known about the existence of the secret drawer.

An incident which served to further publicise Swedenborg's abilities occurred at a dinner in Gothenburg, on the western coast of Sweden, on 19 July 1759. At six o'clock he suddenly stood up and left the party. He returned looking pale and shaken, claiming that a fire had broken out near his house in Stockholm, hundreds of miles away on Sweden's east coast. The fire had started in the Södermalm district, and it was moving towards his home. During the next couple of hours he remained anxious, and reported that the fire was destroying the home of a friend and near neighbour. At eight o'clock, however, his mood lifted. He announced that the fire had been extinguished just three houses away from his own. News of this incident quickly spread, and Swedenborg was summoned to see the Governor the following morning to describe what he 'saw' of this fire. Two days later, a messenger arrived from Stockholm, carrying a message from the Board of Trade. It contained a description of a fire in Stockholm that matched Swedenborg's vision, down to details such as it being extinguished at eight o'clock.

In early 1772, when Swedenborg was eighty-four years old, he wrote a letter to the preacher and founder of Methodism, John Wesley, after being informed in the spirit world that Wesley wished to speak to him. Wesley replied that he did indeed desire an interview. He was about to embark on another of his lengthy preaching tours of the country, but he would be delighted to come and see him when he got back. Swedenborg replied that this was a great shame. He would not be available to meet Wesley on his return, because Swedenborg knew he was due to die in a month's time, on 29 March 1772.

A serving girl in the house in which Swedenborg was staying, Elizabeth Reynolds, also said that he had told her the exact date of his own death. She said that he seemed as happy about it as if he was 'going on holiday or to some merrymaking'. On the morning of the predicted day, he was ill in bed, and visited by his friend Pastor Ferelius. Realising that time was short, Ferelius asked Swedenborg if he wanted to recant. There were those who thought that everything he had written was mere invention, created to bring Swedenborg fame and notoriety. Was there anything, perhaps, that he wanted to confess to God?

Swedenborg raised himself up on his bed, put his hand on his heart, and said, 'As truly as you see me before your eyes, so true is everything that I have written; and I could have said more had it been permitted. When you enter eternity you will see everything, and then you and I shall have much to talk about.'

He died that afternoon, as predicted.

*

It might be assumed that Blake would have been a lifelong supporter of Swedenborg's work. It argued, after all, for the reality of the angels and spirits that Blake regularly communed with, offering a readymade defence against claims that he was deluded or mad. But Blake wasn't looking for a defence. The spiritual world was so self-evidently real to him that he felt no need to argue for it. If someone thought there were no angels to be found in London, that was their problem.

Blake's notes in the margins of Swedenborg's books are considered and respectful, with phrases like 'Mark this' or 'Excellent' next to passages found to be particularly important. Blake could also be pleasingly waspish, for example by amending a section about the unknown nature of man with the comment, 'This was known to me & thousands.'

The more Blake studied Swedenborg's writings, however, the more doubts he began to have. While there was much in Swedenborg that Blake recognised and accepted, there were also elements that he did not agree with. The idea that someone could be granted visions and yet still get things wrong was troubling.

As a source of authority, Blake looked to his own experience and nothing more. If anything differed from this, it was by definition wrong. Seeing as pretty much every philosophy and system differed from his experience, he had no choice but to reject them all. As he would write in *Jerusalem*:

I must Create a System, or be enslav'd by another Mans
I will not Reason & Compare: my business is to Create

In 1790, Blake began work on an illustrated book that serves as a critique of Swedenborg. In attempting to explain where Swedenborg was wrong, Blake produced an account of his own theology that was short, profound, funny and shockingly out-rageous. Its title alone defines his main difference of opinion with the Swedish mystic. Swedenborg's best-known and most readable book was titled *Heaven and Hell*. In reaction, Blake gave his work the theologically extraordinary title of *The Marriage of Heaven and Hell*.

For Swedenborg, heaven and hell were different and separate things. A soul after death would know one but could never know the other. Blake, in contrast, joined the two in holy wedlock because, as he scribbled in the margins of one of Swedenborg's books, 'Heaven & Hell are born together.' His love of contraries and the dynamic tensions between them were found to be sorely lacking in Swedenborg. As he saw it, the concept of heaven without hell, or hell without heaven, was meaningless.

Blake found absurd the idea that a human soul could know one but not the other, because heaven and hell were both internal states. An individual would no doubt favour one over time, but both were always available. A kind, compassionate individual always had the opportunity to dive gleefully into the selfish world of isolated individualism, just as a cruel-hearted narcissist could awaken at any moment to the peace and light of selfless unity.

The Marriage of Heaven and Hell begins with the bombastic, heavy metal line 'Rintrah roars & shakes his fires in the burdend air'. Here Rintrah is the personification of just wrath. Blake, clearly, is not mess-ing around. The poem that follows is a warning about false gurus, which is easy to read as an attack on Swedenborg's supporters. It details a just man being led away from the correct path into barren climes, while the trickster who laid the false path feigns innocence:

Now the sneaking serpent walks
In mild humility.
And the just man rages in the wilds
Where lions roam.

After the warning of this tone-setting prelude, Blake wastes no more time and gets down to business. The next page begins with a couple of sentences which, for most modern readers, will need unpicking:

> As a new heaven is begun, and it is now thirty-three years since its advent: the Eternal Hell revives. And lo! Swedenborg is the angel sitting at the tomb; his writings are the linen clothes folded up.

To help us out Blake wrote '1790', the date he composed that first line, above it in the copy of the book owned by his patron Thomas Butts. Thirty-three years before 1790 was 1757. According to Swedenborg, the Last Judgment – that much debated staple of Judaic, Christian and Islamic thought – had already happened, and took place in the year 1757. Most people didn't notice because it occurred exclusively in heaven, he claimed, although the spiritual transformation it generated would, in time, affect all of humanity.

The year 1757 was, therefore, when a new form of consciousness appeared on earth and, it just so happened, it was also the year that William Blake was born. You can imagine how this scenario pleased him. While he was quick to dismiss Swedenborg in areas that he disagreed with, he had no problem with his ideas when they appealed. In these lines, he declares this new era to be hellish and specifically identifies Swedenborg as the angel who announces it. For Blake, of course, 'hellish' is not necessarily a bad thing, especially when he wanted to balance Swedenborg's pro-heaven prejudice. Swedenborg's writings are described as 'linen clothes folded up', suggesting dry, dusty, corpse-like ancient texts, and not the vibrant living words that we now needed. You won't find any exclamations like 'Rintrah roars!' in Swedenborg.

Blake does not hide or sugar-coat his issues with Swedenborg:

Now hear a plain fact: Swedenborg has not written one new truth: Now hear another: he has written all the old falsehoods.

And now hear the reason. He conversed with Angels who are all religious, and conversed not with Devils who all hate religion, for he was incapable thro' his conceited notions.

Unlike most of Swedenborg's critics, Blake was not questioning the reality of Swedenborg's visions. Instead, he argued that his accounts of them were flawed and of little value. They suffered from the limitations inherent in the worldview of successful, privileged authority figures. Swedenborg was too comfortable in his own reality tunnel to question how limited it was. We all have our blind spots, of course, but not everyone wants to discover them.

To show what Swedenborg was missing, Blake dedicated much of *The Marriage of Heaven and Hell* to exploring infernal wisdom and knowledge. He includes a lengthy section called 'Proverbs of Hell', which lists the sayings he heard when he was 'walking among the fires of hell, delighted with enjoyments of Genius; which to angels look like torment and insanity'. The hellish proverbs include some of his most quoted lines:

The road of excess leads to the palace of wisdom.
The cut worm forgives the plow.
A fool sees not the same tree that a wise man sees.
Prisons are built with bricks of Law, Brothels with bricks of
    Religion.
What is now proved was once, only imagin'd.
One thought. fills immensity.
The tygers of wrath are wiser than the horses of instruction
Expect poison from the standing water.

You never know what is enough unless you know what is more than enough.

If others had not been foolish. we should be so.

The 'Proverbs of Hell' also includes statements that you might think belonged to a more heavenly culture:

The most sublime act is to set another before you.
The bird a nest, the spider a web, mankind friendship.
The soul of sweet delight. can never be defil'd.

These proverbs were intended to be universal truths. They may contain wisdom that you won't hear from the mouths of angels, but that doesn't stop them from being true.

Blake included accounts of meetings with angels, but the stories were chosen to display the limits and failings of angelic understanding. As he confessed, 'I have always found that Angels have the vanity to speak of themselves as the only wise; this they do with a confident insolence sprouting from systematic reasoning.' To modern eyes, there is something very funny about a sentence as otherworldly and profound as this starting with the mundane phrase 'I have always found...' It is tempting to suspect that he was mocking Swedenborg, who displays a very similar attitude in his written accounts of heaven and hell. It seems more likely, though, that the similarity of prose stems from similar experience. As we know, to both Blake and Swedenborg, visions were everyday experiences. Even conversations with angels can become commonplace.

Having expressed the failings of Swedenborg's limited understanding, Blake has no choice but to set out how things are, at least as he sees them. It is this which makes *The Marriage of Heaven and Hell* so important, raising it above a literary spat. Blake does not argue for his personal perspective; he simply states it as fact. It is from this work that we get some of the clearest statements of his philosophy, many of which we have already talked about or will discuss soon:

> Without Contraries is no progression.
> Energy is Eternal Delight
> Those who restrain desire, do so because theirs is weak enough to be restrained
> Opposition is true Friendship.
> Thus men forgot that All deities reside in the human breast.
> God only Acts & Is, in existing beings or Men.
> For every thing that lives is Holy
> Man has no body distinct from his Soul for that called Body is a portion of Soul.

The Marriage of Heaven and Hell repeatedly highlights the importance Blake places on contraries. For example, at one point he divides humanity into two types of people: the Prolific, who produce and create, and the Devourers, who consume. Other writers might praise the Prolific and condemn the Devourers, but Blake understands that both types are needed to keep the world turning: 'These two classes of men are always upon earth, & they should be enemies; whoever tries to reconcile them seeks to destroy existence.' Not one to miss a sharp kick at religion, he adds, 'Religion is an endeavour to reconcile the two.'

For all that Blake argues that both these opposites are needed, he doesn't do so in a way that those of us raised in the postmodern twentieth century might expect. He is not saying that both are in some way equal, neither is he taking a relativistic approach about their virtues. When he stresses the wisdom of hell, he is not saying that there is no difference between heaven and hell. Nor is he arguing that they are both as bad as each other. He writes very clearly that: 'Good is Heaven. Evil is Hell.'

For Blake, stressing the need for contraries in no way disturbed his moral compass. If anything, recognising that things do not make sense without their opposites – whether that is heaven and hell, love and hate, spirit and matter or the Prolific and the Devourers – automatically highlights which way this moral compass should face. Should you focus on heaven and ignore hell, you mistakenly believe that heaven is everything. If you understand both, in contrast, you truly grasp why it is you choose to face heaven. Blake never forgot that it was the dynamic struggle between the two that matters, for this is the power that turns the engines of the universe. This is what keeps creation alive, vibrant and constantly dancing. This is why anyone who 'tries to reconcile them seeks to destroy existence'.

Swedenborg could only agree with heaven. Hellish thought was invisible to him. Blake grasped both, rejected neither and, by marrying heaven and hell, truly understood good and evil.

Thus wept the Angel voice & as he wept the terrible blasts
Of trumpets, blew a loud alarm across the Atlantic deep.
No trumpets answer; no reply of clarions or of fifes,
Silent the Colonies remain and refuse the loud alarm.

On those vast shady hills between America & Albions shore;
Now barrd out by the Atlantic sea: call'd Atlantean hills;
Because from their bright summits you may pass to the Golden world
An ancient palace, archetype of mighty Emperies,
Rears its immortal pinnacles, built in the forest of God
By Ariston the king of beauty for his stolen bride.

Here on their magic seats the thirteen Angels sat perturb'd
For clouds from the Atlantic hover oer the solemn roof.

7.

ONCE, ONLY IMAGIN'D

For Blake and Swedenborg, the imagination was a faculty which could be exercised and strengthened, and which ultimately became a path to the land of vision. But what, exactly, do we mean when we say 'imagination'? It is a common, everyday word, yet tricky to define. Examining what has been written about the imagination over the years, it is clear that the concept is understood in a number of different ways.

Many notable figures have described the imagination in exulted terms. The French poet Charles Baudelaire called it 'the queen of the faculties' and insisted that 'Imagination created the world'. Pablo Picasso told us that 'Everything you can imagine is real'. In the eyes of the Pulitzer Prize-winning American poet Wallace Stevens, 'imagination is the only genius'. The British philosopher Owen Barfield, who founded the Inklings writers group with C. S. Lewis and J. R. R. Tolkien, warned of the need for a 'responsibility of the imagination', based on the awareness that things we imagine in our minds do not necessarily stay there. The great proto-feminist author Mary Wollstonecraft wrote that: 'The imagination is the true fire, stolen from heaven, to animate this cold creature of clay, producing all those fine sympathies that lead to rapture.' In 1931, Albert Einstein wrote that: 'Imagination is more important than knowledge. For knowledge is limited, whereas imagination embraces the entire world, stimulating progress, giving birth to evolution.'

Claims like this are usually made by artists, poets, mystics and the occasional scientist of rare genius. They serve as a reaction against the opposing trend in Western thought, which is more frequently expressed by philosophers, intellectuals, politicians or academics. This tradition argues that the imagination is of little value compared to the rational intellect. Imagination, from this perspective, is just the brain at play. It is entertaining in its own way but of no real use.

This dismissal goes all the way back to Plato, whose dialogue *Phaedo* included the argument that 'a theoretical inquiry no more employs [mental] images than does a factual investigation'. In Platonic philosophy, imagination belonged on the lowest rank of mental faculties. Aristotle also argued that 'imaginings are for the most part false'. Later philosophers took a similar dismissive view. The English philosopher John Locke argued that there 'was nothing in the mind that was not first in the senses'. The German philosopher Edmund Husserl did not see imagination as a 'productive' act, because measurable things that exist externally, in time and space, were important in a way that things that exist internally were not. This way of thinking was, according to Husserl, 'the natural standpoint'.

Perhaps the philosopher most dismissive of imagination was the French existentialist Jean-Paul Sartre, who viewed the world of imagination as a non-existent 'anti-world'. According to Sartre, imagination was a 'nothingness of being' that could not be cured of its 'essential poverty'. His stance was more than a little disingenuous, however, as he had personal experience of imagination's vividness and power. In 1926, Sartre took what turned out to be, with hindsight, an excessive dose of mescaline. As a result, he spent many years hallucinating sea creatures, who made a nuisance of themselves while he attended to his duties. As he told the political science professor John Gerassi in 1971, 'after I took mescaline, I started seeing crabs around me all the time. They followed me in the streets, into class. I got used to them. I would wake up in the morning and say, "Good morning, my little ones, how did you sleep?" I would talk to them all the time. I would say, "OK, guys, we're going into class now, so we have to be still and quiet," and they would be there, around my desk, absolutely still, until the bell rang.' That Sartre had to persuade figments of his imagination not to be noisy during lectures suggests that they should be regarded as something more than nothing. Of course, Sartre took the view that everything suffered from a lack of meaning or value, and he was never going to make an exception for imagination.

Opinions on what imagination is and how it should be valued have clearly varied wildly over the centuries. It may seem curious that what some consider to be the most vital aspect of our minds should be seen by others as so unimportant. This does, however, serve as a reminder of the extent to which the world as we perceive it is a self-portrait. Philosophers and intellectuals are proud of their rationality and believe that the external world works logically. Artists, on the contrary, value their imagination, and perceive the world to be a place where it is of primary importance.

The difference of opinion is heightened because we have traditionally had difficulty defining exactly what imagination is. In many accounts, imagination, fantasy, hallucination, consciousness and even memory blur into one another, and the terms are sometimes used interchangeably. The American philosopher Edward S. Casey is one of the few academics who have attempted to define what we mean when we talk of imagination. According to Casey, much of the philosophic and artistic discourse around the subject is vague, undefined and can safely be discarded.

Casey believed that the arguments among Greek philosophers about where imagination ranked in the scheme of mental faculties were essentially meaningless. The hierarchical models of mind used in the classical world fail to understand that the brain is a network, with different facilities interacting with and affecting each other at the same time. 'A recognition of the multiplicity of the mental', he argues, 'must replace a vertical view of the mind if we are to avoid the harmful consequences of thinking in exclusively hierarchical terms.' Casey also believed that poets have overstated the association between imagination and creativity. While the two terms are clearly linked, they do not refer to the same phenomenon. It is possible for imagination not to be creative; many everyday acts of imagination prove to be banal and repetitive.

Imagination, Casey tells us, is unusual in that it is separate from other forms of thought. Memory, perception and abstract intellectualising easily flow into each other, but an act of imagination is a stand-alone experience. It can be either spontaneous or self-controlled, and it occurs in the mind in imaginal space and time, on a mental stage.

In a similar manner to Swedenborg, Casey classified acts of imagination into different types, which he called 'imaging', 'imagining-that' and 'imagining-how'. The three names are so similar that they are easily confused, but Casey's categories do provide considerable insight into how imagination becomes deeper and more powerful.

Imaging, Casey's first category, is when you bring something to mind. You might, for example, mentally produce an image of the detective Sherlock Holmes. This usually presents itself in the mind's eye as the image of a thin-faced man with a deerstalker hat and a large magnifying glass in his hand, although the actual form this image might take will vary from person to person. Some might see an image of the actor Benedict Cumberbatch in modern clothes, for example, while others may see the character from the Sidney Paget illustrations that originally accompanied Arthur Conan Doyle's stories. Some will see a still image while others will see a moving one, but all will have a self-contained image of Sherlock and nothing else. We are unlikely to imagine a world around this character, unless we actively decide to conjure one.

Imaging is usually visual, but the term also applies to other sensory acts of imagination, such as imagining bird sounds or the smell of fresh coffee. We not only see with the mind's eye, we can also smell with the mind's nose and taste with the mind's tongue. Sherlock Holmes can also be brought to mind in an abstract way, with no visual or other sensory aspects, because we can experience non-sensory imaging as well, as we will see later.

After imaging comes imagining-that. Not just the simple act of bringing a specific single object or person to mind, it is about imagining a more complex scene, with specific dynamics and relationships being acted out among its constituent parts. It is what Casey calls 'a state of affairs'. Imagining Sherlock Holmes and Professor Moriarty struggling above the Reichenbach Falls is an example of imagining-that. It is a scene that plays out over time, and one which is possible to imagine unfolding in numerous ways. Imagining-that is more complex than imaging, although it is still a scene that we witness in our mind, as if we were a nearby, impartial observer. In this scenario, the mind is watching the mind.

Imagining-how is more complex still. It involves working out the details of how a scene is going to develop in real time, perhaps to rehearse a task or solve a puzzle. The person doing the imagining does not remain a separate entity who objectively views the action from a distance in their mind's eye. Instead, they place themselves in the scene. They become an active participant, deciding how to feel, think, act or behave in the scene as it unfurls. An example would be imagining how you could escape from Moriarty's attack above the waterfall, if you were Sherlock Holmes. You could imagine how the detective might grab on to a tree branch as Moriarty goes to push him over the edge, leaving him dangling over the side but avoiding the fall. Or perhaps you imagine how you as Sherlock elegantly sidestep Moriarty's attack, resulting in your nemesis toppling alone over the falls.

In imagining-how, it is necessary to enter the scene either as yourself or, as in this case, as a surrogate for a different character. The difference between imagining-that and imagining-how is like moving from watching a film to donning a virtual reality headset and playing a game. In this way, you can try out scenarios and rehearse different approaches for dealing with a situation. Again, imagining-how can occur using the mind's eye or other senses, or it can occur non-sensuously; for example, when a computer programmer imagines how an algorithm they are writing will work.

As we move from imaging to imagining-that and imagining-how, the act of imagination grows in complexity. We find ourselves being drawn into it, moving from passive observer to active participant. We are no longer the audience watching the mind, but an actor taking part in the play. This development mirrors that reported by Swedenborg during his journey from dreaming scientist to full-blown mystic. The contents of his imagination became more complex and compelling, until he fell into them completely.

Casey, then, shows how imagination is not a single, fixed activity, but something that grows deeper as the person imagining becomes more involved in their mental creation and increasingly blind to the exterior world. The Swiss psychologist Carl Jung developed a similar system. The practice of 'active imagination' was an important part of Jung's therapeutic work, and he classified different types of fantasy as either voluntary, passive or active.

Voluntary fantasy was superficial and trivial, he thought, while the imagination begins to take over during passive fantasy, and unexpectedly overwhelms the mind without being summoned. In active fantasy, however, there is a 'positive participation of consciousness', and the conscious self becomes a central part of the imaginative act, in a process that seems identical to the imagining-how that Casey describes.

How, though, can this deep imagination lead to the vision states that Blake and Swedenborg describe? A clue may be the overwhelmingly fantastical nature of what they imagined. In Blake's mythological system and Swedenborg's tours of hell or alien worlds, there was little that involved autobiographical memory or worldly scenarios which require the brain's default mode network to be active. As we saw earlier, deep involvement in a task that does not require much assistance from the default mode network can lead to a loss of the sense of self. This, in turn, seems to be a key to visionary experience. A similar process can be found in the practice of transcendental meditation, in which the mental repetition of a mantra works to quiet the chattering mind. This mantra is a collection of syllables which are meaningless in English and which practitioners keep secret, in order not to connect the word with any real-world experiences. As a result, there is nothing for the mind to snag on to when it is repeating the mantra, as there are no mental connections associated with it. It does not trigger trains of thought that distract from the meditation and activate the default mode network. That Blake's mythology was his alone and had no associations to his wider culture may, perhaps, have kept social and autobiographical parts of his brain quiet and allowed him to reach deeper states of mind.

Based on Casey and Jung's models, it is possible to see how an increasingly complex and rich imagination could reach a point where the mind forgets all about the everyday world and experiences what it is imagining as vividly, or even more so, as it does the real world. Their models do not go any further than this. Blake's accounts of his visions, however, suggest this is only the start, and that it is after this point that things get interesting. His 'fourfold vision', for example, implies the existence of a state of imagination more extreme than those in Casey's work.

As mentioned earlier, the psychedelic counterculture of the 1960s thought that the fourfold visions Blake reported were similar to states of mind that could be induced through the use of psychedelic compounds such as LSD. Such experiences are worth considering here because they go further than Casey's model in reporting increasingly deep states of imagination and consciousness. One of the more useful models of extreme forms of consciousness comes from the infamous Harvard psychologist and LSD advocate Dr Timothy Leary.

Leary was originally an academic who excelled at systematic thinking. Over the course of decades of psychedelic drug use, he developed and refined a model of the different states of mind experienced during expanded awareness. He called this the eight-circuit model, where each of the eight 'circuits' describes a different level or style of mental activity. Describing specific mental activity as brain 'circuits' is now considered an outdated metaphor, because the brain works very differently to a computer. Leary's model dates back to the emergence of cybernetics, however, when such computing metaphors were all the rage.

The first four of these 'circuits' are uncontroversial and are largely borrowed from existing models of psychological development. They cover basic survival, recognition of power, manipulation of symbols and awareness of sexuality. It is not until the fifth circuit that we encounter the mind in a non-everyday state.

The fifth level is called the neurosomatic circuit and deals with feelings of bliss, pleasure, wellbeing and the recognition of beauty.

It involves sensual awareness of the body and is sometimes called the rapture circuit. Logic, purpose and utility become irrelevant in the face of overwhelming aesthetic experience. Importantly, there is a sense of detachment from the worldly concerns of the first four circuits. Our past and future, and our worries and responsibilities, fade away until they seem of little importance. The sense of self produced by the default mode network and other brain structures is being dialled down and weakened. This circuit matches what Blake called Beulah, a state of grace likened to a temporary earthly heaven. Beulah was a place of dreams, moonlight and love, and its function was to separate the material world that Blake called Ulro from Eternity above. This fits well with Leary's model, in which the detachment of the fifth circuit acts as a buffer between the worldly concerns of the first four circuits and the higher levels of consciousness to come.

Leary believed that this state could be deliberately switched on through use of cannabis, tantric sex or certain types of yoga and meditation. Blake would have argued that the creative exercising of the imagination was the real key, although the fact that Blake, Swedenborg and Leary were all highly sexed may be significant. Both Blake and Leary insisted that this buffer stage, for all its seductive appeal, should not be a goal in itself. Passive pleasure can be welcomed when it arrives, but our lives need more purpose.

After the neurosomatic circuit comes the sixth level, which Leary called the neuro-electrical circuit. This is the circuit that we most associate with the psychedelic sixties; it is what everything from psychedelic music to 1960s poster design was trying to express. It is an explosion of perspectives and connections that can be thrilling or overwhelming, and which can be triggered by a psychedelic drug such as LSD. The self, though greatly reduced, is still present at this level, but the rules of the physical world have become very different.

Blake has described experiences which sound very similar to being thrown into Leary's sixth circuit. When he was sitting for the portrait painter Thomas Phillips in 1807, he described an encounter with the archangel Gabriel which we've already noted. In this account, the moment when the roof of his study opened and he was thrust upwards into the heavens sounds much like an account of the sixth circuit activating. Blake seems to be trying to describe experiences like these when he talks of 'fourfold vision'.

This circuit is also sometimes referred to as the meta-programming level. Leary believed that this was a state of consciousness in which the mind became aware of how it works and could consciously rewrite itself. On the sixth circuit, the 'mind forg'd manacles' that dictate how you react to the world are revealed, and religions, prejudices, beliefs and social structures appear arbitrary and changeable. Here the self understands that it is just a story, rather than something real or fixed, and that it is able to rewrite itself if it so wishes. Blake's declaration that 'I must Create a System, or be enslav'd by another Mans' is evidence of this state of awareness.

The 'meta-programming' made possible by this state of awareness helps explain why modern therapists have gained promising results from psychedelic drug therapy for the treatment of issues such as alcoholism and post-traumatic stress disorder. It is also why psychedelic drug use can be dangerous, and why the 1960s and 1970s produced so many 'brain-fried acid casualties', to use a common description. Rewriting your assumptions about the world is not something to be done casually or even accidentally. There were many who came down from recreational drug experimentation with new beliefs that were wild, paranoid and entirely at odds with the rest of society.

Although the sixth circuit still leaves you clinging on to an awareness of the physical world, this is left behind at the seventh circuit. Leary called this the neurogenetic circuit. What remains of the self is in a place outside of time and space. It is here that ancestors are encountered and the history of life is laid out before you. This is the realm of the archetypes, the collective unconscious that Jung wrote about. Swedenborg's travelogue of heaven and hell seems to be the product of a similar state of consciousness, as do Blake's references to Eternity.

The eighth circuit, which Leary added to his model late in life, involves the complete annihilation of the self. It is entering the light at the end of the tunnel in a near-death experience. It is far beyond description, and as such there is little that can be said about it here.

If Blake is to be believed, these higher states of consciousness reported by mystics, saints, poets and psychedelic pioneers can be triggered by exercising the imagination. Of course, both Leary's structured list of states of expanded awareness and Blake's visionary mythology are models – they are simplified framings of much richer and more complex phenomena. We can accept them as useful guides, but we shouldn't confuse them too literally with the mental territory that they are trying to record and describe. Yet the fact that they fit together so well, despite the centuries and experiences that separate their authors, suggests that they describe a universal mental experience.

As we have seen, imagination varies greatly in terms of depth and involvement. But it also varies in how it is experienced, as neurologists are only just discovering. The experience of the 'mind's eye', it has recently been realised, is very different from person to person.

If you ask several people to close their eyes and imagine a cow, the results will differ significantly. For most, an image of something roughly cow-like will appear in their mind's eye. It may be vague and indistinct, and it may soon fade, but they will see something. This is not true for everyone.

Some people will see nothing at all, which indicates a condition known as aphantasia. Even if you asked an aphantasic to mentally picture something extremely familiar, such as their own kitchen, they would not be able to do so because they have no faculty for mental imagery. Most aphantasics find this normal, and struggle to imagine how it could be otherwise. They tend to assume that the concept of a 'mind's eye' is simply metaphorical, because although they couldn't see a cow or a kitchen if you asked them to imagine one, they were still thinking about those things. Aphantasics are more likely to have difficulty recognising faces and often have weak autobiographical memories of events in their lives. Roughly 2–3 per cent of the population is aphantasic, which makes it a surprisingly common condition.

At the opposite end of the spectrum are people with a condition called hyperphantasia. If you could glance inside a hyperphantasic's mind when you asked them to imagine a cow, what you saw might shock you. A hyperphantasic would see a cow in their mind's eye as vivid and real as if it was standing just in front of them. They would not only be able to see the cow in pin-sharp focus, but they would also be able to smell its damp hide and feel the heat from its breath. To a hyperphantasic, images are not things that you think, they are things that you encounter.

Scientists have only just begun to study these extremes of mental imagery vividness. The term 'aphantasia' was first coined by the neurologist Adam Zeman and researchers at the University of Exeter in a 2015 paper. Studies of the condition are currently in their infancy, but there are already some interesting correlations being reported. Hyperphantasics tend to spend more time daydreaming than the average person. They are more prone to emotions such as regret, longing and nostalgia; they experience both greater anxiety and greater empathy than most; and they can find reading about a gory incident extremely distressing. Research into hyperphantasia is producing techniques that can help syndromes like post-traumatic stress disorder. Patients suffering from intrusive memories, it has been discovered, can be calmed by being presented with alternative strong visual imagery, such as playing the game Tetris – the mind can only hold one mental image at a time, and the vividness of the new image overwrites the old intrusive one.

Although retrospective diagnoses of historical psychological conditions are problematic, the case for Blake being a hyperphantasic is strong. As we have already noted, Blake insisted that everything he painted he saw first in his mind. His contemporaries also commented on this. Thomas Phillips wrote how Blake 'always saw in fancy every form he drew'. This situation was tested by a series of experiments Blake undertook around 1820 with the watercolour painter John Varley. He encouraged Blake to draw portraits of famous spirits that he saw, including Moses, Julius Caesar, William Wallace and Edward III. A cynic may say that these portraits, known as the 'visionary heads', owe more to memory than vision, because a number of his drawings of historical figures resembled previous portraits that Blake would probably have seen. The accounts of Blake producing these images, however, suggest that whatever their original source, Blake was indeed sketching people who appeared vividly in his mind's eye.

Sessions took place at night, usually starting around 9 or 10 p.m. and sometimes lasting until 3 or 4 a.m. Varley would suggest a historic figure, and after a brief moment, Blake would cry, 'There he is!' and get to work. As he sketched, Blake would occasionally look up, as if he had a real sitter before him. Sometimes he would abandon a portrait mid-sketch, saying, 'I can't go on, it is gone! I must wait till it returns.' When he was asked to sketch the monstrous spirit from his famous painting *The Ghost of a Flea*, Blake started drawing the spirit he 'saw' but ran into a problem when it moved position and opened its mouth. He had to abandon his first sketch and start again next to it, this time showing the new position of the creature's features. This suggests that he was sketching what he saw vividly in his mind's eye, rather than making up the image as he went. From the many similar accounts, it seems that Blake was telling the truth about drawing what he 'saw' in vision.

There are other aspects of Blake's life which support the possibility that he was hyperphantasic. When people discuss the great moral problems of the day – in the modern world issues like climate change, inequality and biodiversity collapse – they can usually remain dispassionate and calm. Blake couldn't; the issues of his age, which included slavery and child labour, pushed him into anger. For an hyperphantasic person, talking about the cruel conditions that plagued child chimney sweeps would conjure vivid visions of the suffocating, claustrophobic darkness that these young children were forced to endure. When talk of these issues causes the reality of those situations to play out in your mind's eye, a reaction of righteous anger is natural. Blake was always quick to express fury about confinement. In the poem 'Auguries of Innocence' he writes:

A Robin Red breast in a Cage
Puts all Heaven in a Rage
A Dove house filld with Doves & Pigeons
Shudders Hell thro all its regions

The increased empathy and anxiety experienced by hyperphantasics suggests a link between Blake's politics and moral outrage and the strength of his imagination.

Many hyperphantasics are highly creative, and a striking number are drawn to visual art. It is not the case, however, that they paint to record what they see in their mind's eye. The contemporary London artist Clare Dudeney is an example. Dudeney is hyperphantasic and her condition can affect her profoundly. 'When people describe things, especially gory things, I visualise them so vividly it's like I'm experiencing them first-hand,' she has explained. 'A few years ago, I was on the train reading a passage about someone who got a nail stuck in their foot and I passed out.' Yet she does not have similarly strong spiritual experiences in religious settings, such as churches or cathedrals. Hyperphantasia does not seem to directly coincide with a tendency to experience deep mystical states, such as Blake's 'fourfold vision'.

The work of different hyperphantasic artists is as varied as you would expect from any random group of artists. While they tend to view their hyperphantasia as an asset, it is not the case that they feel compelled to record their internal visions on canvas. If there is a connection, it seems to be one of intent, rather than results. Dudeney, who has the strange ability to draw with both hands at once, produces work that is predominantly abstract, energetic, and focused on colourful shapes colliding. She describes the motivation behind her own work: 'My practice considers how the subjective experience of "being" might be shared with another [...] Imagining "the self" as a network of relationships in flux: fragmented, uncertain and complex. The works map subconscious thoughts and feelings.' This also serves as a perfect description of the works of William Blake.

The vividness of the hyperphantasic imagination, however, does fit with the idea that Casey's imagining-how can tip into Leary's higher circuits. When the experience of imagining-how is so vivid and real, awareness of both the self and the external world falls away. At this point awareness is focused on only the imagination, which interacts with nothing but itself, and a path to the world of vision is revealed.

This would still be a rare occurrence, of course. It is not

something that every hyperphantasic would experience. But occasionally there will be an individual like Blake with the temperament, upbringing and background for whom deep imagination lessens their sense of self and tips them into expanded states of awareness. In his letter to Thomas Butts from Felpham, Blake described how the twofold vision that was with him always turned into the delight of the threefold vision of Beulah and, finally, the 'supreme delight' of fourfold vision. Leary required psychedelic drugs to lessen the sense of self and undergo a similar experience. For Blake, however, the key was vivid, deep imagination.

While hyperphantasia may provide insights into the mind of William Blake, the study of the contrary condition of aphantasia suggests reasons to be wary of being swept along by Blake's understanding of imagination.

In 2019, an exhibition of work by artists with aphantasia and hyperphantasia was held in the Tramway gallery, Glasgow. Called *Extreme Imagination: Inside the Mind's Eye*, the roots of the exhibition lay in the realisation that a surprisingly large number of both the aphantasics and hyperphantasics that Zeman and his team were studying were creative. This was perhaps most surprising in the case of aphantasics, for whom a lack of a mind's eye might seem like a barrier to imaginative visual art. Instead, aphantasics were drawn to creating images on canvas or as sculptures, often as a direct compensation for their lack of ability to create them in their mind.

As the aphantasic Canadian artist Sheri Bakes has explained, 'Recently, I've been thinking that maybe not being able to see things in my mind ... maybe that's a good thing. The paintings have become my brain. The paintings have become the picture inside that I can't see.' Other aphantasic artists talk about painting as a way to reveal what the imagination is hiding from them. As the British artist Michael Chance explained: 'I must physically work on a drawing or painting in order for my imagination to become visually manifest[...] Largely bypassing conscious decision making, the way images (usually figures) emerge from my subconscious is akin to dreaming, and the resulting work is often just as strange, surprising and revealing as that would suggest.' A surprisingly high percentage of animators at Pixar are aphantasic, and so is Ed Catmull, the former President of Pixar and Walt Disney Animation Studios.

For aphantasics, creativity is not limited to the visual arts. The aphantasic writer Dustin Grinnell describes writing as a form of collage, building his work through the assembly of individual ideas. 'From my perspective, a writer without a mind's eye writes by patchwork, using multiple sources and collected ideas and concepts to build something original,' he has explained. The biotechnologist Craig Venter believes there is a connection between his aphantasia and his scientific achievements. 'I've known many people with photographic memories for facts who can't even remotely combine them conceptually like I can,' he has said. The lack of an ability to visualise in the mind, clearly, does not limit intellectual achievement.

Bringing something vividly to mind quickly and easily is not something that aphantasics are able to do, so instead of relying on this handy mental shortcut they find other ways of understanding and thinking about things. These usually focus on the context and connections between objects and concepts. As a result, their thinking may be slower, but it can also be richer and deeper. To a visionary, the vividness of their mind's eye is usually a quality they treasure. It is an ability that marks them out as special, different, and perhaps even chosen. It is not unusual for a prophet or a mystic to feel that they are in some way more important than the great majority who are unable to experience visions. From an aphantasic's point of view, however, being distracted by the surface dazzle of a mental image sounds like a limitation, rather than a blessing. The mind's eye seems, to them, like a distraction from deep thought and imagination. It is like someone trying to convince a blind person that the most important thing is 20:20 vision. The blind person, who can understand the world and navigate it perfectly well without the benefit of sight, is unlikely to find such an argument convincing.

Because we take imagination for granted, we rarely stop to think about what a strange phenomenon it is. What we imagine is often trivial or useless and easily dismissed. It is the realm of dreams when we sleep, or daydreams when we are bored, and those fantasies and nightmares are frequently little help in paying the mortgage. Imagination, as intellectuals and philosophers claim, can appear to be a lesser thing than intelligence or reason. Yet when you examine those higher, more celebrated forms of cognition, you realise that they too are dependent on imagination.

An engineer requires a plan of something that does not exist before they can start to physically construct it. The theory of relativity began when Einstein attempted to imagine how the world would appear if he were travelling on a beam of light. The discipline of philosophy is a centuries-long tradition of imaginative thought experiments. Before a verbal, spoken language can evolve and develop, someone needs to imagine a connection between concepts and sounds. Should you attempt to think of an activity, pursuit or cause that can be described as more important than the ephemeral act of imagination, you soon realise that without imagination it would be impossible. The ability to voluntarily or unwittingly conjure in our minds what does not exist, it turns out, is a necessary part of all the different abilities that differentiate us from the animals.

Imagined ideas that arise unbidden, which don't seem to be

beholden to the laws of cause and effect, are perhaps the only situation in which we genuinely get something for nothing. This aspect of imagination can legitimately be described as godlike, because it is the ability to create something that did not previously exist. It is not a physical act of creation, of course, but that is not the same as it being nothing. We live our lives surrounded by a physical world, including chairs, desks, houses, laptops and clothes, which would not exist if the idea and design of them hadn't first formed in somebody's mind. We can add things like language, fashion, culture, economics and laws to this list of things that began in an act of mental creation. We can also add angels, demons, gods and other wonders. These are the flora and fauna that grow in the human imagination.

Because imagination seems such a trivial, effortless, daft thing that we do, to declare it to be the most precious quality of our world, as Blake did, might seem anticlimactic. But as we have seen, there are varying levels of imagination. What is trivial in our everyday lives can, in the mind of someone such as Blake or Swedenborg, be profoundly powerful and overwhelming.

Humanity is the only phenomenon we know capable of experiencing the light of imagination. It appears to be an unlimited resource, and we have only just begun to explore it. If the world of imagination was a vast continent, then we have only wandered along the shore – we still have no idea of the marvels that await us upriver. Imagination is required for that most important and vital quality of life, the generation of enthusiasm. The word 'enthusiasm' means to be inspired by the gods, and the gods, Blake reminds us, come from the imagination. It is through the imagination of human minds that purpose, meaning and relevance enter this universe.

For this reason, Blake viewed the imagination as divine. True, some may have hoped for a concept of divinity that grants power and control over the material world, which imagination alone may not be capable of. But even power and control could not exist without imagination. We think of a black hole as powerful and controlling, but in a dead, pointless cosmos it is meaningless and irrelevant, and as much a random quirk of the physical world as everything else. It is only the human mind that can add qualities like awe and dread to a black hole. Likewise, there would be no concept of divinity itself without imagination.

The Canadian poet and musician Leonard Cohen told us that there is a crack in everything, which is how the light gets in. From a Blakean perspective, imagination is Cohen's crack in Urizen's closed, limited, finite universe, a way in which something new can appear, as if by magic. It is how the inspired, the world changing and the mundane can arrive from out of nowhere. More importantly, it is a direct challenge to Urizen's belief that he is the creator god of all that exists. This explains why, in Blake's mythology, imagination is the key to freeing Urizen from his delusions and shattering the self-imposed limitations on his perception. It is through imagination, Blake promises us, that we will be redeemed.

8.
SEEK LOVE THERE

In 1781, the twenty-four-year-old Blake was at the house of a friend discussing a recent failed relationship. A dark-haired, bright-eyed nineteen-year-old named Catherine Boucher was also present, and she listened intently. She responded with the forthright declaration that she 'pitied him from the heart'.

'Do you pity me?' queried Blake. 'Yes! I do, most sincerely,' came the immediate reply. 'Then I love you for that,' he told her.

The word 'pity' has negative connotations in the modern world. People now resent being pitied, because it implies being looked down upon. But in the late eighteenth century, and in this context, it implied sincere compassion and empathy. In *Jerusalem*, Blake describes 'Wrath' and 'Pity' as 'the Two Contraries of Humanity'.

Catherine was the daughter of a market gardener from Battersea, on the south side of the Thames. She and William were married the following year and remained together until his death forty-five years later. She was illiterate and signed her marriage certificate with an 'X'. Her lowly social position was perhaps the reason Blake's father was unhappy about the union. Because of this friction, William and Catherine moved to 23 Green Street (now

Irving Street, by Leicester Square) after their marriage, and only returned to Broad Street after Blake's father's death in 1784. Given the choice between obeying his father and following his heart, Blake was always going to choose the latter.

Catherine's new husband taught her to read and write and to assist him in many different aspects of the printing process, from removing impressions from the press to hand-colouring the printed pages. In later years, they were viewed as a devoted team, with Catherine described as an 'excellent Wife (a true Helpmate!)', who was fiercely loyal to William and the reality of his visions. In 1830, the Scottish poet Allan Cunningham said that: 'She seemed to have been created on purpose for Blake:– she believed him to be the finest genius on earth; she believed in his verse – she believed in his designs; and to the wildest flights of his imagination she bowed the knee, and was a worshipper. She set his house in good order, prepared his frugal meal, learned to think as he thought, and, indulging him in his harmless absurdities, became, as it were, bone of his bone, and flesh of his flesh.' In 1802, Blake's patron William Hayley wrote that: 'They have been married more than seventeen years & are as fond of each other as if their Honey Moon were still shining [. . .] The good woman not only does all the work of the House, but she even makes the greatest part of her Husbands dress, & assists him in his art – she draws, she engraves, & sings delightfully & is so truly the Half of her good man that they seem animated by one Soul.' As William said to Catherine on his deathbed, 'You have ever been an angel to me.'

Catherine's devotion to her husband also resulted in her being described as the 'madder of the two'. Cunningham noted that while she did not understand everything Blake wrote, 'she was sure [his poems] had a meaning, and a fine one'. It is perhaps unfair to interpret this as a criticism of her because no one has ever understood everything that Blake wrote, possibly including Blake himself. But as Obi-Wan Kenobi asks rhetorically in *Star Wars*, 'Who's the more foolish, the fool, or the fool who follows him?'

Because most of our accounts of Catherine Blake are observations recorded by other men, the image we have of her can tend to be a two-dimensional archetype: that of the devoted, loyal assistant. This is a portrait that owes much to the gender politics of the day. She is seen as some form of angel, albeit one with the suggestion of madness. We very rarely get to hear her own words or sense the fullness of her personality. There are, however, moments in Blake's work when we may be able to detect a deeper understanding of her life and personality, particularly during the 1790s, when the marriage was strained. The main cause of the stresses of the Blakes' relationship was, it seems, the result of William's attitude to sex.

'Those who restrain desire, do so because theirs is weak enough to be restrained,' wrote Blake in *The Marriage of Heaven and Hell*. Statements like this have earned him the reputation as a champion of sexual freedom and liberation. He saw sex as something holy and good, and often attacked the Church for its attempts to control the sensual side of people's lives. 'Prisons are built with stones of Law, Brothels with bricks of Religion [...] The lust of the goat is the bounty of God,' he wrote in the same work. In 'The Garden of Love', a poem from *Songs of Experience*, he describes how:

> Priests in black gowns, were walking their rounds,
> And binding with briars, my joys & desires.

The tendency of religion to deny and forbid sexuality was, for Blake, a clear sign that religion was corrupt, foolish and unholy. As he wrote in *Jerusalem*, 'We are told to abstain from fleshly desires that we may lose no time from the Work of the Lord. Every moment lost, is a moment that cannot be redeemed every pleasure that intermingles with the duty of our station is a folly unredeemable & is planted like the seed of a wild flower among our wheat.' The thought of all those lost and forbidden moments of pleasure filled him with horror.

One of the best-known stories about Blake and his wife involves them being visited by his patron Thomas Butts during the 1790s, when they lived south of the river in a little terraced house in Lambeth. Butts found them naked in the garden and claiming to be Adam and Eve living in Eden, 'a little to the scandal of wondering neighbours'. This story was known to be circulating in the Royal Academy during Blake's lifetime, and it formed the basis of Jack Shepherd's 1989 play *In Lambeth*, in which the naked Blakes are interrupted by Thomas Paine. The 1993 BBC adaptation of the play featured Mark Rylance as William Blake. Sadly, this lovely story is now treated with suspicion by Blake scholars. Several of Blake's close friends insisted it was nothing more than – in the words of the painter John Linnell – 'a malicious invention'. As the artist Samuel Palmer wrote in 1864, 'Mr. Butts' visit to "Adam and Eve" had grown in the memory, I think. I do not believe it: it is unlike Blake.'

Palmer's belief that the event has 'grown in the memory' is plausible. It is easy to imagine Butts calling on Blake when he was changing and Blake citing Adam and Eve as an excuse for Butts not to be embarrassed. The tale would then 'improve' with subsequent retelling. Despite this, it seems unlikely to disappear from popular accounts of Blake, because it fits so perfectly with our sense of who we want him to have been: a joyful, liberated, sexually honest individual, entirely unconcerned by the constraining forces of society. It is also pleasing to hear a carefree, happy account of Catherine that differs from her usual portrayal as dutiful and serious. Blake did see desire as something to be acted on and he believed that repression was psychologically unhealthy. 'He who desires but acts not, breeds pestilence,' he wrote, a century before the field of psychiatry emerged.

He took this belief to an extreme end in his most controversial and troubling proverb: 'Sooner murder an infant in its cradle than nurse unacted desires.' Blake scholars are in general profoundly uncomfortable with this line and often attempt to explain it away, for example by arguing that 'murder an infant in its cradle' is a metaphor. Blake did tell Crabb Robinson that he 'had committed many murders', for example, and no one believes he was speaking literally. This has not prevented the line being picked up on by libertarians and Satanists, who argue for their right to total liberty and who believe that nothing should be allowed to stop them from doing whatever they wish.

Blake's intended message in that proverb seems to be that 'nursing' unacted desires, as in feeding them and helping them grow, is a negative act. Unfortunately, his attempt to express this seems to us to be extreme and tasteless, to the extent that it undermines his point. His choice of words here is perhaps best looked on as a mistake to be learnt from – even great writers make mistakes. As he had written earlier in the section: 'The road of excess leads to the palace of wisdom', and, 'You never know what is enough unless you know what is more than enough.' We only learn how far we can go, in other words, after we have gone too far. Certainly, the idea that the right to act on your desires should allow you to make others suffer is not found in the rest of his work, and actively contradicts much of his writing. Among the same list of proverbs, for example, he states that: 'The most sublime act is to set another before you.'

Finding the right balance between acknowledging desires and treating those close to him well does not seem to have been easy. There is evidence of friction in the early years of their marriage, seemingly concerned with William's unhappiness about the sexual aspect of their relationship. We don't know if this was because Blake's desire for other women was too strong for the monogamous world of marriage, or whether William's and Catherine's sex drives were simply mismatched, or whether he found Catherine to be a passive and unresponsive partner. Regardless of the reason, Blake's sexual life did not initially seem to be the joyful, life-enhancing, spiritual union that he craved. Gilchrist seems to have known more about this, but, mindful of his Victorian readership, he kept a respectful veil over the subject. All that he lets slip was that the cause of the strife was 'jealousy on her side, not wholly unprovoked'.

Some Blake scholars have argued that Blake wanted to take a mistress and include her in his and Catherine's Lambeth home, and that as justification for this he may have cited the biblical story of Abraham and his wife, Sarah. When Sarah was unable to have a child, she offered her husband her Egyptian slave Hagar in her place, and Abraham went on to conceive a child with Hagar. If it is true that Blake made this suggestion, it seems to have hurt Catherine deeply.

Support for this scenario comes from his poem 'William Bond', which can be read as an autobiographical account of these events. The name William Bond is here understood to be William Blake bound by the vows of marriage. In this and other poems of the time, a character called Mary is thought to represent Catherine:

O William if thou dost another Love
Dost another Love better than poor Mary
Go & take that other to be thy Wife
And Mary Green shall her servant be

Yes Mary I do another love
Another I Love far better than thee
And Another I will have for my Wife
Then what have I to do with thee

For thou art Melancholy Pale
And on thy Head is the cold Moons shine
But she is ruddy & bright as day
And the sun beams dazzle from her eyne

Mary trembled & Mary chilld
And Mary fell down on the right hand floor
That William Bond and his Sister Jane
Scarce could recover Mary more

In the poem, Mary's despair and collapse triggered a moment of clarity for William which brought about a deeper appreciation of their union. The potential relationship with 'Sister Jane' was abandoned. In life, it seems that William's desires for other partners caused a great deal of upset for Catherine, but it's worth noting that there is no evidence that these desires were ever acted upon.

Given the importance William placed on sex and the delight he took in children, the fact that his marriage was childless has often been commented on. This may simply be the result of infertility, and it is interesting to note that none of William's brothers or sisters had children. Another explanation, however, may be inferred in a curious illustrated poem Blake composed in the late 1780s called 'The Book of Thel'.

According to Gilchrist, this poem is 'a strange mystical allegory, full of tender beauty and enigmatic meaning'. It was written in the years between *Songs of Innocence* and *Songs of Experience*, and it has the same tone of childlike kindness as *Songs of Innocence*. It tells the story of Thel, a beautiful spirit in a heavenly realm who is the youngest daughter of angelic creatures. Thel is troubled by the transient nature of existence, describing herself as:

Like a reflection in a glass. like shadows in the water.
Like dreams of infants. like a smile upon an infants face,
Like the doves voice, like transient day, like music in the air;

If Thel descends to the earthly material realm, she realises, her existence will be one of decay and meaninglessness. She discusses her situation first with the 'Lilly of the valley', a small, weak 'watry weed' that does 'love to dwell in lowly vales', then with a passing cloud that will dissolve in the act of watering the valley, and finally with a clod of clay that nurses a newborn worm. All three understand the role they play in the larger picture of natural balance, and all tell her that they consider their existence blessed because of this. As the cloud explains, 'every thing that lives, Lives not alone, nor for itself'. Thel, in contrast, can't see how she fits into the physical world. She is from a place called the Vale of Har, and in Blake's emerging mythology Har represented self-love or self-interest. She can only understand meaning centred on herself, rather than the wider ecosystem.

Then we come to the last page, where there is a sudden shift in tone. The penultimate page ended with the clod of clay inviting Thel to enter her earthly home, in order to understand it better. We then turn the page and are told:

The eternal gates terrific porter lifted the northern bar:
Thel enter'd in & saw the secrets of the land unknown;
She saw the couches of the dead, & where the fibrous roots
Of every heart on earth infixes deep its restless twists:
A land of sorrows & of tears where never smile was seen.

The reference to moving through the northern gates in the first line, in Blake's wider mythology, means to enter the world of the imagination. This dark, joyless vision is how Thel imagines the physical world. She then finds her own grave and hears a voice lamenting the power of the physical senses. It is at this point that the poem comes to a sudden and surprising conclusion.

> The Virgin started from her seat, & with a shriek.
> Fled back unhindered till she came into the vales of Har
>
> The End

Until this point most readers would have assumed that Thel was going to learn about life on the physical plane and come to terms with it, perhaps even becoming eager for the cycle of birth, sex, motherhood and death she was discovering. The sudden retreat at the end breaks all expected narrative laws. It makes the poem unsatisfying, and seemingly pointless. Why write about a spirit about to descend to earth who then changes their mind at the last minute and decides not to?

Given the ending, it is tempting to interpret the 'Book of Thel' as the story of a miscarriage or stillbirth. The last page is believed to have been written at a slightly later date than the rest of the poem, and as such may be a different ending to the one originally planned. It is possible that the poem started as the story of a pregnancy told from the point of view of the baby's spiritual self, unsure of their transition from the higher realms to the earthly one. When the pregnancy was not a success, the spiritual child fled in horror from the world of men. Such an original and unexpected perspective would be entirely in keeping with Blake's work.

Support for the idea that Catherine had difficult and unsuccessful pregnancies comes from a record of a 'Cath.e Blake' registered as a patient at the British Lying-In Hospital in London, which would indicate a period of recovery after a miscarriage. The record is dated 26 Aug 1796, about six years after 'The Book of Thel'. We cannot be certain, however, that this Catherine Blake was William's wife and not another Londoner with the same name.

In 1795, William produced a mysterious and extraordinary colour print called *Pity*. It showed a woman lying on the ground with her hands clutched to her breast and her head tipped back. Above her a cherubin is riding through the air on a pale horse, who leans down and takes away a newborn babe. While there is great sorrow on the woman's face, the babe has its arms spread wide with joy. This was a common conceit in Blake's descriptions of souls leaving their earthly bodies behind at death. He spoke about his brother Robert's soul leaving his body and floating upwards 'clapping its hands for joy'.

The strange title of *Pity* is a reference to *Macbeth*. In Act 1, scene 7, Macbeth is considering how people would react to the murder of Duncan, his well-respected king:

[...] Duncan
Hath borne his faculties so meek, hath been
So clear in his great office, that his virtues
Will plead, like angels, trumpet-tongu'd against
The deep damnation of his taking off;
And Pity, like a naked new-born babe,
Striding the blast, or heav'n's cherubi hors'd
Upon the sightless couriers of the air,
Shall blow the horrid deed in ev'ry eye;
That tears shall drown the wind

Blake had not produced an illustration of the play *Macbeth*. His *Pity* is not a visual interpretation of a general considering regicide. He was instead drawn to a metaphor used in the play, in which the emotions caused by a too-early death are personified as a babe taken away into the air by a horsed cherub, and he chose to illustrate that metaphor instead. With Blake, it is always the emotions behind things that interest him, rather than the earthly consequences.

In Shakespeare's metaphor, the babe represents the emotion of pity. Blake departs from the *Macbeth* quote to show it being taken away from its mother, the ultimate source of this pity-babe. Perhaps because Catherine's first words to William were a declaration of how he triggered the emotion of pity to emerge from her heart, it is tempting to see Catherine here, enduring the loss of a child. If this was the case then the picture is another reminder that the word 'pity', in eighteenth-century usage, was an expression of empathy and compassion.

There are a few drawings of an unambiguously sexual nature in Blake's notebooks. One shows a crowned woman with a cathedral or a temple between her legs. Another shows three kneeling, praying women worshipping a giant, erect penis. The message of both is clear: sexuality was linked with spirituality and divinity.

There is a logical connection here. For many people, the most vivid and potent form of imagination is the sexual imagination. It may be difficult to utilise the type of imagination that leads to creative works or new inventions, but most people find that slipping into sexual imagination is, in comparison, no trouble at all. This is, presumably, a by-product of evolution; our ancestors with an overactive sexual imagination would have been more likely to have sex and pass on their genes.

Blake, as we have discussed, believed that the imagination was divine. As such, to strengthen and explore it was a spiritual act. It follows that, for those who want to empower and improve their overall imagination, sexual fantasy is the simplest and most effective place to start. From this perspective, sexual imagination is a holy act, regardless of what the more puritanical preachers might say. Physical bliss, in Blake's mind, was no different to spiritual bliss. Ecstasy was ecstasy and labelling it as either spiritual or sexual was irrelevant. Central to all this was Blake's belief that the physical body was not a separate entity from the human soul, which is a subject we will return to.

There has been much speculation about whether those two sexual sketches were representative of a much larger body of sexualised artwork which has since been lost. The question arises due to the actions of the painter Frederick Tatham. Tatham befriended Blake in later life and looked after Catherine after her husband died, nominally employing her as a housekeeper to keep her from destitution. After Catherine died in 1831, a great quantity of William's manuscripts, letters and other work was controversially retained by Tatham. He then became a follower of the Scottish preacher Edward Irving, who believed that the second coming of Christ was imminent. As William Michael Rossetti, the brother of the artist Dante Gabriel Rossetti, recorded: 'The fact is – so I have been informed – that Swedenborgians, Irvingites, or other extreme sectaries, beset the then youthful custodian [Tatham] of these priceless relics, and persuaded him to make a holocaust of them, as being heretical, and dangerous to those poor dear "unprotected females" Religion and Morals. The horrescent pietists allowed that the works were "inspired"; but alas! The inspiration had come from the Devil.'

Under the influence of Irving and other religious fanatics, Tatham set about destroying Blake's 'satanically inspired' work. Countless papers and manuscripts went into the fire, and the engraved copper printing plates for his illuminated manuscripts were melted down into scrap. As Rossetti reported, 'Notebooks, poems, designs, in lavish quantity, annihilated: a gag (as it were) thrust into the piteous mouth of Blake's corpse.' This incident is known as the 'Tatham holocaust' in Blakean circles and talk of it fills many with a sense of cosmic horror. We simply don't know how many works have been lost. The question of whether Blake's sexual drawings were common among his wider manuscripts is unfortunately now unanswerable.

The importance of sexuality and imagination as pathways to spiritual experience was not lost on several eighteenth-century religious sects, even if the pursuit of such things often led to scandal. Blake's mother, for example, had been part of a Moravian congregation in her younger years, led by the controversial Count Nikolaus Ludwig von Zinzendorf. This sect was accused by Swedenborg and others as being a front for orgies.

The Moravian congregation was then divided into male and female 'choirs', with a separate choir of married members. Zinzendorf wrote how members of the married choir were 'to teach sexual procedures and practices to newly wedded brothers and sisters'. As the American historian Aaron Fogleman has explained, 'The instructions emphasised the importance of consent by both parties in marriage, properly informing young men and women before and after marriage about sex, how and why their sexual organs were made holy by Jesus, the methods of sexual intercourse and how often it should be performed.' The permitted methods were sitting, for which use of a chair and a towel was approved, or lying down, for which a pillow was recommended. Male ejaculation was understood to be the husband blessing the wife, after which the couple prayed and discussed the event in terms of an act of worship with other members of the congregation.

The Moravians preached that union with Christ could be achieved through both marital and extramarital sex and gender transgression. Each individual Christian was considered to be the bride of Christ, and therefore female in terms of spiritual sexuality. They practised visualisation exercises, which focused on the wound in Jesus' side, in order to better understand the spiritual nature of being penetrated by the male Christ. Zinzendorf preached that the congregation 'must become sinners in order to be saved', and that, 'It is only the sinner, such as Mary Magdalen, who is saved. The self-righteous saint must first be made a thief in order to be saved by the power of the wounds.'

A petition by Blake's mother to join the Moravian congregation in Fetter Lane begins: 'My Dear Bretheren & Sistors, I have very littell to say of my self for I am a pore crature and full of wants but my Dear Saviour will satisfy them all I should be glad if I could allways lay at the Cross full as I do know thanks be to him last Friday at the love feast our Saviour was pleased to make me Suck his wounds and hug the Cross more than Ever and I trust will more and more till my fraile nature can hould no more.' Blake's mother left the Moravian congregation after the death of her first husband. When she remarried and started a family with William's father, her decision to keep William from school and educate him at home was in keeping with Moravian teaching.

Zinzendorf's sexual teachings eventually led to scandal, both in London and Germany, as word spread beyond Fetter Lane and was turned by rumour into wild stories of church-based public orgies. In response, the sexual aspect of their teachings was excised, and the Moravian Church gradually returned to respectability. Purged of the taint of sexual scandal, it is still going strong today.

Blake's perspective on women is complicated. In the opinion of the Blake scholar Helen P. Bruder, Blake was 'by turns a searching critic of patriarchy but also a hectoring misogynist'.

One incident is commonly raised in the case against Blake. Gilchrist recounts an episode when William and Catherine were living with William's brother Robert in Broad Street, after the death of their father. According to Gilchrist, a dispute broke out between Catherine and Robert and, in the heat of the argument, Catherine 'used words to him'. As wonderful as it would be to know what those words were, for they may have revealed much about Catherine, they were not recorded. They did, however, cause William to interrupt the argument and demand that she 'Kneel down and beg Robert's pardon directly, or you will never see my face again!' His tone, and his character, clearly indicated that this was a threat he meant.

Catherine, as Gilchrist wrote, 'thought it very hard, as she would afterwards tell, to beg her brother-in-law's pardon when she was not in fault! But being a duteous, devoted wife, though by nature nowise tame or dull of spirit, she did kneel down and meekly murmur, "Robert, I beg your pardon, I am in the wrong." To which Robert replied, "Young woman, you lie! *I* am in the wrong!" ' With this, the air was cleared.

In William's defence, the only person you could imagine him ever siding with in a conflict with Catherine was his beloved brother Robert. Nevertheless, the incident illustrates Blake's belief that men were primary and women secondary. He did not have a regular education and instead grew up reading the Bible, in which woman was created out of man when Eve was created out of Adam's rib. This male-first cosmology was neither controversial nor commonly questioned in the eighteenth century. Blake himself wrote, in the margins of a copy of *Aphorisms of Man* by Johann Lavater, 'let the men do their duty & the women will be such wonders, the female life lives from the light of the male. See a mans female dependents [and you will then] know the man.' In his unfinished manuscript *The Four Zoas*, he described the moment a female spirit is expelled by a male:

One dread morn of gory blood
The manhood was divided for the gentle passions making way
Thro the infinite labyrinths of the heart & thro the nostrils
   issuing
In odorous stupefaction stood before the Eyes of Man
A female bright.

In Blake's own mythology the mind or soul is divided into four separate beings, which are the 'zoas' mentioned in this work's title. These represent reason, creativity, emotion and sensation. We have already met one of these zoas – Urizen, the personification of limited reason. All four of the zoas are male, but each has a separate female companion who is described as their 'emanation'. As with the biblical account of Eden, the male comes first, and the female is created from them.

This idea was buried so deeply in the Christian culture of eighteenth-century Europe that not even Blake questioned it. But that is not to say that opposing ideas were not in the culture or that they were not present in authors that Blake studied. In *Conjugial Love* (1768), for example, Swedenborg stressed that in marriage partners were equal. The commonly held belief in male superiority and female subordination, he believed, had no basis in the spiritual realm.

To twenty-first-century eyes, the culture of eighteenth-century Britain was shockingly patriarchal. The reaction to that pioneering work of proto-feminist philosophy, Mary Wollstonecraft's *A Vindication of the Rights of Woman*, illustrates this clearly. The conservative aristocrat Thomas Taylor was the first person to translate the complete works of Aristotle and Plato into English, so he was regarded as an intelligent man. Yet he responded to Wollstonecraft's work by writing a satire entitled *A Vindication of the Rights of Brutes*. In this he argued that if women should be granted rights, then so should animals. Taylor's reactionary pamphlet was intended to dismiss women and the idea of human rights in general. Ironically, it is now seen as one of the first arguments for modern animal rights. Taylor, it is probably fair to say, would have been furious about this.

Blake probably met Wollstonecraft and he was certainly familiar with her work, because her publisher Johnson commissioned him to produce engravings for her book *Original Stories from Real Life*. For all Blake's unquestioned male-first beliefs, he still seems to have understood and approved of her pioneering feminism. Indeed, when you look at some of the women in his work, it is startling to see just how far ahead of his times he could be. This is particularly apparent in his illustrated poem 'Visions of the Daughters of Albion' (1793), which explores how the social norms of marriage constrain and repress the healthy sexual appetites of women, explicitly comparing joyless marriage with the slavery still being practised in America. This is, clearly, an extraordinarily progressive perspective for a male writer in the eighteenth century.

'Visions of the Daughters of Albion' is the story of a woman called Oothoon, who represents thwarted love. The poem begins with her lines:

I loved Theotormon
And I was not ashamed

The object of Oothoon's desire is Theotormon, and she sets out to claim him. Her line 'I was not ashamed' immediately marks her out as someone who values emotional honesty above the social norms of the day. But those cultural norms prove to be unavoidable, as Oothoon lives in a place called the Vale of Leutha, which represents guilt, sin and, in the words of Blake scholar S. Foster

Damon, 'sex under law'. It is here that she decides to 'pluck a flower' to symbolically act upon her desires. Oothoon, as imagined by Blake, is not one of the idealised, decorative women typical of the era. She is a character who has agency.

Oothoon sees her chosen flower with the same twofold vision that Blake saw his argumentative thistle, seeing it simultaneously as a flower and a beautiful nymph. At first, she questions whether she has the right to take what she wants, but the nymph assures her it will cause no harm:

> Art thou a flower! art thou a nymph! I see thee now a flower;
> Now a nymph! I dare not pluck thee from thy dewy bed!
>
> The Golden nymph replied; pluck thou my flower Oothoon
>   the mild
> Another flower shall spring, because the soul of sweet delight
> Can never pass away. she ceas'd, and closd her golden shrine.
>
> Then Oothoon pluck'd the flower saying, I pluck thee from thy
>   bed,
> Sweet flower. and put thee here to glow between my breasts
> And thus I turn my face to where my whole soul seeks.

Oothoon had hoped that taking the flower would lead to her claiming her true desire, her intended husband, Theotormon, but she instead finds herself with a very different character called Bromion. Bromion represents law and reason and lacks the emotion that she craves. He sees Oothoon – 'this harlot here on Bromions bed' – as something to conquer. He impregnates her in an act not of love but of rage, and the pair are then 'Bound back to back' in a loveless marriage:

[...] she who burns with youth. and knows no fixed lot; is
  bound
In spells of law to one she loaths: and must she drag the chain
Of life, in weary lust!

The following morning, however, Oothoon finds herself pure
again, rather than defiled. Because her heart and mind were pure,
she has no reason to feel any shame. But her beloved Theotormon
is unable to see this, because Oothoon has become invisible to him.
Now that she has been legally claimed and is sexually active, it is
as if she does not exist, and so he pines for the woman he has lost.
Oothoon also symbolises the 'soft soul of America' and as such her
conquest by Bromion appears to Theotormon like the claiming of
America by European slavers. Outside Bromion and Oothoon's
cave he hears in the far-off distance:

[...] beneath him sound like waves on the desart shore
The voice of slaves beneath the sun, and children bought with
  money.

To Oothoon, who is unashamed and unchanged by her time with
Bromion, his reaction makes little sense. She ponders how different
the world must look to those who conquer compared to those who
are claimed.

There are echoes of this situation in a remarkable passage in
Blake's later work *Jerusalem*, in which Joseph discovers that Mary
is pregnant with a child who is not his. At first Joseph 'spoke in
anger & fury', asking, 'Should I Marry a Harlot & an Adulteress?'
Mary, however, then spoke to him about the nature of forgiveness,
and here we gain an insight into why Blake believed forgiveness
was one of the most important Christian values. For Blake, it was
so profound and transformative that we should be grateful for

the existence of sin, because without sin there can be no blessed forgiveness. As Mary exclaims:

> There is none that liveth & Sinneth not!
> [...] O Mercy O Divine Humanity!
> O Forgiveness & Pity & Compassion! If I were Pure I should
>   never
> Have known Thee; If I were Unpolluted I should never have
> Glorified thy Holiness, or rejoiced in thy great Salvation.

Blake's conception of the 'Virgin Mary' is clearly different to that of mainstream Catholicism. In a similar way, Oothoon understands that if Theotormon practised Christian forgiveness he would be redeemed and he would not consider her impure. His blinkers would be removed, and he would be able to see her again. The rift in their relationship, then, is his fault and not hers; his hypocrisy and jealousy have created all this heartache and strife:

> Such is self-love that envies all! a creeping skeleton
> With lamplike eyes watching around the frozen marriage bed.

She is insistent that in choosing to pluck a flower she has done nothing wrong, for joy and desire are ultimately expressions of divinity:

> The moment of desire! the moment of desire! The virgin
> That pines for man; shall awaken her womb to enormous joys
> In the secret shadows of her chamber; the youth shut up from
> The lustful joy. shall forget to generate. & create an amorous
>   image
> In the shadows of his curtains and in the folds of his silent
>   pillow.

Are not these the places of religion? the rewards of continence?
The self enjoyings of self denial? Why dost thou seek religion?
Is it because acts are not lovely, that thou seekest solitude,
Where the horrible darkness is impressed with reflections of
    desire.

Oothoon wants only joy for Theotormon and promises that she would feel no jealousy if he were to take other partners, even offering to procure some for him. She tells him that she will:

[. . .] catch for thee girls of mild silver, or of furious gold;
I'll lie beside thee on a bank & view their wanton play
In lovely copulation bliss on bliss with Theotormon:
Red as the rosy morning, lustful as the first born beam,
Oothoon shall view his dear delight, nor e'er with jealous cloud

But being invisible to blinkered Theotormon, her pleas cannot reach him. Only other women, the daughters of Albion, understand what she is going through. She remains chained to Bromion in her loveless marriage, while her heart's desire despairs that he has lost her. The power of 'sex under law' in the Vale of Leutha is such that she will be forever denied the holy act of bliss.

In its critique of marriage and monogamy, 'Visions of the Daughters of Albion' seems directly inspired by Mary Wollstonecraft. But Blake went further than Wollstonecraft, and his plea for the right of women to be sexually fulfilled was an extraordinarily progressive idea for the 1790s. It was, arguably, nearly two hundred years ahead of its time.

There is a more cynical reading of the poem, however, which argues that the character of Oothoon represents a gender-swapped version of Blake himself. In this reading, the whole poem was an attempt by Blake to persuade his wife to give her blessing to extramarital affairs, perhaps with the woman referred to as 'Sister Jane' in the poem 'William Bond'. Whether this was true or not, he did at least argue that the sexual liberty he desired applied equally to all, regardless of sex or gender. Women might be created out of men in Blake's cosmology, but they had an equal claim to experiencing bliss and ecstasy. Oothoon's final rallying call in 'Visions of the Daughters of Albion' falls on deaf ears, but it is addressed to male and female alike:

Arise and drink your bliss, for every thing that lives is holy!

If we could accept the right of all to 'drink their bliss', unhindered by law or jealousy, then Blake believed we would find a path to heaven. The key here, once again, is the all-important act of forgiveness. As he wrote in a poem called 'The Gates of Paradise' the same year:

Mutual forgiveness of each Vice,
Such are the Gates of Paradise

Towards the end of the eighteenth century, however, the subject of sexual liberation became less prominent in Blake's work. At the same time, William and Catherine's relationship appears to have developed into a stronger one, and all accounts of the couple's relationship from 1800 onwards paint them as a solid, perfectly matched, deeply loving pair. Whether the shock to their marriage caused by his desire for other partners eventually brought them closer, after the couple had worked through these issues, or whether William grew less self-centred, is not entirely clear. It may simply be that his declining libido in his middle years was better suited to Catherine's temperament, and the self-centredness of youth gave way to a more mature understanding of relationships.

8. SEEK LOVE THERE

In 'William Bond', Blake wrote openly about his desire for a woman where the 'sun beams dazzle from her eyne', rather than a wife whose head 'is the cold Moons shine'. But at the end of the poem, he speaks with a calmer, deeper appreciation of love. It is here, perhaps, that we find the mature voice of Blake, chastising his selfish younger self, offering the hard-won truths that experience had taught him about the human heart:

I thought Love lived in the hot sun Shine
But O he lives in the Moony light
I thought to find Love in the heat of day
But sweet Love is the Comforter of Night

Seek Love in the Pity of others Woe
In the gentle relief of anothers care
In the darkness of night & the winters snow
In the naked & outcast Seek Love There

9.
THEIR FORMS ETERNAL EXIST

Imagination may have been central to the philosophy of Blake and Swedenborg, but they were swimming against the intellectual fashion of their time. The wider society of the age was becoming increasingly focused on rationality. Through the application of reason rather than imagination, it was felt, we could understand the world of matter.

By the eighteenth century, proto-scientific experiments, measurements and theories had begun to give a more accurate description of the world than that offered by the Church. An example of this was the debate about heliocentrism – the theory that the earth revolved around the sun. Measurement and observation eventually revealed that the earth was not the centre of the cosmos, as had been claimed. It was hard for the Church to maintain its role as the ultimate authority on truth after its claims about such fundamental issues were revealed to be arbitrary. It made sense that enquiring people would look at the world from a mechanical, materialistic perspective instead, to see if any certainty could be found that way.

This led to the rise of a philosophical position called deism. The name is derived from the Latin word for god, *deus*, revealing the nervousness people felt about stepping away from religion. With a name like 'godism', you would be forgiven for assuming that this philosophy was nothing at all like atheism. Technically, this was true. Deists claimed to believe in God and agreed that God created the universe. Beyond this claim, however – and on a practical level – deism and atheism were remarkably similar.

Deists believe that God created the universe as a form of machine, which he switched on and left alone. This 'universe machine' then continued to operate according to its original design, even though God was not present or making decisions about its operations. This made it possible to study and understand the universe without making any reference to Him. There was no revelation or divine intervention in this model of the universe, nor indeed any need for them. As a deist, you could study the cause and effect of events within this machine-like material universe exactly as an atheist would, without risking the social condemnation that coming out as an actual atheist would then have caused.

It's no coincidence that the rise of deism in the Age of Enlightenment was accompanied by a fad for automatons. The most famous was the Mechanical Turk (1770), a robot wearing a turban that appeared to be able to play chess, and the Digesting Duck (1739). The robot duck had over 400 moving parts in each wing alone, and when switched on it appeared to eat grain, drink water and defecate. While the actual chess playing and duck defecation were faked, the automatons still suggested a new way to think about life. They were clockwork machines that looked and behaved like living things, despite clearly not having a soul or immaterial essence. As such, they give an insight into the universe as the deists, and the abstracting, rational Urizenic part of our minds, perceived it. Urizen was picturing the universe in his own image, as something law-bound, self-referential, and separate from the observer. If the universe was nothing more than a machine, it followed that the animals and people it contained should be understood as machines also. The more people explored the idea of a machine universe, the more it seemed complete and comprehendible. Suddenly, the immaterial world of soul or spirit was no longer required.

By the mid-eighteenth century, deism had developed into a significant and threatening body of thought which the religiously inclined felt necessary to condemn. In 1754, the English Presbyterian minister John Leland published *A View of the Principal Deistical Writers*, which detailed leading deist thinkers and their heresies. The Scottish philosopher David Hume, whose essay *The Natural History of Religion* was published in 1757, the year of Blake's birth, was brave enough to argue for a position somewhere beyond deism, but at this point there were very few who dared go all the way into full-blown atheism. For the enquiring intellectual who wished to avoid being ostracised by a largely religious society, deism was a philosophy that was treated with suspicion, but which still provided plausible deniability from the damning accusation of atheism. By claiming you were studying God's handiwork, it was possible to investigate the workings of a godless universe.

Western philosophy and culture, from the Pythagoreans onwards, had proceeded on the understanding that both the material and the immaterial worlds exist. This position is known as dualism, and it fits our everyday experience of life well. There is a problem, however, and it concerns the interaction between these two worlds. How do the world of solid, physical matter and the world of intangible thoughts and feelings relate to each other? How can a thought that has no physical presence affect the material world?

In theory, there should be no way that something with no material aspect could impact a physical system. However, this happens all the time, for example when the idle thought, 'I wonder what's in the fridge?' results in a physical human walking across the kitchen, opening the fridge and eating some cheese. This was a problem that deeply troubled the French philosopher René Descartes. Eventually, he managed to hand-wave it away by claiming, with no real justification, that the immaterial and material interacted through the pituitary gland in the brain. In the centuries that have followed, much effort has been expended in seeking a less arbitrary answer.

Our current model of what's going on is that, however it happens, it is all the brain's fault. Although we have no idea how the electrochemical mush of a physical brain interacts with, or creates, the immaterial realm of consciousness, the assumption is that somehow it does. Because of this assumption, it is a common belief that the immaterial world of consciousness only exists inside our brains, and that there is no immaterial aspect to the universe outside of our skulls.

Some hardcore rationalists argue that the best way to solve the problem of consciousness's ability to impact matter is to deny that it does. The appearance of it doing so must therefore be an illusion. In this scenario, there is no reason to think that the immaterial exists at all. This position – that there is only a material universe, and that the existence of anything immaterial is meaningless, delusional and false – is called materialism. Although a materialist might acknowledge that we do not currently understand what consciousness is, they typically assume that one day everything, including consciousness, will be explained in a materialist framework, because ultimately everything is only matter. This is something of a circular argument.

The opposite philosophy of materialism is called idealism, which is the belief that only the immaterial exists and that matter is an illusion. This illusion of the physical world is created out of the immaterial mind of God in much the same way that Urizen created our limited, physical world out of a void of formless potential. An eighteenth-century proponent of idealism was the Irish philosopher George Berkeley, Bishop of Cloyne. As the politician Lord Chesterfield noted, Berkeley 'has written a book to prove that there is no such thing as matter, and that nothing exists but in idea [...] His arguments are, strictly speaking, unanswerable; but yet I am so far from being convinced by them, that I am determined to go on to eat and drink, and walk and ride, in order to keep that *matter*, which I so mistakenly imagine my body at present to consist of, in as good a plight as possible.'

Just as the modern world leans towards a philosophy of materialism without entirely accepting it, so too did the religiously inclined in the early eighteenth century lean towards idealism, usually without fully swallowing it. Here the idealist Bishop Berkeley has much in common with the modern American materialist philosopher Daniel Dennett, who has argued that consciousness is an illusion. Both Berkeley and Dennett were strikingly original and brave thinkers who could construct elegant and impressive arguments in favour of their purist models of the universe. And yet, for all their talents, neither could quite convince the general public of their idealist or materialist philosophy. Just as our everyday experience of the material world prevented those in the eighteenth century from being convinced by idealism, so too does our experience of immaterial consciousness prevent us from accepting materialism. For all our inability to explain how the material and immaterial can interact, we generally believe in both and remain at heart dualists.

Dualism, however, is a philosophical position not without its schisms. We may accept the reality of both the material and the immaterial, but people have been profoundly split on which came first. Which is primary – mind or matter?

In the secular twenty-first-century West, the accepted answer is that the material world came first. The physical universe came into existence for no reason 13.8 billion years ago. It was a lifeless, material chaos with no immaterial aspect. In time, the simple, light elements of matter formed into stars, which fused into heavier elements, which became the building blocks of planets. On at least one of those planets, life emerged out of the mineral world in all its wild and glorious forms. Consciousness somehow sparked into being inside life and, more extraordinarily still, it evolved into self-consciousness. In this way, the immaterial became aware of itself.

It was from within the mysterious world of consciousness that the immaterial world – ideas, spirits, the experience of emotions and so on – was born. It logically follows, then, that for the billions of years that it took for matter to form into life capable of consciousness, the immaterial was entirely absent from the universe. This is, admittedly, a model of the universe that doesn't fit well with a number of interpretations of quantum mechanics, which require a conscious observer for anything fixed and definite to occur. That aside, this is our scientific culture's current best model, and there are many scientific and astronomical measurements to back it up.

The idea that the material world preceded the immaterial one is relatively new, however, and in the eighteenth century few would have been prepared to put their names to such a godless position. That deism was as close as you could publicly get to atheism is a reminder that, for most of history, people believed that it was the immaterial world that came first, and that matter was created out of it. This was the understanding of much of the world's religions and thinkers up until the time of Blake, Swedenborg and the Age of Enlightenment. As the Bible told us, in the beginning was the Word, and this Word was clearly something immaterial. A word is not a material object.

For most of the world's great religions, mind preceded matter.

The immaterial came first. This immaterial thing was God, or the universal spirit, or Brahman, or the Tao, or whatever name individual cultures preferred. After an eternal period of solitude, this immaterial spirit eventually decided to produce the world of matter. This physical world was usually described as an 'emanation' from the fundamental immaterial reality.

Just as a material world with no immaterial aspect is problematic in quantum mechanics, so too does the idea of an immaterial universe with no material aspect raise questions. Not least of these is the issue of what God was doing for the uncountable eons before he decided to make the universe. The idea that God sat around for many trillions of years doing nothing strikes many as deeply odd. In the beginning there was the Word, we are told, but what sort of Word could that be when there was nothing for that Word to refer to?

Whether the material or the immaterial came first looks suspiciously like a trick question. Both appear to be meaningless concepts without each other. Like Blake's contraries, it may be that neither can exist in isolation, and that both the immaterial and the material are, like two sides of a coin, incomplete without their opposite. Perhaps they are necessary aspects of some other larger reality, in the same way that time and space were believed to be separate, contrasting things before Einstein realised that they were both part of something more fundamental, which he called spacetime. The idea that the material and the immaterial are two aspects of the same, hidden substance has been given the slightly disappointing name of dual-aspect monism.

Both Blake and Swedenborg, however, believed that the immaterial world had primacy over the material. To them, the divine light of spirit came first, and it logically followed that this was more important than the cold, dense world of matter. This belief is common to those who have experienced mystical states, as William

James noted in his ground-breaking study *The Varieties of Religious Experience*. As we discussed earlier, those who undergo a visionary experience frequently report that the world they saw was *more real* than the everyday world they left behind – in a way that they can't quite explain, but which they are entirely certain about. This was a belief expressed by Swedenborg and countless visionaries, mystics and religious leaders across centuries, from the mystery schools of the classical world to the religions, occult schools and traditions that followed.

If the mind or spirit feels 'more real' than the physical world to those who have experience of it, then it would seem self-evident that mind came first and that it has primacy over matter. After all, how could the world of matter produce something that seemed more real than itself? As we have already noted, however, this may be a side effect of the mind operating without a sense of self. When an idea appears in the mind normally, the thinker is aware of what has happened and is present to critique that idea. With the thinker absent, the arrival of an idea can feel more like revelation than thought, and it is unquestioningly accepted.

While those who immerse themselves in the immaterial world find it self-evident that mind or spirit is more fundamental than matter, modern scientists who immerse themselves in the material world are equally convinced that physical reality is more real and more important than feelings or imagination. In the famous 'double slit' experiment in particle physics, light behaves as a wave when we measure it as a wave, and it behaves like a particle when we measure it as a particle. In a similar way, consciousness is more fundamental than matter when the world is explored spiritually, and matter is more fundamental than mind when the world is examined scientifically. Whichever truth you wish to find about the nature of things, the universe is happy to show it to you.

*

Belief in the primacy of the immaterial lies behind one of the key ideas in Swedenborg's theology, which is the concept of correspondences. As Swedenborg saw things, everything in the physical world corresponded to something glorious and wonderful in the spiritual realm. Things only exist down here because there is a spiritual equivalent existing up there in splendour. This is an idea that has strong parallels with hermetic and magical thought, although Swedenborg denied that he had read earlier mystical writers such as the German philosopher Jakob Boehme, with whom his philosophy shares many similarities. Blake had read Boehme, however, and rated him highly. His influence is clear when Blake writes that 'every Natural Effect has a Spiritual Cause', or that, 'We who dwell on Earth can do nothing of ourselves, every thing is conducted by Spirits, no less than Digestion or Sleep.'

There are similarities between Swedenborg's correspondences and the Platonic theory of forms. In a number of his dialogues, Plato argued that for an object, such as a chair, to exist in the physical world, there must first exist an idealised, perfect chair in some immaterial abstract realm. A 'Platonic form' like this remains unaffected by the fate of chairs on earth. This was one aspect of Platonic philosophy that Blake agreed with. As he wrote in *Milton*:

The Oak is cut down by the Ax, the Lamb falls by the Knife
But their Forms Eternal Exist, For-ever.

Swedenborg believed that correspondences were not always a simple one-to-one match. Indeed, it might not be immediately apparent what a physical earthly thing was a representation of in the world of spirits. The light and warmth of the sun on your face, for example, did not correspond to a giant ball of light in heaven's sky. Instead, it corresponded with divine love and truth.

Because everything in the material world ultimately corresponded with some higher spiritual event, as Swedenborg believed, it logically followed that the study of earthly reality could reveal much about the nature of the heavens. Each letter and number, for example, would have their own spiritual origin and meaning. This meant that even the most mundane sentence in the Bible could contain profound wisdom, if only the true nature of correspondences was understood. For Swedenborg, everything was a sign: the physical world was a language to be read. This is the logic that gave rise to practices like numerology and astrology. It is also why materialists and dual-aspect monists dismiss them. Even committed idealists can admit that seeing every aspect of this world as a coded message from the spirit world can soon become exhausting.

Swedenborg tended to favour simple, literal associations between aspects of earthly life and spiritual things. This is why the heaven he described was so similar to earth, and why angels had jobs, prepared food and lived in houses. To the modern mind, it might appear that this is the wrong way around. Swedenborg's spiritual version of domesticity seems more plausible as a reflection of earthly domesticity, not least because angelic jobs and chores don't really make a lot of sense in a world where space and time don't work like they do on earth. But Swedenborg believed that the immaterial was more real and therefore primary. Life on earth, in this scenario, must be a reflection of the angels and not the other way around.

This may explain why Swedenborg's angels were sexually active. According to his theory of correspondences, sex on earth must correspond with something in heaven, and the powerful, emotionally involving and overwhelming nature of sex suggested that it must relate to something important. Swedenborg decided that the correspondence in this case was simple and literal, for what else could human sex represent but loving relations between angelic couples? Because of this, he argued in favour of tolerance of a wide variety of human sexual practices on the grounds that these too were echoes of heavenly love. These included pre-marital sex and the taking of other partners by married people should their sexual life with their spouse be, for whatever reason, unsatisfying. It is possible that Swedenborg's beliefs in this area influenced Blake's attempt to take a partner other than Catherine in the 1790s. It is also possible that the emotional hurt this caused was the reason the older, wiser Blake told Henry Crabb Robinson that Swedenborg's 'sexual religion is dangerous' thirty years later.

Swedenborg's concept of correspondences has been incredibly influential. Charles Baudelaire published his most famous volume of poetry in 1857, *Les Fleurs du mal* (*The Flowers of Evil*). It included a poem called 'Correspondances', which was Baudelaire's attempt to express Swedenborg's ideas in a poetic form. It begins with the metaphor '*La Nature est un temple*' (Nature is a temple), and goes on to describe how we live in a forest of symbols. 'Correspondances' is often credited as the beginning of Symbolism, one of the more important artistic movements of the nineteenth century.

Baudelaire also wrote about a condition now called synaes-thesia, in which the senses can be blended so that a person hears colour, or perhaps sees music. The most common form of synaes-thesia is called grapheme-colour synaesthesia, in which different letters and numbers are perceived to be associated with different colours. The French poet Arthur Rimbaud experienced letters in this way and wrote about it in his poem 'Voyelles' ('Vowels'). Many other creative people were or are synaesthetes, including Nikola Tesla, Vladimir Nabokov, David Hockney, Richard Feynman, Billy Joel, Joanne Harris and Aphex Twin. The musician and producer Pharrell Williams wrote about his condition on the N.E.R.D. album *Seeing Colours*.

Neurologically, it is not well understood, although we know it is lifelong, stable, involuntary and has a genetic component. Around 4 per cent of the population experiences some form of synaesthesia, and the condition can sometimes be experienced by non-synaesthetes through the use of psychedelic drugs. It is possible that Blake experienced a similar condition to synaesthesia, because he wrote of 'seeing' words in the air around him. Some synaesthetes, incidentally, not only report seeing the words people say to them in conversations, but also that words in different accents appear in different fonts.

Neurologists acknowledge that the condition of synaesthesia is not well defined and refers to a broad number of different experiences which may have differing neurological causes. We can say, however, that Blake was extremely comfortable with inner states being expressed in multiple ways through different senses. Metaphor was one of his greatest strengths, from the 'mind forg'd manacles' to the 'arrows of desire' or the 'forest of the night'. In a world where text and images and music are now routinely combined, it can be hard to grasp just how ground-breaking were his illustrated books, in which poetry, design and, for *Songs of Innocence* at least, music were all created at the same time and understood to be part of the same artistic expression.

Thanks to Symbolist art and early twentieth-century psychologists such as Sigmund Freud and Carl Jung, the idea that an object in the world symbolises something immaterial is common in the twenty-first century. We understand that different rules apply in the material and immaterial realms. In the physical world and in the 'single vision' that Blake hated, it is the case that one object is just one object and nothing more. But in the immaterial world of the mind, things are very different. The immaterial world is a place of metaphor. One thing can be many, and many things can be one.

The world of vision is not neat or easily catalogued. Recognising this is important for understanding Blake's work where, for example, a figure such as Orc is understood to be a human-like character and, simultaneously, the urge towards violent revolution. These multiple levels of meaning become increasingly evident in Blake's work, particularly in, as we shall see, his later epic work *Jerusalem*.

Given how heavily Blake used metaphor and symbolism in his work, and his constant efforts to stress the importance of the imagination at a time when people favoured reason, it is easy to assume that Blake agreed with Swedenborg, and believed that this was absolutely a world that existed as the emanation of God. Yet if you read him closer, it becomes apparent that it is not that simple.

In *The Marriage of Heaven and Hell*, Blake states his belief that, 'God only Acts & Is, in existing beings or Men.' The immaterial, spiritual world requires the imagination of physical humans in order to exist. Without people, in other words, there would be no God. This is a logical consequence of his belief that we create gods by our imaginative powers and that, as he wrote in the same work, 'All deities reside in the human breast.'

To Blake, asking whether the spiritual or physical world came first would have seemed a meaningless question. As we have already seen, the boundary between the interior and exterior worlds was blurred in Blake's philosophy. As far as he was concerned, the imagination of man was the source of everything, both physical and spiritual. By taking this stance, Blake sidestepped the categories of idealism and materialism, and he avoided the dualist question of whether the physical or the immaterial had primacy. As always, he had no interest in perceiving the universe through the categories used by academia.

In Blake's philosophy, God creates man and man creates God. This is, for most, an alien way of thinking and it is one of the reasons why Blake's work is so easily misunderstood. The immaterial imagination is the source of everything, yet this imagination requires a flesh-and-blood human in order to manifest. It seems as if this is an unsolvable paradox. When thinking in standard categories, it is.

Yet as we have noted, time and space originally appeared to be unrelated concepts, so different that they could almost be said to be opposites. Or at least they did, until Einstein proved they were opposite sides of the same coin – indivisible aspects of a larger cosmological substance he called spacetime. In a similar way, a dual-aspect monist believes that the material and immaterial qualities of the universe are also the opposite sides of a cosmological coin. They could not exist without each other and are both aspects of a higher aspect of the universe we lack the perspective to see.

In the mind of Blake, this was the same as the relationship between God and man. Neither could exist without the other, for they were both aspects of a larger unperceived reality. And if they were both necessary aspects of the same unseen thing, then man and God had to be considered as equally important. Blake was far outside contemporary thought here, exploring territory a long way from standard theology. With this key idea in place and the value of humanity radically reappraised, he was able to channel these ideas into his work. What followed was an extraordinary creative flowering.

9

Enitharmon slept,
Eighteen hundred years; Man was a Dream!
The night of Nature and their harps unstrung:
She slept in middle of her nightly song,
Eighteen hundred years, a female dream!

Shadows of men in fleeting bands upon the winds:
Divide the heavens of Europe:
Till Albions Angel smitten with his own plagues fled with his bands
The cloud bears hard on Albions shore:
Fill'd with immortal demons of futurity:
In council gather the smitten Angels of Albion
The cloud bears hard upon the council house; down rushing
On the heads of Albions Angels.

One hour they lay buried beneath the ruins of that hall;
But as the stars rise from the salt lake they arise in pairs,
In troubled mists oerclouded by the terrors of struggling times

10.
APPEARD AS ONE MAN

William Blake spent most of the 1790s in a small brick terraced house with a garden in Lambeth, south of the Thames, were he lived with Catherine and a large wooden printing press. It was a decade of extraordinary creative productivity and relative stability – arguments about extramarital affairs aside.

The decade began with the printing of *The Marriage of Heaven and Hell* in 1790. In this, he casually states, 'I have also; The Bible of Hell: which the world shall have whether they will or no.' Blake scholars generally consider the name 'Bible of Hell' to refer to the bulk of the illuminated books he produced during this decade. There has been much academic debate about exactly which works should be thought of as part of Blake's Bible of Hell and which are outside the Hell Bible 'canon'. The short works that explore characters from Blake's emerging personal mythology – *The Song of Los* (1795), *The First Book of Urizen* (1794), *The Book of Ahania* (1795), and *The Book of Los* (1795) – are generally accepted as included, while arguments have been made to include the longer works *Europe a Prophecy* (1794) and *America a Prophecy* (1793), as well as *The Marriage of Heaven and Hell* itself.

Alongside the work that makes up the Bible of Hell, he produced 'Visions of the Daughters of Albion' (1793) and *Songs of Experience* (1794) in the same decade, as well as much paid engraving work for other people that generated the bulk of his income. Disappointingly, he could only find a handful of buyers for his own illuminated books. Most typically achieved sales in single figures. This made his revolutionary printing technique a little redundant, as it was designed for mass reproduction. Yet a lack of audience did not deter him from his labour, and it is hard not to be impressed by the quantity and quality of work he generated during this inspired and productive decade – even before you factor in the watercolours and other artworks he produced. These include some of his most famous, including *Newton* and *Nebuchadnezzar*, which were first produced in 1795.

At the start of the decade, Blake was still optimistic that his new printing technique would be the key to financial success. In October 1793, he produced a prospectus headed 'TO THE PUBLIC', which detailed his various works for sale. It begins with the declaration, 'The Labours of the Artist, the Poet, the Musician, have been proverbially attended by poverty and obscurity; this was never the fault of the Public, but was owing to a neglect of means to propagate such works as have wholly absorbed the Man of Genius. Even Milton and Shakespeare could not publish their own works.' Blake then outlines his new printing method, which he claims 'produces work at less than one fourth of the expense'.

'If a method of Printing which combines the Painter and the Poet is a phenomenon worthy of public attention, provided that it exceeds in elegance all former methods, the Author is sure of his reward,' he wrote. He then listed the prices of various works, ranging from 3 shillings for *The Book of Thel* to 7 shillings and sixpence for *The Marriage of Heaven and Hell* or 'Visions of the Daughters of Albion'. *Songs of Innocence* and *Songs of Experience* were still listed as separate works at this point, available for 5 shillings each. If the public proved receptive, it had all the makings of a profitable venture.

Unfortunately, they were not. Only a handful of copies found buyers. Even *Songs of Innocence and of Experience*, his best known and most accessible work, only sold around thirty copies in his lifetime. As the 1790s rolled on, it gradually became apparent that Blake's career was not taking off to the same extent as those of his peers from the Royal Academy. At the start of the decade, when the Blakes moved into their new Lambeth home, they were financially comfortable enough to hire a maid. They let their maid go after a few years, however, and were never in a position to employ help again. In the struggle that was the world versus William Blake, it was increasingly apparent that he was now the underdog.

Blake was not being commissioned as a professional engraver as much as he would have liked, presumably owing to his unusual personality rather than the quality of his work. He narrowly missed out on opportunities, such as the funding to study in Italy that launched the careers of some of his contemporaries. His friend the sculptor John Flaxman, for example, went to Italy with the intention of studying for two years, on a trip partly funded by the potter Josiah Wedgwood. A rash of commissions while in Rome extended his voyage for seven years, and when he returned home to London in 1794, he was on his way to becoming one of the most successful and influential English artists of his day. Blake, in contrast, remained at home, aware that the paid work that came his way was starting to dry up.

Still, the end of a decade meant that a new century was about to begin, with all the potential and possibilities that this opened up. Whatever life threw at him, Blake never lost his capacity for optimism. The new era in Britain, however, was a time of expansion, commerce and Empire, where the rational 'single vision' of science proved to be a valuable tool for industry, profit and power. The nineteenth century was when the Enlightenment ideas of the eighteenth century were set free and ran to their logical conclusion. Rationality, an emerging middle class and mass production reshaped the material world at the expense of craftsmanship, tradition and the human soul. Although there were original ideas and thinkers in the nineteenth century, such as Marx, Darwin and Freud, their impact would be mostly felt in the twentieth century. The nineteenth century was, in essence, a faster and more competitive version of the eighteenth, and its basic outline was in place right from the beginning. It was not an era in which Blake was going to thrive.

The year 1800 marked a significant event in Blake's life. For the first and only time, he and Catherine moved out of London. This was because of an opportunity presented by a wealthy poet, biographer and patron of artists, William Hayley, who had a country home in the village of Felpham, near Bognor on the Sussex coast.

Hayley had an illegitimate son, Tom, who was dying of a spinal disease. He wanted an engraving of his son produced, based on a portrait by the historical painter Henry Howard, and John Flaxman recommended Blake for the job. The commission did not go smoothly. Blake left Hayley waiting many weeks for the engraving, the finished result was considered a poor likeness and Blake had to rework the image before it was accepted. Not, on the face of it, a promising start to their relationship.

Blake was experiencing a period of depression at the time. He confessed to George Cumberland that he had fallen into a 'Deep pit of Melancholy, Melancholy without any real reason for it, a Disease which God keep you from & all good men'. This is one of Blake's earliest references to the state of his mental health, although they would shortly become more common. His recognition here that depression was 'a Disease' shows an understanding which was far ahead of his time.

After Hayley's son Tom died on 2 May 1800, Blake wrote a remarkable letter of condolence. This seems to have affected Hayley deeply:

> I know that our deceased friends are more really with us than when they were apparent to our mortal part. Thirteen years ago I lost a brother & with his spirit I converse daily & hourly in the Spirit & see him in my remembrance in the regions of my Imagination. I hear his advice & even now write from his Dictate. Forgive me for Expressing to you my Enthusiasm which I wish all to partake of Since it is to me a Source of Immortal Joy: even in this world by it I am the companion of Angels. May you continue to be so more & more & to be more and more persuaded, that every mortal loss is an Immortal Gain. The Ruins of Time builds Mansions in Eternity.

After this letter, Hayley took a greater interest in Blake and looked for ways that he could help support the struggling artist. He attempted to promote Blake's work among his wealthy social circle, with occasional success. He also knew of a thatched labourer's cottage near his home in Felpham which faced south, looking over the fields to the sea. He suggested that Blake and Catherine might move to this cottage, where he could work under Hayley's patronage, for example by producing engravings for Hayley's biography of the poet William Cowper.

Blake considered Hayley's offer the answer to all his problems. As any freelancer will admit, an offer of guaranteed financial support after a lengthy period of insecure grifting is deeply appealing. As he wrote in a letter to his lifelong friend George Cumberland at the beginning of September, 'I have now better prospects than ever

The little I want will be easily supplied he has given me a twelve-months work already, & there is a great deal more in prospect I call myself now Independent. I can be Poet Painter & Musician as the Inspiration comes.' He ended the letter with a few lines that expressed his feelings about leaving London:

> Dear generous Cumberland nobly solicitous for a Friends welfare. Behold me Whom your Friendship has Magnified: Rending the manacles of Londons Dungeon dark I have rent the black net & escap'd. See My Cottage at Felpham in joy Beams over the sea a bright light over France, but the Web & the Veil I have left Behind me at London resists every beam of light; hanging from heaven to Earth Dropping with human gore. Lo! I have left it! I have torn it from my limbs I shake my wings ready to take my flight! Pale, Ghastly pale: stands the City in fear

A 'Dungeon dark [...] Dropping with human gore' is, by anyone's standards, a bleak way to view your hometown, but it gives an insight into the depression Blake was suffering.

The Blakes moved to Felpham on 18 September 1800. It was a major undertaking, requiring their printing press to be disassembled and the parts packed away, along with all his engraved copper plates, into a total of sixteen crates. These then had to be taken by carriage for the sixty-mile journey from Lambeth to Felpham. The journey went smoothly, however, and the beautiful weather on the way south seemed to promise a new, blissful period in his life.

Blake's surviving letters show that he found Sussex life joyful, at least at the start. 'Sussex is certainly a happy place & Felpham in particular is the sweetest spot on Earth at least it is to me & My Good Wife,' he wrote in May 1801. 'The Villagers of Felpham are not mere Rustics they are polite & modest. Meat is cheaper than in London but the sweet air & the voices of winds trees & birds & the odours of the happy ground makes it a dwelling for immortals,' he wrote shortly after arriving. In a letter to John Flaxman around the same time, he makes it clear that he thinks the change of environment will intensify his visions: 'Felpham is a sweet place for Study. because it is more Spiritual than London Heaven opens here on all sides her golden Gates her windows are not obstructed by vapours. voices of Celestial inhabitants are more distinctly heard & their forms more distinctly seen.' When he looked out of his cottage windows, over the fields down to the sea, he saw angels mixing with labourers in the fields.

Blake described a remarkable vision in verses he sent to Thomas Butts in October 1800, soon after arriving in Felpham. It was triggered by watching the sun from the yellow sands of the beach, which sent him to a place 'Remote from Desire'. As Blake watched, each individual jewel-like particle of light revealed itself to be a tiny man, as did each grain of sand, and every stone, mountain and hill.

My Eyes more & more
Like a Sea without shore
Continue Expanding
The Heavens commanding
Till the Jewels of Light
Heavenly Men beaming bright
Appeard as One Man

Taken together, these countless tiny men were also one man. The universal man folded Blake into his arms and spoke gently, telling him that he was a 'Ram hornd with gold':

And the voice faded mild
I remaind as a Child
All I ever had known
Before me bright Shone

That the experience had turned Blake into 'a Child' suggests a return to the innocent state of consciousness he experienced wandering the countryside as a youth. Of course, such an elated and ecstatic vision coming so soon after the 'Melancholy' he experienced in London would now be thought of as bipolar or manic-depressive symptoms. Such a condition may have been a factor in his awareness of contraries.

The strange idea at the heart of this vision, that every particle of the universe is a little man, and that collectively they make up a universal man, is one that can be found in Swedenborg. In the years before his visions, as we've noted, Swedenborg was what we now think of as a proto-scientist. He attempted to understand what the universe was made of, on both micro and macro levels. Through his studies, he concluded that the cosmos was, to borrow a much later word, a hologram.

With a hologram, the entire image is encoded at every point of the picture. If you were to cut in half a regular photograph and discard the left half, what would remain would be the right-hand part of the image, and nothing more. If you were to cut a hologram in half and discard one part, however, you would be left with a smaller version of the same image. Continue cutting and you would get smaller and smaller holograms, all of which would contain the entire image. There are many modern physicists who take the idea of a holographic universe seriously, although they arrived at this conclusion for very different reasons to Swedenborg.

Swedenborg believed that everything in the universe worked like a hologram. The sun, for example, would be made up of countless tiny versions of the sun, each of which could be further subdivided into endless smaller suns. Likewise, the sun could be thought of as being a constituent part of some larger, vaster sun.

Swedenborg lived at a time when chemistry was in its infancy. The idea that the universe was built from tiny building blocks, called atoms, had been around since the ancient Greek philosopher Democritus, but it would take until 1905 before Albert Einstein proved that atoms existed. We now know that a lump of a natural element such as gold can be endlessly divided, down to an atomic level, into smaller and smaller pieces of gold, as Swedenborg believed. But most things are created from a mix of different elements, rather than being a unique substance. The sun is not made of smaller and smaller elements of sun, for example, but out of a combination of helium and hydrogen atoms, with a few other elements. In his attempts to explain the materiality of the universe, Swedenborg has been shown to be wrong, but, given what was then known about the nature of things, his theory was certainly interesting.

When his attention moved to spiritual matters, Swedenborg again applied the logic of his holographic, fractal-like cosmos to the higher realms. Heaven is made up of angels, and thus must be a giant angelic figure itself. Likewise, the highest and most important thing in the physical universe is humanity, and hence the universe itself must be an immense person – a figure usually referred to as the Grand Man or the Universal Man. As Swedenborg described the situation, 'The Whole Heaven, Grasped as a single Entity, Reflects a Single Individual.' This idea is not unique to Swedenborg, but it was important for him and he leans on it heavily in his writings. A similar fractal-like relationship between the microscopic world and the macroscopic world is central to hermetic and alchemical thought, which describes the situation with the maxim 'as above, so below'. As the vision Blake wrote about to Thomas Butts shows, it was an idea that fitted into Blake's philosophy also. As we shall see, it is of central importance to his greatest work.

The idea that the universe is a giant person may be hard to reconcile with a twenty-first-century worldview. Think of the enormity of the cosmos, of the stars and immense black holes and the vast distances between them. Think also of the intricacy of life on this planet, of the ecosystems in rivers and forests and the slow creativity of evolution. Think of the totality of creation, of the scorching temperatures inside supernovas and the dark emptiness of the voids between. How can such a vast cosmos be inside some form of giant person? The idea seems absurd.

Yet the cosmos you were just then experiencing was not physical reality. It was nothing more than your imagination, the one you have created inside your mind. In this example, you were the Universal Man or Woman inside which that immense cosmos existed. It is this universe, which fools you into thinking it is a physical world when it is nothing more than mind, that Swedenborg and Blake are describing. Recall these lines from *Jerusalem*:

> [...] in your own Bosom you bear your Heaven
> And Earth, & all you behold, tho it appears Without it is Within
> In your Imagination [...]

Once again, we see how the division between the interior and exterior worlds are blurred in Blake's philosophy, and how the universe we perceive is a product of both ourselves and the cosmos. It would not exist otherwise.

There are precedents for ideas like this in the Christian faith. The Gospel of Luke includes an account of Jesus being asked for concrete details regarding the kingdom of God and when it would arrive. This kingdom, Jesus replied, would not be something physical that people would be able to point at: 'Neither shall they say, Lo here! or, lo there! for, behold, the kingdom of God is within you.' Established Churches did not tend to explore this idea, however, and neither do they stress that gods, angels, heavens and demons were the product of the internal world. Blake, in contrast, was clear that God can only exist where the human mind is present; to mention again what he wrote in *The Marriage of Heaven and Hell*: 'God only Acts and Is, in existing beings or Men', or more simply, 'men forgot that All deities reside in the human breast'.

From this perspective, the universe is indeed inside a great cosmic figure, and that person is you. Blake and Swedenborg describe the figure as being male because they themselves were male, but of course this Universal Human will match the gender of whoever perceives it. In theological terms, this position has dramatic implications. No longer is mankind small, pitiful and at the mercy of a cruel and vengeful God. Instead, humanity has been vastly raised in power and importance. Here we recall the Blakean concept discussed in the last chapter, in which God and man were indivisible and, in some way, dependent on each other.

This pro-mankind stance leads us to another heretical position, and one which perhaps more than any other differentiates Blake from other Western cosmologies. Blake believed that there was no separation between the body and the soul. Instead, the body was part of the soul. Again, he is clear about this in *The Marriage of Heaven and Hell*. 'Man has no Body distinct from his Soul', he wrote. 'The notion that man has a body distinct from his soul, is to be expunged.' This is a distinct break from the dualism which has coloured Western thinking from Plato onwards, in which the immaterial and material aspects of the universe were thought of as separate and incompatible.

The way we thought about our bodies was starting to change in Blake's era. Flesh was previously seen as something corrupt, weak and foul. Diets and standards of hygiene were poor and sores, insect bites and potent body odours were considered normal. Diaries and letters of the period reveal the deep repugnance many people felt about both their own flesh, and about that of others. The elaborate wigs and powders worn by the upper classes may now seem comical, but they reflected the desire for refinement and elegance over physical reality.

Our view of the body started to change in the second half of the eighteenth century. A culture that previously saw plump fleshiness as a sign of status and vitality began moving towards more narcissistic ideas of exercise and controlled diets, such as those favoured by Lord Byron. But this was still a long way from viewing the body as being on a par with the soul.

Many early Christian thinkers saw the material body as the prison of the immaterial soul, and hence something to be despised. The practice of self-flagellation which runs throughout Christian history is a product of ideas such as this, although thankfully few took it to the lengths of the third-century Christian theologian Origen of Alexandria, who is said to have castrated himself for God.

The teachings of Augustine a couple of centuries later softened these ideas. He argued that original sin was the cause of all our woes, and not simply the flesh itself. This shifted the spiritual battleground from the body to the will, and argued that we had the ability to resist physical temptation. Augustine's excuse for bodily sins was in agreement with the Gospel of Matthew: 'the spirit is willing, but the flesh is weak.'

None of these developments questioned the centuries-old idea that body and soul were two different things. As we've noted, this dualism is central to Western thought, so to find alternatives you need to look outside of Europe. Western, Chinese and Indian Vedic thought all differ in how they conceptualise the fundamental nature of the universe, and hence all have very different perspectives on the subject.

In Vedic philosophy, the ultimate reality of the universe is called Brahman. A key concept in many schools of Indian thought is that *atman* equals *Brahman*, where *atman* refers to the self or the soul. If an individual looked within themselves, it was thought, they would discover that there was no separation or difference between themselves and the eternal unchanging nature of the universe. Deep inside, the soul and the physical world were ultimately the same. As we saw earlier, this is a philosophy not of dualism, but of dual-aspect monism. It is also an idea that agrees with Blake's philosophy. As he wrote in *The Marriage of Heaven and Hell*, 'The philosophy of the east taught the first principles of human perception.'

This need to go deeply within to discover the true nature of things was absent in Chinese thought. The Chinese had no interest in ideas like abstract, eternal souls. Instead, their fundamental principle was called the *Tao*, which was everywhere and everything. The Tao is the way of things, and a path that those in harmony with nature would follow.

In Europe, by contrast, philosophers after Pythagoras insisted on a dualist position in which soul and matter were two entirely separate things. In his dialogues, Plato talked of physical objects being poor reflections of perfect immaterial forms which existed elsewhere, in some unreachable heaven. The distinction between soul and matter has since been reframed as the distinction between mind and matter, but the general principle of a fundamental separation remains.

Here, then, are three very different starting points for the foundation of culture and philosophy. If your idea of the fundamental principle of the universe was *Brahman*, you would expect to find this deep inside an object. If your fundamental principle was the *Tao*, then the object itself would be part of the *Tao*, and there would be no need to look inside to find it. But if your fundamental principle was dualist, and you considered matter and soul to be separate, then the thing you would be looking for would not be part of the physical object. It would be away somewhere in an unreachable immaterial realm. This is the idea that sits at the heart of the European worldview.

For Blake to insist that the body was part of the soul was to go against centuries of Western assumptions and philosophy. His contemporaries and peers educated at Oxford and Cambridge placed great authority in ancient Greek and Christian ideas. With a dualist education, they were always going to struggle to understand his worldview. The assumptions that lay at the heart of Western philosophy were buried so deeply in their mental models of the world that they had become invisible, and as such could not be questioned. In those circumstances, Blake's baffling position was never going to make any sense. To the classically educated, it could only be categorised as madness.

But Blake was not bound by their categories or habits of thought. He was free of those particular 'mind-forg'd manacles', which are adopted early in Western education. He was able to describe the universe as he perceived it, rather than how he was taught it should appear. His perspective offered a radical new framing of the relationship between man and God.

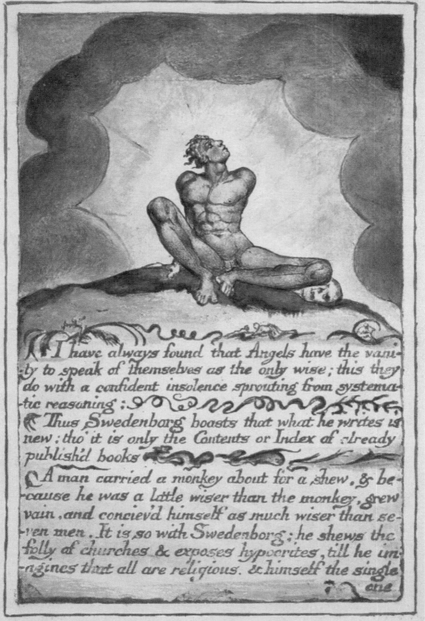

I have always found that Angels have the vanity to speak of themselves as the only wise; this they
do with a confident insolence sprouting from systematic reasoning:

Thus Swedenborg boasts that what he writes is
new: tho' it is only the Contents or Index of already
publish'd books

A man carried a monkey about for a shew, & because he was a little wiser than the monkey, grew
vain, and conciev'd himself as much wiser than seven men. It is so with Swedenborg; he shews the
folly of churches & exposes hypocrites, till he imagines that all are religious. & himself the single
one.

11.

GREEN & PLEASANT LAND

Blake's years away from London hold a special place in his story, because it was here that he started writing the words we now know as the hymn 'Jerusalem'. The 'green and pleasant land' of Sussex became, in time, the archetypal description of England. Other countries see themselves as bold, passionate, courageous, welcoming, strong or beautiful; only England dreams of being thought 'pleasant'.

The poem begins with two of Blake's most famous lines:

And did those feet in ancient time,
Walk upon Englands mountains green:

As ever with Blake, he doesn't pause to make his meaning clear. Whose feet is he talking about? Blake knows, so he assumes that everyone else will know as well. It is an attitude that makes his writing a glorious puzzle.

Frequent references to feet appear in his work, particularly after his time at Felpham. In *Milton*, for example, we are presented with the spirit of the poet John Milton falling from the heavens in the form of a star and entering Blake's body by landing on his foot. The symbolism of the foot can be explained by Blake's views on the relationship between body and soul. For Blake, the body is an aspect of the soul, as we've seen. The foot, therefore, is the lowest part of the soul. It is this that we use to step into the 'vegetative world' of the physical realm. The feet in ancient times were the vehicle that brought the divine spirit to the otherwise material realm of England's mountains green.

The words we now know as the hymn 'Jerusalem' are taken from the preface to the poem *Milton: a poem in 2 books* (and not, to confuse matters, from his other epic work *Jerusalem: The Emanation of the Giant Albion*). In England at least, these are now the most well-known lines that Blake wrote, but he discarded this preface and did not include it in later printings of *Milton*. When the poem beginning 'And did those feet' is seen in the context of the preface, its meaning is revealed to be very different to its popular interpretation. Perhaps Blake found it, with hindsight, too hectoring and political.

In the preface, Blake does not waste time warming up before delivering his opinions. It starts as a full-on rant. The opening paragraph begins:

> The Stolen and Perverted Writings of Homer & Ovid: of Plato & Cicero. which all Men ought to contemn: are set up by artifice against the Sublime of the Bible.

For Blake, the enemy was the rational, dualist interpretation of Greek philosophy that was drilled into students at the universities of Oxford and Cambridge. What was needed instead was the sublime inspiration of the Bible, and the great works which drew from it, which for Blake included the English writers Shakespeare and Milton. Blake believed that rote university learning of abstract ancient Greek arguments needed to be replaced by engaged creativity. As he put it in the preface, 'the Daughters of Memory shall become the Daughters of Inspiration'. This is the same argument made by the education reformer Sir Ken Robinson in his 2006 TED talk 'Do schools kill creativity?' It has been highly influential, and at the time of writing is the most watched TED talk of all time.

The preface very quickly becomes a rabble-rousing rallying cry to all those who want to overthrow the insipid, uninspired establishment of Britain, and replace it with the inspired and the brilliant:

Rouze up O Young Men of the New Age! set your foreheads against the ignorant Hirelings! For we have Hirelings in the Camp, the Court, & the University [...] We do not want either Greek or Roman Models if we are but just & true to our own Imaginations, those Worlds of Eternity in which we shall live for ever; in Jesus our Lord.

At this point, Blake switches to verse and asks whether divine inspiration has ever found a home on these damp islands. He calls for mental weapons, such as 'arrows of desire', along with physical weapons, such as a sword which won't sleep in his hand. These weapons are needed to overthrow the existing order and turn this bewildered land into paradise:

And did those feet in ancient time,
Walk upon Englands mountains green:
And was the holy Lamb of God,
On Englands pleasant pastures seen!

And did the Countenance Divine,
Shine forth upon our clouded hills?
And was Jerusalem builded here,
Among these dark Satanic Mills?

Bring me my Bow of burning gold:
Bring me my Arrows of desire:
Bring me my Spear: O clouds unfold!
Bring me my Chariot of fire!

I will not cease from Mental Fight,
Nor shall my Sword sleep in my hand:
Till we have built Jerusalem,
In Englands green & pleasant Land.

It is hard now to separate these words from the stirring, patriotic music that Sir Hubert Parry composed in 1916, while the First World War raged on. That this hymn is a favourite of English public schools is one of the great ironies of the William Blake story, because in the context of the preface it is basically a demand that such institutions be overthrown. Parry, it seems, understood the radical nature of the hymn better than his audience. He gifted the copyright to the National Union of Women's Suffrage Societies.

In the modern world, the reference to 'Jerusalem' being built in Britain may need explaining, given that Jerusalem is a city in Israel currently claimed by both Israel and the Palestinian National Authority. The spiritual significance of the city comes from it being the site of the temple of Solomon, which was the original temple the Israelites built for their god around 960 BCE. Inside this temple was an inner sanctuary called the Holy of Holies, which was revered as the single holiest place in the world. Only the high priest was allowed entry, and then only on one day a year. It was here that the Ark of the Covenant was kept. If ever there was a place on earth where it could be said that God resided, this was it. Around this sanctum and temple grew the city, so Jerusalem was thought to be the city in which God resided.

After invading Babylonians conquered the city and burnt the

temple to the ground in 587 BCE, the Israelite elite were transported to Babylon. For all Babylon's grandeur and strange temples to the god Marduk, it did not contain the Holy of Holies. The exiled Israelites, therefore, found themselves in a city in which God could not be said to live. Here is the reason why the names of these two cities continued to have spiritual resonance many centuries later. Jerusalem was a spiritual city where the divine dwelt, and Babylon was the city where God was absent. Numerous religious figures looked at the state of London in the eighteenth century and saw it as Babylon. Their mission, they felt, was to turn it into a New Jerusalem.

The 'dark Satanic Mills' of the poem are often commented on. The phrase is usually interpreted as an early condemnation of the factories of the Industrial Revolution, which were then starting to appear across the country, particularly in the north. Blake would have been familiar with these thanks to Albion Mills, a steam-powered flour mill in Southwark, not far from where he lived in Lambeth. The mill opened in 1786 and burnt down in 1791. It seems likely that Blake would have found the name of the factory deeply symbolic, and that he would have been horrified by the inhuman nature of working conditions in this mill and in the Industrial Revolution in general.

The 'dark Satanic Mills' can be interpreted differently, however. They are sometimes said to refer to Oxford and Cambridge, the great universities of the age that were churning out constrained, uninspired minds blind to the divine nature of human imagination. When we read on past the preface, we discover that the rest of the poem keeps returning to this key Blakean image. We find references to the 'Starry Mills of Satan' which churn continuously beneath the shell of the physical world. Satan himself is 'Prince of the Starry Wheels' and 'The Miller of Eternity', grinding time and space into their constituent parts. The fine particles of dust produced are separate, broken and have lost their spiritual component. It is these Starry Mills of Satan that generate the 'Single vision & Newtons sleep' that drive the Age of Enlightenment. This is also the same process that generates the universities of Oxford and Cambridge and the mills of the Industrial Revolution, so it could be said that all common interpretations of this phrase are valid in their own way.

The poem is usually interpreted as a reference to the myth that a young Jesus Christ once visited Britain in his youth. Jesus was accompanying his uncle Joseph of Arimathea, a trader of copper and tin, on his travels. In this reading, 'those feet' are the feet of Jesus as a child. That Blake asks whether 'the holy Lamb of God' was 'On Englands pleasant pastures seen' confirms this interpretation for many. The idea that Jesus once walked upon the gently rolling hills of southern England is, understandably, an appealing one to English Christians, even those who find it historically unlikely.

This is an interpretation that has been questioned, not least because the story that Jesus came to Britain can only be found from the end of the nineteenth century onwards, over ninety years after Blake wrote those lines. For this reason, the leading Blake scholar Professor Jason Whittaker has speculated that Blake intended 'those feet' to be those of Joseph of Arimathea. Blake certainly knew of the medieval legend that Joseph visited Britain because he produced the 1773 engraving *Joseph of Arimathea among The Rocks of Albion* when he was a teenage apprentice. In this legend, Joseph arrived after the death of Jesus, and hid the Holy Grail somewhere in Britain, possibly around Glastonbury. He also preached an early form of proto-Christianity to the pagan Brits. In the mid-1790s Blake produced a colour printed etching called *Joseph of Arimathea Preaching to the Britons*, which depicts exactly this. Could it be that the hymn 'Jerusalem' refers not to Jesus in Britain, but his uncle bringing the earliest, uncorrupted form of Christianity to these islands?

There is another candidate for the owner of those feet, who we'll meet when we examine Blake's later epic poems. For now, though, it's worth noting that the matter is complicated by Blake's understanding of Jesus, and what it meant for someone to be part human and part divine. Blake always saw himself as a committed Christian, and he frequently proclaimed the Christian doctrine that it was only through Jesus Christ that we would find redemption. Yet his understanding of the nature of Jesus was very different to that of the Church, because he also believed that the divine part of Jesus came from the imagination. Blake wrote in *Milton* about 'the Human Imagination / Which is the Divine Body of the Lord Jesus. blessed for ever', for example. 'Christianity is Art [...] Jesus & his Apostles & Disciples were all Artists,' he wrote a couple of decades later. 'The Eternal Body of Man in the Imagination, that is God himself, The Divine Body: Jesus we are his Members.' If Jesus' divinity came from the imagination, as Blake believed, then it was theoretically accessible to others. It was, perhaps, theoretically accessible to all.

Theologically, Jesus was neither a god nor a man, but a combination of both; a perfect illustration of Blake's belief that humanity and divinity were codependent. From Blake's perspective, Jesus' dual qualities were not unusual. Being part man and part god was normal, even if regular people weren't as aware of their divine element as Jesus was.

For traditional Christians, Jesus was unique, a one-off gift from God that showed us what perfection would look like. We could never hope to be like him, of course, but by believing in the divine nature of this mortal man we would keep that potential perfection alive in our minds. This, in time, would help us to find redemption. By interpreting Jesus as a man illuminated by divine imagination, however, Blake saw Jesus as the first, not the only. Within us all was the potential to understand the world in the way that he did. In more modern times this idea is known as 'Christ consciousness', or sometimes by the less controversial phrase 'higher consciousness'. It has many similarities with the Buddhist notion of enlightenment, which was also something that was never supposed to be possessed by the Buddha alone.

Just as Buddhism believes that we all have the potential to become enlightened like the Buddha, so too did Blake believe that Jesus, being divine through the imagination, was an example we could emulate. The worship of Jesus was not the lowering of oneself in front of unattainable divinity. It was keeping your higher goal alive in your mind, an act of intention focused on spiritual attainment. As the musician George Harrison described the situation in 1967: 'Everyone is a potential Jesus Christ, really. We are all trying to get to where Jesus Christ got.'

In this context, the identity of the feet in the poem is not particularly important – they are the soul stepping into the vegetative world. What matters is the extent to which the owner of those feet was illuminated by divine imagination. In this interpretation, the poem asks if the ancient Britons were once as inspired as Jesus, and then declares that we should use our mental and physical weapons to become so again. This was the message of those lines that have, stripped of their original context, become the unofficial English national anthem.

The extraordinary popularity of 'Jerusalem' has made Blake a favourite of English patriots, but his actual views on his homeland are more interesting than simple nationalism. Blake saw the value in people from all nations. As he once wrote:

And all must love the human form,
In heathen, turk or jew.
Where Mercy, Love & Pity dwell,
There God is dwelling too

Lines like this were a reaction to the divisive attitudes displayed by members of the established Church, such as the eighteenth-century minister and prolific hymn writer Isaac Watts. Watts's 'Song VI: Praise for the Gospel' begins:

LORD, I ascribe it to thy Grace,
And not to Chance as others do,
That I was born of CHRISTIAN Race,
And not a Heathen or a Jew.

Blake had no time for anyone who considered their country or creed to be inherently 'better' than anyone else's. For Blake, Albion was an enchanted island, and London a heavenly city, because his imaginative vision made them so. Any other city or nation on earth would have equal claim to the status of the New Jerusalem, if they had been seen with Blake's eyes, or lay under Blake's feet. If all the people of the world could learn to see through the eyes of divine imagination, then all the world would be Jerusalem.

This is not to say that Blake didn't think Britain was a special place, nor that he thought that all places were equal. On the contrary, he felt it was necessary to recognise the unique personality of individual places. 'To Generalize is to be an Idiot,' he wrote, bluntly. It is in the specifics that things reveal themselves, because, as he writes in *Jerusalem*, 'General Forms have their vitality in Particulars.' Other nations had spiritual aspects, not just Britain. His works contain references to Erin, the spiritual form of Ireland, and Shiloh, the spiritual form of France. Like all countries, these had a unique personality and a unique role to play in the unfolding story of humanity. As we shall see, in Blake's view Britain did have a pivotal role to play in the spiritual evolution of mankind. As he wrote in *Milton*, 'All things begin & end in Albions ancient Druid rocky shore.'

*

When the French Revolution began in 1789, it was seen by its many supporters as a beacon of rationalism and humanity. It did not take long, however, until that wave of optimism collapsed before the horror of the Reign of Terror. In September 1792, hundreds of Parisian workers broke into the jails, dragged out the prisoners and butchered them in the streets. About 1,400 people were murdered by the common citizenry, in the name of safeguarding the revolution. Attention then turned to counter-revolutionary threats outside of France. As the politician Jacques Pierre Brissot declared in the Legislative Assembly, 'We cannot be calm until Europe, all Europe, is in flames.' This led to the military rise of Napoleon Bonaparte and French control of large parts of western Europe. A revolution undertaken in the name of rationality and Enlightenment values had produced frenzied, irrational slaughter and hatred. This was the process which Blake personified with his mythic character Orc.

In May 1803, Britain declared war on the French. Napoleon was to be crowned Emperor, and the British establishment feared both revolution from the common people and invasion by the emerging French Empire. They were paranoid and scared, and draconian laws were introduced in an attempt to stamp out any possibility of public dissent. Troops were billeted across the south coast of England, ready for any French invasion. On 12 August 1803, Blake walked out of his cottage and found one of these soldiers, Private John Schofield of the First Regiment of Dragoons, leaning against a wall in his garden.

Blake did not realise that Schofield had entered the garden after being asked by Hayley's gardener for assistance, and he asked the soldier to leave. As he described the encounter, Schofield responded with 'an impertinent answer. I insisted on his leaving the Garden he refused I still persisted in desiring his departure he then threatend to knock out my Eyes.' As the exchange became heated, Blake grabbed the soldier and pushed him out of the garden. There is an echo here of Blake as a young apprentice in Westminster Abbey being bullied by public schoolboys and responding, not with fear, but by knocking his assailant onto the stone floor. Blake did not seek confrontation, but he did not fear it when it arose.

Once out of the gate, Schofield continued to threaten and swear at Blake: 'I perhaps foolishly & perhaps not, stepped out at the Gate & putting aside his blows, took him again by the Elbows & keeping his back to me, pushed him forward down the road about fifty yards he all the while endeavouring to turn around & strike me & raging & cursing which drew out several neighbours.' In this way, Blake delivered the furious soldier to the door of the nearby Fox Inn, where he had been billeted.

Schofield's account of the encounter focused on what he claimed Blake said to him, which was to damn the soldier, his cause and king and country. 'The English know within themselves that Buonaparte could take possession of England in an hour's time, and then it would be put to every Englishman's choice for to either fight for the French or have his throat cut,' Schofield alleged that Blake said. 'I think I am as strong a man as most, and it shall be throat cut for throat cut, and the strongest man will be the conqueror. You will not fight against the French. Damn the King and Country and all his subjects. I have told this before to greater people than you. Damn the King and his Country; his subjects and all you soldiers are sold as slaves.' Schofield added that Catherine Blake emerged from the house to see what the fuss was about, and on hearing the debate claimed that she would fight 'for Bonaparte as long as I am able'. Based on this, Schofield filed a complaint against Blake. The charge was sedition, which could, in theory, have led to the death penalty.

Blake found himself in the long, slow process of a legal trial.

The indictment was read out before a jury in Petworth in October, with the charges becoming more frightening and hysterical when seen in legal language written during a paranoid time: 'William Blake late of the said Parish of Felpham in the said County of Sussex being a Wicked Seditious and *evil* disposed person and greatly disaffected to our said Lord the King and wickedly and seditiously intending to bring our said Lord the King into great hatred contempt and Scandal.' His trial, however, would not take place for over a year, in January 1805, until which time Blake had to live with the stress and scandal as best he could.

Blake pleaded not guilty to the charges. He argued that Schofield had invented the seditious conversation as revenge for the humiliation of being forcefully marched out of the garden and down the road by a much smaller man in front of several witnesses. Of all the villagers interviewed in the course of the trial, none claimed to have heard this seditious speech, and thanks to this lack of corroborating evidence Blake was found not guilty. It is noticeable, however, that the seditious talk does not seem wildly out of character, and it is some coincidence that these allegations are largely in keeping with Blake's view and beliefs. The quote from Catherine was likewise plausible, for she is known to have said at a later point that 'if this Country does go to War our King ought to lose his head'.

Blake's beliefs were not rigorously examined during the trial. None of his associations with political radicals, such as Joseph Johnson, were used against him, and none of his politically revolutionary illuminated works were examined (it was probably wise that he did not put his name on *The Marriage of Heaven and Hell*). Despite Blake's insistence on his blamelessness, he did not provide an alternative to the words that passed between them. It is tempting to suspect that there may have been some truth to Schofield's account, however exaggerated it may have become. If

214

this is the case, the testimony of the villagers suggests that their claims not to have heard anything may reflect a fondness for Blake and perhaps a dislike of Schofield and the other soldiers who had arrived in their village.

The incident with Schofield marked the end of William and Catherine's time away from London. Even before they encountered the soldier, the Blakes were already planning their return, in part because the lease on the cottage was due to expire. Another factor was Catherine's health. She suffered from ailments described as 'ague' and rheumatism. It was thought that the damp in the exposed coastal cottage was the cause, although her health did not improve when they were back in London. Even without these factors, it was time for Blake to make a change in his circumstances. The patronage of Hayley had not proved to be the independence he hoped for.

William Hayley was a very different person to William Blake. Educated at Eton and Cambridge, his personal wealth kept him in a social bubble removed from the constant struggle experienced by the majority of his countrymen. He had an affected manner and mildly eccentric habits, such as attempting to use an umbrella to keep the sun out of his eyes when riding his horse, which often resulted in a fall. According to Gilchrist, he saw the world through a 'fog of amiability'. He saw himself as generous and good intentioned, but others found him controlling with an ingrained, delusional sense of superiority and a need for flattery and compliments. Blake had thought that his patronage would give him creative independence, but the reality was more like a job with Hayley as his overbearing boss.

To his credit, Hayley had introduced Blake to the local gentry, including Lord Egremont of Petworth and Lord Bathurst of Lavant, and this did result in some commissions. He also encouraged him to try his hand at miniature portraits, for which there was a ready market. However, Blake found that the work he had in Felpham was uninteresting, the workload excessive, and the pay poor. His escape to the blissful country had come to feel like a damp, cold trap that left him isolated from his family and friends in London.

Beneath all this was the reality of his commercial situation. Work had been drying up before he left Lambeth, and his growing reputation as some form of lunatic meant it was becoming hard to earn enough money to keep his wife at the level of comfort she deserved. The commissions he got from regular patrons such as Thomas Butts had a whiff of charity about them. Being largely dependent on Hayley for income was a very different scenario to being a professional tradesman constantly in demand by a broad circle of clients. In such circumstances it would be easy to resent Hayley, especially as Hayley's privilege kept him from seeing the situation from Blake's perspective.

Blake and Hayley spent a lot of time together in Felpham, and Blake was a frequent visitor to Hayley's library. Superficially, it sounds like they were good friends, but in Blake's notebook and letters, we find many attacks on his patron.

> To H ——
> Thy Friendship oft has made my heart to ake,
> Do be my Enemy for Friendships sake.

> To H
> You think Fuseli is not a Great Painter Im Glad
> This is one of the best compliments he ever had

These stand in contrast to Hayley's letters, where Blake is usually referred to fondly as 'good Blake', 'kind Blake' or 'excellent Blake'.

Hayley did prove to be a good friend to Blake when his legal problems began, offering him much needed legal and financial help. This awkward fact seems to have caused Blake to question his resentment. 'If a Man offends me ignorantly & not designedly surely I ought to consider him with favour & affection. Perhaps the simplicity of myself is the origin of all offences committed against me,' he wrote to Thomas Butts. '[B]urn what I have peevishly written about any friend.'

Despite this, it was time for his exile in the green and pleasant land to end. In September 1803, William and Catherine moved back to London. They may have thought that a return home would reset their lives and get them back on track. In this, they would be disappointed. The years ahead would be dark, both in terms of Blake's career and his mental health.

12.
WHEN I SPEAK I OFFEND

In 1788 the subject of madness, and how it was understood, became an issue of great political importance. King George III, it was widely reported, had gone mad. Bouts of mania left him frothing at the mouth and unable to stop talking for hours at a time. He was taken to Cheltenham Spa in order to recover, but his doctors had no real understanding of what was happening and could do little beyond bloodletting and restraining the King for his own good. A monarch was believed to represent the nation state symbolically, so for the crown to be on the head of a babbling, straitjacketed lunatic was a big problem.

With the head of state incapacitated, politicians found themselves struggling with enormous constitutional issues made more difficult by the lack of medical knowledge about mental health. A key question was whether an afflicted person might recover. The rival politicians William Pitt the Younger and Charles James Fox debated establishing a Regency period, in which the crown would pass from George III to his son, but they did so cautiously. They knew it would lead to enormous changes in the current balance of power, which would shape Britain for a generation.

While the debate dragged on, the King recovered and the crisis was averted – temporarily at least. Although retroactive diagnosis of illness from historical records is generally problematic, it is now commonly believed that George suffered from porphyria, a genetic blood disease whose symptoms include seizures and confusion. It was not recognised at the time, but what the King was suffering from wasn't 'madness' as it was then conceived. George's illness flared up again in 1804, however, and the Prince of Wales was eventually made Regent in 1811.

The Age of Enlightenment caused people to question existing ideas about the nature of mind and disease. The old practice of blaming such afflictions on witches, demons or God was no longer satisfactory, but doctors still lacked better models to explain these conditions. Before it suddenly threatened the nation's constitution, many people had been content to ignore the problem. The 'mad' were simply said to be 'mad', and there was little else to be added. Nowadays we avoid derogatory and unspecific terms like 'mad' or 'madhouse', but such terminology illustrates how these matters were viewed in Georgian England.

The mentally ill had always been part of society and were looked after and tolerated in various ways. Some were said to be slow, while others were said to have lost their wits. Communities felt a general responsibility to look after them as best they could. The Vagrancy Act of 1714 made specific mention of such people, in its attempt to deal with the problem of wandering masterless men. The law dictated that homeless people who appeared to have lost their reason could be restrained and confined, subject to the opinion of a medical practitioner. In London in the eighteenth century, for all but the wealthiest, this usually meant confinement in the oldest and most notorious asylum in history: the Bethlem hospital, known to all as Bedlam.

Bedlam wasn't a hospital in the modern sense of the word; it did not claim to heal people. It was simply a 'madhouse', and no real attempts were made to cure the inmates. They were housed, fed and confined, and this was felt to be all that could be done for them. Patients also received bloodletting, were purged by vomiting and were given opium, but this was to make them easier for the wardens to deal with. The form filled out on admission shows how unsophisticated mental health care was at the time. Of the four questions asked, only one was concerned with the nature of the patient's illness. This question simply asked whether the patient was 'melancholy, raving or mischievous'.

Bedlam was a large, impressive looking building at Moorfields. The gates were topped with two sculptures in Portland stone by the fashionable Danish sculptor Caius Gabriel Cibber, with a figure representing melancholy on the left and a figure representing raving madness on the right. Despite this impressive façade, the building was poorly built and maintained. It lacked foundations and had been built on a rubbish heap. It soon began to deteriorate, with subsidence, cracked walls and leaking roofs rendering the building a symbol of the people inside in architectural form.

For a suitable donation, visitors were allowed to observe the inmates, with the wilder and more distressed proving especially popular. Bedlam became one of London's leading tourist attractions, and its patients were essentially exhibits in a heartless human zoo. There was little concern about how this might impact them, although preachers were banned from visiting on the grounds that their sermons tended to make the inmates madder. One Swiss traveller described his visit in 1725, when he saw 'dangerous maniacs, most of them being chained and terrible to behold. On holidays numerous persons of both sexes, but belonging generally to the lower classes, visit this hospital and amuse themselves watching these unfortunate wretches, who often give them cause for laughter.' This profitable entertainment was eventually stopped in 1770.

One of the unfortunate people who was incarcerated in Bedlam was a Welsh tea broker named James Tilly Matthews, who was committed in 1797. Matthews has the honour of being the first recorded paranoid schizophrenic in the medical record. His case is worth looking at, because it demonstrates how the Age of Enlightenment was creating entirely new forms of mental health problems, which in turn impacted on how Blake was seen by his contemporaries.

Matthews had been arrested after entering the public gallery of the Palace of Westminster and calling out 'treason!' during a speech by Lord Liverpool, the President of the Board of Trade. Such behaviour risked a charge of sedition and a potential death penalty in those nervous times, but Matthews was judged to be insane and hence not fit for trial. When asked to explain himself, he talked of grand conspiracies involving the crowned heads of Europe and of being sent by Lord Liverpool to France to prevent war. He also talked about how there was a figure of a man on top of Bloomsbury church, who carried a copy of the Domesday Book. This contained a complete account of all history, he explained, which only Matthews could read. Strangest of all, however, was his account of the air loom gang.

The air loom, he explained, was a machine housed in a large, damp, airless basement of a secret building, somewhere near London Wall. Powered by windmill sails, the machine manipulated pressurised gases, pneumatic chemistry and strange mesmeric fluids, including such unwholesome substances as 'stinking human breath' and 'gaz from the anus of the horse'. These were used to 'weave' the air like a loom, in such a way that it would send signals which could spy into people's minds. It could also direct them to talk and act in ways dictated by the people controlling the machine. It was the machine that propelled him into parliament, he insisted, and caused him to yell 'treason!' against his own wishes and better judgement.

When under the influence of the machine, Matthews claimed, he was able to see the mysterious 'gang' of seven people that controlled it. He gave them nicknames and studied them over time. A sharp-faced woman wearing gloves operated the controls directly, and he referred to her as Glove Woman. A character in a wig who took copious notes was called Jack the Schoolmaster. Other members of the gang worked further away from the machine and were harder for Matthews to see clearly. The group included the guffawing Sir Archy, who was fond of dirty jokes and may have been a cross-dressing woman, and a character Matthews called The Middle Man who kept repeating the strange, David Lynchian phrase, 'Yes, he is the talisman.' Overseeing all these people was the boss of the operation, Bill the King, who only appeared when extremely sensitive or important work was being carried out, and a woman called Augusta, who liaised with other gangs hidden around London. The final figure was Charlotte, a half-naked French girl who was a chained prisoner of the gang. In this way, the shadowy people behind the air loom exerted sinister control over politicians and public figures in order to shape European politics to their own ends. Matthews, a talented draughtsman, drew detailed illustrations of the air loom, in the hope that this would help win his freedom.

Matthews would now be immediately recognised as suffering from classic paranoid delusions, but at the end of the eighteenth century this was all entirely new. Since Matthews, the medical establishment has encountered many patients who believe that unseen others are conspiring against or controlling them using the latest cutting-edge technology, such as messages delivered through television sets, viruses controlled by 5G telephone masts, or information being beamed into radios hidden in their fillings. So common are cases like these that the idea of a 'tin foil hat' which blocks controlling signals is used to mock paranoid people and conspiracy theorists.

Matthews would now be said to have been suffering from a persecution complex, because he was convinced that he was being persecuted by high-level politicians intent on stopping him preventing war in Europe. To complicate matters, however, this part of his story was true. He had repeatedly travelled to revolutionary Paris in an attempt to negotiate peace between England and France – given the turbulent events of the time, this was an incredibly courageous thing to do.

Matthews's efforts had resulted in him being placed for a time in a Parisian jail. This appears to be the point when the stress became too much, and his mind gave way. It was here that he heard about the then-fashionable pseudoscience of mesmerism, which claimed to be able to put thoughts in people's heads and to control their actions. The concept of mesmerism, which is now more commonly called hypnotism, provided Matthews with a much needed solution to the question that so troubled him. A convinced believer in Enlightenment thought and republicanism, Matthews couldn't understand how such rational concepts had led to so much fury and slaughter. Neither could he explain why the continent was marching to war when no countries wanted war. The idea that dark hypnotic powers were controlling people's minds and actions explained a great deal in these circumstances and helped calm the cognitive dissonance he was experiencing. Given the huge advances being made in science and engineering, the idea that a machine could harness these strange hypnotic powers and force people to damage society against their better intentions seemed more or less plausible. More importantly, it could explain a bewildering, chaotic world. His mind latched onto this story because it was the only explanation he had which preserved his pre-existing belief system.

Before the nineteenth century, there is an almost complete absence of accounts of schizophrenia. It may be that we don't possess adequate records of early sufferers, and that cases were simply recorded in vague terms such as mania, a lack of wits or religious revelation. However, some historians of medicine argue that the schizophrenic family of illnesses did not exist before this time. At the start of the nineteenth century there were around 5,000 people confined in British asylums and madhouses, and by the end of the century the number had grown to over 100,000. There are many factors in this growth, from an increase in the size of the population to changes in the treatment and medical understanding of mental health issues. Even with these issues acknowledged, there remains at least the suspicion that societal changes such as those caused by the Industrial Revolution, the growth of Empire and a more scientific, rational worldview had a damaging impact on mental health.

In a similar way, the move to our current networked world has been accompanied by an increase in mental health issues, especially among the young. The huge increase in anxiety reported by teenagers who have never known a world without constant mobile online access is an obvious example of this. The evolution of society, as it becomes increasingly distant from the historical environment our minds evolved to deal with, puts increasing pressure on our minds. Madness is understood to be the opposite of sanity, and sanity is defined as the possession of a clear and accurate understanding of reality. As our changing understanding of reality causes the nature of sanity to shift, so too does the nature of madness change.

During the Age of Enlightenment, the common societal understanding of reality shifted from a spirit-haunted world to a rational machine-like universe. It was in this period that we see the rise of what we would now call paranoid conspiracy theory. The first popular conspiracy work, *Memoirs of Jacobinism* by the French Jesuit Augustin Barruel, was translated into English in 1797. Lurid tales about secret societies such as the Freemasons and the Illuminati found a ready audience in a readership unable to understand the rapidly changing world or, like Matthews, grasp why the French Revolution had taken such a dark turn. Just as Matthews's mind needed to invent the air loom in order to keep its understanding of the world from shattering, so too did people latch onto Barruel's claim that sinister plotters were masterminding political events from the shadows. Such an idea was more comforting than the idea that world politics was meaningless, random chaos and that no one was in control.

The behaviour of people in the eighteenth century can seem strange to us now. It was a time, for example, in which weeping in public was considered entirely normal. It was also a time when the King of England had to be restrained in a straitjacket, the former prime minister Pitt the Elder sat in silence in a darkened room when official business reduced him to fits of trembling, and the Lord Chancellor, Charles Yorke, was so overwhelmed with anxiety that he cut his own throat. Fortunately by the end of the century the issue of mental health was, perhaps for the first time, finally being recognised as a subject worthy of study and investigation.

The Rake's Progress, a hugely popular series of paintings and engravings by William Hogarth, depicted the downfall of a foolish but initially prosperous eighteenth-century gentleman. The final image, which followed the loss of his fortune through gambling and a spell in a debtors' prison, is called *The Madhouse*. Here was the ultimate doomed ending for a person's fall from grace, the worst fate anyone could arrive at other than death. Madness was something that Georgian people truly feared – no doubt encouraged by the decades of visitors who thrilled at the antics of the lunatics of Bedlam.

For William Blake, out arguing with thistles and experiencing visions, it was increasingly apparent that others viewed him as mad and a fit subject for mockery and ridicule – an added stress on top of his financial and career problems and his trial for sedition.

Blake scholars have traditionally fought against the idea that Blake was mad, for fear it would offer an excuse to dismiss him. Aware that his mythology initially appears incomprehensible and devoid of any internal meaning, they have argued for his sanity in order to persuade others that studying his work is worthwhile. This is a notably different stance to that taken by Van Gogh scholars, for whom the painter's troubled mental health is uncontroversial, accepted and seen as an important aspect of his work.

The mental strain of Blake's trial for sedition clearly took its toll. A short verse written in a letter to Thomas Butts shortly after the incident with Schofield shows a sense of despair and self-pity which had previously been absent from his work:

O why was I born with a different face
Why was I not born like the rest of my race
When I look each one starts! when I speak I offend
Then I'm silent & passive & lose every Friend

Blake was aware he was perceived as different, and that this was part of the reason he was overlooked and unsuccessful. In his notebook, he penned a few lines headed 'To F——', where 'F' is presumably his increasingly successful sculptor friend John Flaxman:

I mock thee not tho I by thee am mocked
Thou callst me Madman but I call thee Blockhead

227

Hes a Blockhead who wants a proof of what he Can't Perceive
And he's a Fool who tries to make such a Blockhead believe

After the Schofield incident, Blake began to show signs of paranoia. He seemed to have difficulty accepting that what happened with the soldier was a random, meaningless event. He suspected that an unseen political conspiracy was working against him because of his earlier revolutionary associations, in a similar way to how Matthews believed a conspiracy actively plotted against him. When you believe that everything in this world has spiritual significance, it is easy to elevate an ugly incident into a spiritual melodrama. As Gilchrist wrote, 'Blake used to declare the Government, or some high person, knowing him to have been of the Paine set, "sent the soldier to entrap him"; which we must take the liberty of regarding as a purely visionary notion.'

In 1803, Blake returned from Felpham to London. He and Catherine could no longer afford a property like their former house in Lambeth, which had three floors and a rear garden. Instead, they rented rooms on the first floor of 17 South Molton Street, further west down Oxford Street and closer to the site of the Tyburn gallows. As he wrote in a letter to Hayley in August 1804: 'Money flies from me; Profit never ventures upon my threshold, tho' every other man's doorstone is worn down into the very earth by the footsteps of the fiends of commerce. Be it so, as long as God permits, which I foresee is not long. I foresee a mighty change.'

The sudden switch in tone here between self-pity and blind optimism is representative of Blake's mind at this point. As he began to rebuild his life as a Londoner his mental health was in poor condition, but his determination to understand the strange workings of the mind was never stronger. He knew that his visions separated him from others and led to people thinking him mad, but he also believed that his work could convince people to understand

and even share his reality. In an essay written to promote an engraving, he suddenly lashes out, unprovoked, seemingly at no specific target: 'It is very true what you have said for these thirty two Years I am Mad or else you are so both of us cannot be in our right senses Posterity will judge by our works.'

In those difficult years, Blake clung to the idea that his art would redeem him.

The nineteenth century marks a change in the style and ambition of Blake's illuminated books. The first of these was *Milton: a poem in 2 books*, which, as we've seen, gave us the verses that are now known as the hymn 'Jerusalem'. *Milton* was begun in Felpham but took a further decade to complete. It includes a self-portrait in front of his Sussex cottage conversing with a floating female spirit, and perhaps the spirit-rich atmosphere that Blake initially found at Felpham was a factor in the gear change in his work.

The reason *Milton* took so long was its scale. At fifty printed pages, it was far longer than anything else he had attempted. It was also considerably wordier. Although it had been created using his unique printing technique, which allowed the combination of words and images, many plates consisted of little more than tightly packed text brightened by a wash of watercolours. There were far fewer illustrations accompanying the text than before, and Blake's interest in combining text and pictures to create particular effects had dwindled. Had Blake the connections or ability to do so, it would have made more sense to print *Milton* in the traditional manner. If nothing else, it would have meant that Blake did not need to write out the entire text in mirror writing.

As he worked on *Milton*, his mind seemed unable to move on from his relationship with Hayley. In his notebook we find a short verse entitled 'On H——ys Friendship':

When H——y finds out what you cannot do
That is the Very thing hell set you to
If you break not your Neck tis not his fault
But pecks of poison are not pecks of salt
And when he could not act upon my wife
Hired a Villain to bereave my Life

Blake scholars do not take seriously this suggestion that Hayley hired someone to murder Blake, in order to claim Catherine. It appears to be a paranoid fantasy, and one that probably passed fairly quickly. Blake does not return to the idea, and you would not expect him to drop such an accusation if it was based on a true incident. The line is probably intended as a reference to 'Fair Elenor', an early, Gothic poem of Blake's. But Hayley remained a target for his animosity.

In Blake's eyes, Hayley had become a spiritual enemy, even if he had trouble justifying or rationalising why he thought this way. As far as Hayley was concerned, of course, he had treated Blake with nothing but kindness and was blameless. But as Blake describes the situation in *Milton*, 'Corporeal friends are Spiritual enemies'. Blake was seeking a spiritual reality behind human actions that would fit with his worldview and also explain his lack of earthly success. If the boundary between the internal and external worlds is sufficiently blurred, it becomes easy to project some great spiritual trauma onto an unsuspecting worldly scapegoat. Most of the first third of *Milton*, a sequence known as the Bard's Song, is often interpreted as an attempt to justify his animosity towards his former patron.

The first book of *Milton* begins with Blake petitioning the muses for inspiration, in order to be able to tell the saga of John Milton's spirit returning to our world a hundred years after his death. Blake is specific and unromantic about how a writer becomes inspired, and he does not seek the muses in some far-off astral realm. Instead, he asks the muses to:

> [...] Come into my hand
> By your mild power; descending down the Nerves of my right
>   arm
> From out of the Portals of my brain, where by your ministry
> The Eternal Great Humanity Divine. planted his Paradise,

As always, he is sane enough to be aware that his mind is the source of everything.

The lengthy Bard's Song that follows is the reason why Milton's spirit decides to descend once again to the human realm. The Bard sings of the three types of human: the elect, the redeemed and the reprobate. Only the redeemed and, potentially, the reprobates, Blake tells us, were capable of entering heaven. Blake's concept of the elect here is a mocking inversion of Calvinism and other forms of Protestantism, which claimed that there existed a class of people called the elect who were predestined to go to heaven. Much of the power dynamic in those sects involved the right to declare who was and who was not a member of this elect. Blake turned this whole idea on its head by declaring that 'the Elect cannot be Redeemed'. Rather than being guaranteed entry to heaven, this class of people were damned because 'they cannot Believe in Eternal Life / Except by Miracle & a New Birth.' They could only conceive of redemption as an external gift, rather than something that emerged from their own imagination.

In the Bard's Song, Milton takes the role of the reprobate, a poet named Palamabron is the redeemed, and the elect is none other than Satan himself. However, Blake scholars frequently interpret this as a spiritual reflection of Blake's relationship with Hayley, where the poet Palamabron is intended to represent Blake and Satan is intended to represent Hayley. Hayley's kindness and friendly manner are, therefore, recast as Satanic deceptions. Blake writes of 'Satans extreme / Mildness' that allows Satan to cunningly get his own way, because Palamabron feels compelled to give in to Satan's requests in order not to appear ungrateful. In this, we can see the power structure of boss and employee at work. For those who enjoy their job and are satisfied with their pay and conditions, having a friendly boss whom they get on well with is a perfect situation to be in. For those who resent their work and conditions, or feel trapped in an unsatisfying role, the requirement to fake a reciprocal friendship with a boss can become difficult over time, as it did for Blake.

The bone of contention in the Bard's Song revolves around the right to use a harrow – an agricultural tool that breaks up clods of earth and smooths out the surface of soil. A harrow is typically used on a field after ploughing, which disturbs the soil in a deeper and rougher way than a harrow.

The plough and the harrow in the poem, of course, are spiritual tools. It is the role of 'the Plow & Harrow to pass over the Nations'. The iron plough is driven by the character of Rintrah, who personifies just wrath. This wrath-driven plough churning across the nations is the spirit of revolution violently churning up the long-existing order of priests and kings. It is then that the divinely inspired poet Palamabron needs to pass over the churned land with the golden harrow, gently repairing the damage of the plough and preparing the soil for a new, golden future based on divinely inspired poetic arts. Or at least, that was the theory.

The problem was that Satan was jealous of Palamabron's glorious role, and used his deceitful, weasel-like cunning to persuade him to swap jobs for a day. Satan driving the harrow leads to all sorts of troubles, needless to say, which ripple out from the events in this poem and eventually result in the current fallen state of humanity. In the common interpretation of Satan being

Hayley and Blake being Palamabron, this scenario translates as the uninspired, financially comfortable Hayley being jealous of lowly Blake's divine inspiration and wanting to claim Blake's gift for himself. The one-sided fallout between the two men, from this perspective, is just an unavoidable consequence of the troubles in Eternity being reflected in the earthly realm.

This reading, however, betrays a deeply egotistical side to Blake which is at odds with the rest of his philosophy. Hayley was a competent writer who may then have lacked the mark of true genius, but imagination is a muscle that can be strengthened and, as Swedenborg discovered in his fifties, access to divine imagination can come at any time. A central hope in Blake's work is that all will gain this ability. He ends the preface to *Milton* with a quote from the Bible to this effect: 'Would to God that all the Lords people were Prophets.' Yet the conflict in the Bard's Song is not about everyone rising up to the same level, but a fear that Hayley will take Blake's special gift away from him. In this scenario, only the Blake character can wield the golden harrow and bring about a glorious future, and anyone else undertaking this role will bring disaster and rob Blake of his glorious destiny. Divine inspiration has now become a jealously guarded prize which Hayley must never have, a situation that is the opposite of the message in the rest of Blake's work.

Hayley is Satan and Satan is of the Elect, who by definition can never be redeemed. This may seem harsh, but in *Milton* those 'Who pretend to Poetry' are the greatest enemy there is:

He smiles with condescension; he talks of Benevolence & Virtue
And those who act with Benevolence & Virtue, they murder
    time on time
These are the destroyers of Jerusalem, these are the murderers
Of Jesus, who deny the Faith & mock at Eternal Life:
Who pretend to Poetry that they may destroy Imagination;

You might think that it would take more than someone failing at poetry to destroy Jesus, eternal life, and the divine imagination itself. Nevertheless, this is the logic that the Bard's Song hinges on. It is hard to see this as a great spiritual truth, rather than the earthly justification Blake embraced in order to explain his resentment of his patron.

Blake's mind remained fixated on this one-sided war in the years after Felpham, elevating the clash into mythic forms. Like James Tilly Matthews, Blake found that retreating into warm delusion worked as protection from a cold, indifferent world. Without his new narrative, Blake would have no alternative but to face up to a deeply uncomfortable scenario. In this, he was generally regarded as mad by those who knew him, this madness was what made his work unappealing to the market, despite his obvious talents, and Hayley's patronship was essentially charity, offered to a man who was judged unable to earn money or support his wife. It is understandable, perhaps, that Blake would use his imagination to come up with a far grander and more flattering story.

13.

MY WRATH DID GROW

In 1809, as Blake was nearing the end of work on *Milton*, he staged his only one-man art exhibition. In the same punk DIY spirit that marked his experimental printing, the show was mounted without the support of the art establishment. Lacking a suitable gallery, it was held in the room above his brother's shop, next to the building where Blake had been born fifty-two years earlier.

A leaflet printed to promote the show gives a clear insight into Blake's state of mind at the time:

> The execution of my Designs, being all in Water-colours, (that is in Fresco) are regularly refused to be exhibited by the *Royal Academy*, and the *British Institution* has, this year, followed its example, and has effectively excluded me by this Resolution; I therefore invite those Noblemen and Gentlem[e]n, who are its Subscribers, to inspect what they have excluded: and those who have been told that my Works are but an unscientific and irregular Eccentricity, a Madman's Scrawls, I demand of them to do me the justice to examine before they decide.

This is text written to entice a curious public into viewing his paintings, but it reads as bitter and deluded. As it continues, however, it becomes increasingly Messianic:

> There cannot be more than two or three great Painters or Poets
> in any Age or Country; and these, in a corrupt state of Society,
> are easily excluded, but not so easily obstructed.

The reason that Blake's genius was not recognised owed nothing to bad luck or anything to do with Blake himself, he was saying. It was because of an active conspiracy by the powers that be. This idea is apparent in the annotations Blake made to his copy of *The Works of Sir Joshua Reynolds*. On the title page next to Reynolds's name, Blake has written:

> This Man was Hired to Depress Art. This is the opinion of Will
> Blake my Proofs of this Opinion are given in the following
> Notes

> Degrade first the Arts if you'd Mankind degrade,
> Hire Idiots to Paint with cold light & hot shade:
> Give high Price for the worst, leave the best in disgrace,
> And with Labours of Ignorance fill every place.

Reynolds, who had been knighted in 1769, was the first president of the Royal Academy of Arts and perhaps the most prominent and respected member of the art establishment. Blake had been briefly taught by him during his time at the Royal Academy, which he alludes to on the back of the title page:

> Having spent the Vigour of my Youth & Genius under the
> Oppression of Sr Joshua & his Gang of Cunning Hired Knaves

Without Employment & as much as could possibly be Without Bread, The Reader must Expect to Read in all my Remarks on these Books Nothing but Indignation & Resentment

In his annotations, Blake argues that art and science are the foundations of a nation and empire. It is from these that all else follows, because 'Empire follows art & Not Vice Versa as Englishmen suppose'. It does not make sense that a good government would allow true art to be repressed, he argues, because this is its greatest form of support. That a true artist like Blake should starve, therefore, can only be the result of a conspiracy of tyranny by a corrupt and Satanic establishment. As Blake is one of the few true greats, his determination to continue is, in his opinion, nothing short of heroic. As his advertisement concludes:

> If Italy is enriched and made great by RAPHAEL, if MICHAEL ANGELO is its supreme glory, if Art is the Glory of a Nation, if Genius and Inspiration are the great Origin and Bond of Society, the distinction my Works have obtained from those who best understand such things, calls for my Exhibition as the greatest of Duties to my Country.

As Blake saw it, never had some paintings in a room above a haberdashery shop been of such heightened national and spiritual importance. Yet this dramatic advert did not convince the London public. There were scarcely any visitors and, despite the exhibition being kept open for a couple of months after the intended closing date, none of the pictures sold. The exhibition received only one review, in the 17 September 1809 edition of *The Examiner*. It began: 'If beside the stupid and mad-brained political project of their rulers, the sane part of the people of England required fresh proof of the alarming increase of the effects of insanity, they will be too well convinced from its having lately spread into the hitherto sober region of Art.'

The article's author, Robert Hunt, states his concern that praise for Blake's work from his few well-known and respected friends had led him to mistake his madness for genius, an error that Hunt felt duty-bound to correct. He writes, 'Such is the case with the productions and admirers of WILLIAM BLAKE, an unfortunate lunatic, whose personal inoffensiveness secures him from confinement, and, consequently, of whom no public notice would have been taken...'

For the rest of the article Hunt delights in being vicious, patronising and cruel. He seems intent on putting this working-class creator in his place. It is hard not to see him as one of the uninspired 'Hirelings in the Camp, the Court, & the University' that Blake attacks in the preface to *Milton*. 'The poor man fancies himself a great master,' Hunt wrote, 'and has painted a few wretched pictures, some of which are unintelligible allegory, others an attempt at sober character by caricature representation, and the whole "blotted and blurred", and very badly drawn. These he calls an Exhibition, of which he has published a Catalogue, or rather a farrago of nonsense, unintelligibleness, and egregious vanity, the wild effusions of a distempered brain.'

Just as Decca Records's A&R man Mike Smith is forever remembered as the man who turned down the Beatles, so too is Robert Hunt now only remembered as the critic unable to appreciate the work of William Blake. Given the cruel tone of his review, it is hard to feel bad about this. But it is also fair to say that there would not have been many disinterested observers who, after reading Blake's words and visiting the exhibition, would have come away thinking the artist was sane.

Of the few visitors, one was Henry Crabb Robinson, who would meet Blake at a dinner party sixteen years later and write in his diary: 'Shall I call him Artist or Genius – or Mystic – or Madman?' Robinson paid the one shilling entry fee to James Blake, William's older brother, who escorted him to the upstairs room to see the exhibition. James was a sober, traditional shopkeeper who still dressed in old-fashioned knee breeches and stockings, and so made an unlikely guide into the extremes of imagination on display.

Perhaps the two best-known paintings from the exhibition, which are now owned by the Tate gallery, have the unlikely titles of *The Spiritual Form of Nelson Guiding Leviathan* and *The Spiritual Form of Pitt Guiding Behemoth*. The first depicts the recently deceased Admiral Nelson nearly naked and physically idealised in a similar way to Blake's depiction of Newton. Blake has given Nelson two eyes and arms, and although the painting has become indistinct with age some writers insist he has a prominent erection. The second portrays the prime minister Pitt the Younger as a beatific Christ-like figure. These two establishment leaders are shown controlling the Leviathan and the Behemoth respectively, with these mythological monsters being symbolic of war on the oceans and land.

Exactly how we're supposed to interpret these compositions has been debated at length. Was Blake being genuinely patriotic, or was this a slightly cynical attempt to produce works with popular appeal, even if that meant going against his own political beliefs? Either scenario would be out of character.

A probable clue to understanding his intentions can be found in the Book of Job, which mocks the idea that the great monsters of war can ever be controlled by human will:

Can you draw out Leviathan with a fishhook or press down his
   tongue with a cord?
Can you put a rope in his nose or pierce his jaw with a
   hook? [...]

241

On earth there is not his like, a creature without fear.
He sees everything that is high; he is king over all the sons of
    pride.

In this context, the paintings appear to be mocking the preten-
sions of Pitt and Nelson, those 'sons of pride'. Here Blake's innate
incomprehensibility can be said to have been an advantage, as his
criticism of such powerful men was largely missed at the time. The
paintings did not, however, capitalise on this and find a popular
audience. In the eyes of the general public, seeing their politicians
and admirals commanding monsters while half-naked and Christ-
like was just plain weird.

It is hard now to judge the overall impact of this exhibition,
in part because the central work, a painting called *The Ancient
Britons*, has long been lost. It was described as being 10 by 14
feet in size, making it by far the largest work Blake ever created.
Questions have been raised about how a painting that size could
be installed and displayed in such a small space, a conundrum
which has helped the painting gain the reputation of something
of a magical artefact. Even a sketch of the composition done from
memory in 1866 by the painter Seymour Kirkup has disappeared.
For Blakeans, *The Ancient Britons* is arguably the Holy Grail of his
lost works.

In the lengthy catalogue Blake wrote to accompany the exhibition, which was for sale from James Blake for a half-crown, we
find a few details about the picture. These can, perhaps, help to
conjure it in our imaginations. 'In the last Battle of King Arthur
only Three Britons escaped, these were the Strongest Man, the
Beautifullest Man, and the Ugliest Man,' Blake began. These particular three men are influenced by ancient bardic Welsh folklore,
but they also chimed with Blake's desire to divide the population
into three – there are similarities between these three men and

how he describes the three classes of men in *Milton*. '[T]hese three marched through the field unsubdued, as Gods, and the Sun of Britain set, but shall arise again with tenfold splendour when Arthur shall awake from sleep,' he continued. That these three will 'arise again' when Arthur wakes suggests that they are aspects of this mythological once and future king.

Further details about the composition tell us that it was set in Snowdonia in Wales, in the aftermath of the clash between Celtic ancient Britons and the Roman army: 'The dead and the dying, Britons naked, mingled with armed Romans, strew the field beneath. Among these, the last of the Bards who were capable of attending warlike deeds, is seen falling, outstretched among the dead and the dying; singing to his harp in the pains of death. Distant among the mountains, are Druid Temples, similar to Stone Henge. The Sun sets behind the mountains, bloody with the day of battle.'

Kirkup left us a brief eyewitness account of the painting in which he describes it as 'the finest work of the painter', and recalled how 'the fury and splendour of energy there contrasted with the serene ardour of simply beautiful courage; the violent life of the design, and the fierce distance of fluctuating battle.' Robert Hunt, however, described it as 'a complete caricature: one of the bards is singing to his harp in the pangs of death', and added that 'the colouring of the flesh is exactly like hung beef'.

Blake was fascinated by the subject matter depicted in *The Ancient Britons* because he believed that pure, uncorrupted religion existed in the distant past, including the deep history of Albion. 'The antiquities of every Nation under Heaven, is no less sacred than that of the Jews,' he wrote in the catalogue. In Britain, this original religion was practised by the ancient bards, because it was an expression of imagination and creativity. It would still be recognisable and relevant now, he explained, because it was also 'the religion of Jesus, the everlasting Gospel. Antiquity preaches the Gospel of Jesus.' It is the question of whether this perfect proto-Christianity existed in Britain that he is referring to in that unofficial English national anthem, 'And did those feet in ancient time'.

As Blake saw it, the collapse of this uncorrupted religion was marked by the arrival of the druids. Druidism was experiencing a romanticised revival or reinvention in Blake's time, but he viewed it with disdain. It was too much like priesthood for his liking – the triumph of ritual, hierarchies and dogma over inspiration, revelation and love. He saw stone circle temples and tales of human sacrifice as clear evidence that the original inspired pure religion had become corrupted.

In Blake's eyes, the arrival of the druids was the external consequence of the rise of Urizen in human consciousness. This rise, in his mythology, corresponds with the biblical Fall. It was the moment when we ate from the Tree of Knowledge and our reason cast us out of paradise. Urizen was the rational power who abstracted and divided the exterior world until it became a mental model we could confuse with reality. As the druids watched the movement of the stars and performed rituals at stone monuments aligned with the heavens, they too abstracted the greater reality into a system that they could master, and inside which the stories of their lives could be located and comprehended.

Our Fall began when we started to identify with the mental house of cards that Urizen had constructed, and could no longer see that it was incomplete and approximate. Urizen is, ultimately, deeply insecure. In order to maintain his delusion that he is a creator god, he has to deny, mock or belittle any evidence of a greater world beyond his awareness. Not only must he believe in his model, but he needs other people to believe in it too. Urizen believes he is being rational, but all too often he is just rationalising.

He sets out to convince and convert, an angry zealot who refuses to see other perspectives. As a consequence of this, religions rose, competed and clashed. As centuries passed and we moved from the druids to the Crusades and the Inquisition, Urizen became more and more a slave to power, control and blind faith. In Blake's work, he grew into a dragon form – angry, cruel and cut off from the light beyond.

With Urizen dominant and the human mind unbalanced, society was moulded in his image, with all his prejudices and delusions. Many people in Blake's time struggled to understand how the rational enlightenment ideals that fuelled the French Revolution resulted in the bloodshed and horror of the Reign of Terror, but Blake understood. Urizen was not the whole of our minds. There was something divine beyond reason, he knew. Any model in which this was missing was profoundly flawed and ultimately doomed.

Ancient druids did, however, provide Blake with a link to his beloved Old Testament. 'Adam was a Druid, and Noah; also Abraham was called to succeed the Druidical age, which began to turn allegoric and mental signification into corporeal command, whereby human sacrifice would have depopulated the earth,' he stated confidently. The idea of a link between the Abrahamic religions and druidism was common in the eighteenth century, and Blake would have encountered it when he read the antiquarian William Stukeley. Druids were 'of Abraham's religion', according to Stukeley, and their beliefs were 'near to the Christian doctrine'. Blake claimed that he knew this because it was written in Eden, and he was 'an inhabitant of that happy country'. This, he felt, gave him a far greater authority in historical matters than historians, who he had very little time for: 'Tell me the Acts, O historian, and leave me to reason on them as I please; away with your reasoning and your rubbish.'

*

Another notable work in the exhibition was Blake's depiction of the medieval Canterbury pilgrims from Chaucer's *Canterbury Tales*. This was possibly the first important work to be written in Middle English rather than in French or Latin, which were the languages then used by the nobility, Church and ruling class. As a result, Chaucer's book has become ground zero for the long, rich history of English literature and the English imagination in general. Given Blake's interests and philosophy, returning to the source like this was a logical choice.

But there was a problem. The engraver Robert Cromek had had the same idea. He commissioned the artist Thomas Stothard to create a painting of the pilgrims that would be used for the basis of an engraving. The painting went on a tour of the major cities in England. It was a huge success and became Stothard's best-known work. Prints of the engraving were made available to the public at a price of between 3 and 6 guineas each, and sales proved to be lucrative. This was not the case with Blake's version. Stothard's colourful painting had been executed with the light-hearted gaiety which was then the fashion. Blake's version was, in contrast, restrained and Gothic. This may have been a more appropriate style to render a fourteenth-century pilgrimage, but it appeared old-fashioned. In Hunt's savage review of the exhibition, he dismissively notes that, 'One of the pictures represents *Chaucer's Pilgrims*, and it is in every respect a striking contrast to the admirable picture of the same name by Mr. Stothard.'

'You must know', Cromek wrote in a letter to a friend, 'that I give myself great Credit for thinking of such a glorious Subject – it is true that it was sufficiently obvious – but it is equally true that what is obvious is often overlooked.' In later years, however, Blake would accuse Cromek of stealing the idea from him. Gilchrist took Blake's word on this, but subsequent researchers have been less convinced. This scenario is not borne out by contemporary evidence or letters, and it is not hard to imagine multiple people having the same idea of basing an artwork on such a significant text. But once Blake had decided that the idea was his and that Cromek had stolen it, there's no doubt he convinced himself this was true.

Blake's anger at Cromek also resulted in him cursing Stothard, for reasons that never made a great deal of sense when he tried to explain them. As Gilchrist noted, 'Blake was at no pains, throughout this business or afterwards, to conceal his feelings towards Stothard. To the end of his life he would, to strangers, abuse the popular favourite, with a vehemence to them unaccountable.' When Blake's original drawing of the pilgrimage, which had been on display above his door for a year, was found to have faded, Blake blamed this on a 'malignant spell' cast by Stothard. As the Blake scholar G. E. Bentley, Jr. notes: 'The only period in his life when Blake does not seem to have a firmer grasp than ordinary of the nature and limits of reality is just before and after his 1809 exhibition.'

Blake had a prior resentment concerning Cromek, which is likely a factor in all this. Cromek had branched out from engraving to publishing and, for his first project, issued an illustrated edition of Robert Blair's poem *The Grave*, one of the most popular examples of the mid-eighteenth-century 'graveyard school' of poetry. For this, he commissioned Blake to design the artwork. He did not give Blake the job of engraving these designs, however, instead choosing the Italian engraver Luigi Schiavonetti. Cromek recognised that Schiavonetti's gentler, graceful style would be more popular with a mainstream audience. Blake harboured resentment over this, particularly when the edition of *The Grave* turned out to be a commercial success.

Blake's attacks on people like Hayley, Cromek and Stothard, who had all initially treated him with kindness and tried to support him, helped to alienate him further from London artistic society. Many artists who are thought of as strange can still maintain a career, but that's not always the case for those marked as difficult. His bitter criticism of his peers only highlighted the extent to which his thoughts and beliefs no longer made any sense to others. As Carl Jung would later write, 'Loneliness does not come from having no people about one, but from being unable to communicate the things that seem important to oneself, or from holding certain views which others find inadmissible.'

As we noted earlier, Blake constantly stressed the necessity of forgiveness in his work. Forgiveness was, he argued, the most important Christian act, and the key to redemption. Being unable to forgive was to imprison yourself in what he described in *Milton* as 'A Hell of our own making'. As he wrote in *The Gates of Paradise*:

Mutual forgiveness of each Vice,
Such are the Gates of Paradise.

In this period, however, Blake failed to practise what he preached. Perhaps if Hayley, Cromek and Stothard had indeed wronged him, he may have been able to forgive them. But their crimes were imagined, spiritual and eternal – hence unforgivable. As a result, he condemned himself to the darkest period of his life.

In one copy of *Jerusalem*, a number of words and phrases have been scratched out of the opening address 'To the public' – all refer to love and kindness. For example, when he writes about his former works '...having receiv'd the highest reward possible: the love and friendship of those with whom to be connected, is to be blessed', he has erased the words 'love', 'friendship' and 'blessed'. The thought of Blake actively scoring out these words, presumably no longer seeing any truth in them, is an upsetting one. It suggests a dark state of mind, blinded by paranoia and self-pity.

13. MY WRATH DID GROW

Such an outlook occurred frequently during the first decades of the nineteenth century, but it alternated with bursts of joy that could verge on the manic. In the poem 'I rose up at the dawn of day', he faces up to his poverty during a conversation with the devil:

I have Mental Joy & Mental Health
And Mental Friends & Mental wealth
Ive a Wife I love and that loves me;
Ive all But Riches Bodily.

I am in Gods presence night & day
And he never turns his face away
[...]
Then If for Riches I must not Pray
God knows, I little of Prayers need say
So, as a Church is known by its Steeple
If I pray it must be for other People.

He says if I do not worship him for a God,
I shall eat coarser food & go worse shod
So as I don't value such things as these
You must do Mr Devil just as God please

This positive acceptance of his situation was written in August 1807. It contrasts strongly with another entry written earlier that year in the same notebook: 'Tuesday Jan. 20, 1807, between two and seven in the evening, Despair.'

In the context of Blake's lack of success, his alienation of friends and his reputation for madness, the central conceit in *Milton* must have seemed like pure delusion. After the Bard's Song, which takes up the first quarter or so of the poem, the narrative turns to the spirit of the poet John Milton in Eternity. Milton is so moved by the bard that he makes the decision to leave Eternity, where he had resided for the century since his death. He chooses to return 'into the Sea of Time and Space' to earth, in the hope of redemption, both for himself and humanity. To the horror of the other Eternals, he dives from his position of 'Eternal Life' into the 'Eternal Death' of the human world, falling like a comet from the heavens. Blake is walking in his garden in Felpham when he sees this fall, and Milton's star lands on Blake's left foot. In this way, Blake himself is marked as a continuation in the line of 'Poetic Genius' across the ages, which is mankind's only hope for salvation.

You can imagine how the general public would have reacted to an isolated and unsuccessful artist declaring himself the continuation of Milton's lineage, had this poem found an audience. In the modern world, statements of similar elevated self-worth by Kanye West are constantly mocked, and that is in the context of West's huge commercial success and recognised talent. Now, however, the idea of Blake as a successor to Milton, and a worthy link in the chain of poetic genius being passed down the ages, is seen by many as entirely valid. To lift Blake from the category of a delusional wannabe to his current elevated status required an extraordinarily powerful creative achievement.

This creative achievement did not take the form of just paintings or poems. He constructed that most potent and powerful of all the creations of the human imagination – he created a myth.

Mythology is a term that is widely used but not easily defined. It can often be used interchangeably with folklore, fairy tales, legends, scripture or even history. These differing story categories are used to define the level of perceived truth inherent within. History is believed to be true, for example, but when a story starts out as history and evolves over time to become more fantastical, it becomes classed as legend. The inclusion of supernatural elements means that many folklore stories are understood to be fiction, unless an authority insists on the truth of these tales, at which point they become scripture. Myth, somehow, has elements of all these categories. It is understood not to be true – to say something is a myth is to deny it – and yet it has greater power and authority than fiction. Myth is often concerned with the gods and the origin of the world, or, alternatively, with the end of the world, such as the Norse myth of Ragnarök. It talks not so much about this world, but about the behaviour of the fundamental forces that go on to create it.

British myth is subtly different. It is less concerned with the birth or the end of the world, and more focused on how similarly charged mythic forces act out in individuals. The Arthurian grail quest and the sword in the stone, for example, are stories that belong to the world of myth, but are about psychological challenges and personal epiphanies. While many countries' myths feel safe because they are the sagas of long-dismissed gods far removed from everyday lives, British myths offer strange psychoanalytical stories that, despite their far-off trappings, talk about aspects of ourselves that we may find difficult to confront. Perhaps this is why Britain has an odd, slightly embarrassed relationship with its own rich world of mythology. When Neil Gaiman's *Norse Mythology* and Stephen Fry's book of Greek mythology *Mythos* became bestsellers in 2017, you might have expected another well-respected author to produce a similar book on British mythology. That this did not happen is telling.

Blake's myth was very much a British one, combining the universal with the personal. It was told predominantly in his long illustrated poems *Milton* and *Jerusalem*, as well as the unfinished manuscript *Vala* or *The Four Zoas*. It incorporated the cast of characters from his own complex personal mythology that he had been working on since the 1790s. We now understand the characters that these books introduced us to, such as the patriarchal engineer

Urizen or the fiery revolutionary Orc, to be different aspects of Blake's own psyche. His myth has all the trappings of gods and apocalypses, but it too is fundamentally a story about the struggles of a mind.

Blake's work had always been an exploration of the workings of the mind. Even his early work contained a deep understanding of psychology in poetic form, for example the poem 'A Poison Tree' from *Songs of Experience*:

I was angry with my friend;
I told my wrath, my wrath did end.
I was angry with my foe:
I told it not, my wrath did grow.

And I waterd it in fears,
Night & morning with my tears:
And I sunned it with smiles,
And with soft deceitful wiles.

And it grew both day and night.
Till it bore an apple bright.
And my foe beheld it shine,
And he knew that it was mine.

And into my garden stole,
When the night had veild the pole;
In the morning glad I see;
My foe outstretched beneath the tree.

Blake, from this perspective, can be seen as a psychologist long before the field was founded. When his characters are understood as separate parts of his psyche, the clashes and drama that occurs between them can be seen as Blake trying to understand his own mental landscape. When the angels and demons who appear to be without are understood to come from within, all mythical and theological sagas are revealed to be the clashing energies of the mind.

This examination of competing desires and values was, in part, a form of therapy. It brought to light aspects of the mind that people are often blind to. Given the state of our understanding of mental health at the time, it was extraordinarily advanced and sophisticated. Although it is impossible to prove this beyond doubt, it is perhaps not too fanciful to suggest that writing his epic works was a deep, lengthy work of proto-therapy which helped to bring Blake back from delusion and paranoia.

If this was the case, then it would be entirely appropriate. Blake's myth was, ultimately, a myth of healing.

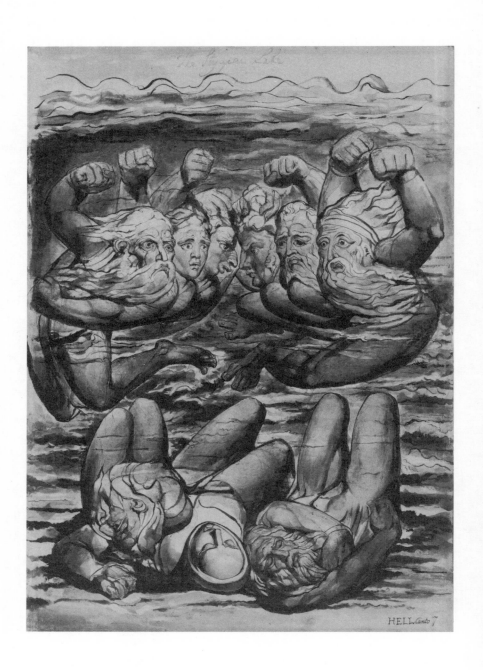

14.

ALTOGETHER HIDDEN FROM THE CORPOREAL UNDERSTANDING

Blake's myth is the story of Albion, a giant.

In British mythology, these islands were originally the home of a race of giants. In the ancient legend of the founding of Britain, as recorded by Geoffrey of Monmouth in the twelfth century, Brutus of Troy lands at Totnes and must defeat all these giants before he can found the city now called London. Brutus then names the island Britain, after himself.

Geoffrey does not mention a giant called Albion, but one appears in Holinshed's *Chronicles* in 1577. In this tradition, Albion is the giant who founded and named this land. Blake takes this idea further, however, and describes him as the father not just of Britain but of all mankind. As he writes in *The Four Zoas*: 'He is Albion, our Ancestor, patriarch of the Atlantic Continent, whose History Preceded that of the Hebrews & in whose Sleep, or Chaos, Creation began.' The giant Albion, then, is the first being. He is, as we will see, a Blakean reinvention of Adam.

The giant Albion is the subject of one of Blake's most famous images – *Albion Rose* (or, alternatively, *The Dance of Albion* or *Glad Day*). A nude male figure with his arms thrown out wide stands in front of glorious streaming coloured light. Blake first produced this image around 1795, and he returned to it repeatedly throughout his life. It is often likened to Leonardo da Vinci's *Vitruvian Man*, due to the similarity of the pose. *Vitruvian Man* has his arms and legs outstretched and is drawn inside a circle and a square in order to show ideal human proportions. These geometric shapes constrain him in Urizen's limited rational world. Blake's Albion, in contrast, is anything but constrained. Where *Vitruvian Man*'s expression is neutral and emotionless, *Albion Rose* radiates joy and vitality. It is perhaps intentional that, where the centre of *Vitruvian Man*'s circle is his navel, the centre of the figure of Albion is his genitals.

Albion is not just a giant, however. As someone who exists in the imagination, he can be symbolic of many different things at once. The most obvious of these is the country itself. Albion is the oldest name we know of for Britain. It is used to refer to the island in its purest form, before any lines were drawn on the map, when it was free of the divisions, politics and tribal factions that would follow. Although it is often thought that Blake uses Albion as the visionary name of England, there are many references to locations in Scotland and Wales in his myth. The name Albion, Blake knew, referred to the whole island, as it was used long before the kingdoms of Scotland and England existed. It has survived longest in Scotland, which is still called *Alba* in Scottish Gaelic, *Albain* in Irish and *Yr Alban* in Welsh.

Albion is often said to derive from the word for 'white', a reference to the white cliffs of the southern coast, although it is odd that the aboriginal British would name their land based on how it appears from beyond their shores. This is what makes the alternative etymology suggested by the French Celtic scholar Xavier Delamarre more convincing. Delamarre has argued that Albion originally meant 'the world above', or the physical world, as opposed to the underworld or world below.

One meaning of Albion, then, is that it refers to the physical island itself. Blake often includes references to rocks when he is referring to Albion as the island, such as 'The Ancient Man upon the Rock of Albion Awakes' or that 'All things begin & end in Albions ancient Druid rocky shore'. The name can, however, also refer to the people on this island. The actions of a country are ultimately the actions of the people that make up that country.

Albion, in Blake's myth, is also understood to be the hermetic concept of the Universal Man, which Swedenborg called the Grand Man and Kabbalists know as Adam Kadmon. This is the immense human inside which the whole cosmos exists, as discussed earlier. This makes Albion far grander than the representation of one island or its people. He is the representation of everyone, and everything. In *Jerusalem*, Blake states that 'Albion covered the whole Earth'.

The myth of Albion also contains details that are taken from Blake's life. There are numerous references to the divine vision appearing at Lambeth and Felpham, for example, and one of the evil Sons of Albion is Schofield, the soldier who accused Blake of treason. Blake has not been able to keep his personal feelings about his accuser out of the poem. Plate 68 of *Jerusalem* begins: 'O Skofield why art thou cruel?' At one point he offers him out for a fight, like a schoolboy:

Go thou to Skofield [...]
Tell him to be no more dubious: demand explicit words
Tell him: I will dash him into shivers, where & at what time
I please: tell Hand & Skofield they are my ministers of evil
To those I hate: for I can hate also as well as they!

Thanks to the inclusion of personal details like this, Albion is also a representation of Blake himself. The Universal Man is also the individual imagining the Universal Man – as above, so below. The myth, from this perspective, is a dramatising of the psychological processes occurring in his mind.

There is some suggestion that Blake's *Albion Rose* painting may be a self-portrait. The paintings and drawings we have of Blake depict him at middle age or older, but he was said to have had a thick head of blond hair in his youth, similar to that depicted in this portrait of Albion. This interpretation would fit with the autobiographical elements in the Albion myth, and explain why the image does not appear to depict a giant. Of course, the issue of scale is tricky in Blake's myth. Although we do not appear to be looking up at a giant figure in the image, it may be that Blake assumes that the viewer has, in the light of the reawakened Albion, become a giant too.

This brings us to another interpretation of Albion, alongside the giant, country, people, cosmos and Blake – that Albion is you, the reader. You are the creator of the universe inside your head, and by reading Blake's work you are seeing it through his expansive eyes. Indeed, when you suspend your sense of self, how could Albion not be you? Whisper it, but there is no 'other'.

Blake's myth of Albion is simple. Long ago, Albion's mind was in balance and he possessed the divine vision, but he was cut off from it by doubt and shame. As a result, Albion falls into the sleep of death. This sorry state is the materialistic world we are in now. But Albion will, we are promised, awaken again, and the world will once again be perceived through divine inspiration.

Although the plot is simple, the telling of the myth is anything but. Blake's narrative appears to come from a place outside the usual constraints of time and place. The fall of Albion, for example, is simultaneously happening right now, about to happen, and has already ended. Blake is not telling the story from the three-dimensional perspective of the human world. He is telling it as it appears in his 'fourfold vision'. He is describing events as they appear from outside normal time and space, in Eternity. It is the way the story is told, and not the simple plot, that gives the poem its challenging reputation.

Blake's myth has an archetypal story structure with many parallels in legend and religion, such as the story of King Arthur. As we saw earlier, Blake referenced the promised return of the 'once and future king' in his description of the lost painting *The Ancient Britons*. Arthur, like Albion, was then understood to be both a person and, as a king, the personification of the land. In the Arthurian legend of the Fisher King, for example, a king suffers a groin wound which results in the land becoming a desolate, barren wasteland. In the world of myth, like the work of Blake, there is always a blurring of the line between the internal and the external worlds. The story of Albion also has clear parallels with the death and resurrection of Jesus, especially as Blake interpreted the half human, half divine figure of Jesus as being the imagination itself.

The sleep and subsequent reawakening of Albion may seem an extremely simple plot for such lengthy poems, but Blake's focus is not on this plot. As always, it was the psychological analysis of events that fascinated him, and it is in this arena that we find Blake's great insights and true genius. To explore the interior of Albion, Blake divided the giant's mind into four separate sections, each of which he personified as an independent male character. As we saw earlier, he called these four aspects of the mind the four zoas.

The word *zoa* is a Greek plural word which Blake used as an English singular. It refers to the four spiritual beasts described by the biblical prophet Ezekiel. This was an important part of the Bible for Blake, because he recognised its disorientating depiction of these strange creatures as being a description of the 'fourfold sight' he had experienced. Like Blake's visions, Ezekiel was confronted by something beyond the regular three dimensions of the material world. He attempted to describe something impossible to visualise, and the effect is unsettling:

> Also out of the midst thereof *came* the likeness of four living creatures. And this *was* their appearance; they had the likeness of a man.
> And every one had four faces, and every one had four wings.
> And their feet were straight feet; and the sole of their feet was like the sole of a calf's foot: and they sparkled like the colour of burnished brass.
> And they had the hands of a man under their wings on their four sides; and they four had their faces and their wings.
> Their wings were joined one to another; they turned not when they went; they went every one straight forward.
> As for the likeness of their faces, they four had the face of a man, and the face of a lion, on the right side: and they four had the face of an ox on the left side; they four also had the face of an eagle.
> Thus were their faces: and their wings were stretched upward; two wings of every one were joined one to another, and two covered their bodies.

The poem *Jerusalem* is likewise frequently disorientating. Like Ezekiel's vision, it is an attempt to describe something witnessed from the higher perspective of 'fourfold vision'.

For Blake, of course, these zoas were not external spiritual beasts but aspects of our own minds. One of them we know well – our old friend Urizen, who represents our cold, rational, reasoning power. He is joined by Tharmas, who represents sensations and the physical body, and Luvah, who is our emotions. These three are joined by Urthona, a zoa who represents creativity and the imagination.

Urthona differs slightly from the others in that when he is active in the human world he changes and becomes Los. This is probably because while intellect, emotions or bodies can exist as abstract ideas in the Eternal realm, creativity and imagination need to be active in the physical world of time and space in order to truly manifest. Los, Blake explains, is 'the Vehicular Form of Strong Urthona'.

Each zoa has a female counterpart called their emanation. Here we again see the influence of the biblical patriarchal worldview, as these female spirits are described as emanating from their male zoa counterparts in the same way Eve emanated from the body of Adam. It can be helpful, however, to not worry too much about the genders of zoas and emanations, not least because eighteenth-century ideas of gender were so different to their twenty-first-century counterparts. If we focus on gender there can be a tendency to project a power relationship between zoas and emanation which the text does not support. Instead, it is more important to notice how zoas and emanations differ not by status but by behaviour.

Emanations are usually described as active, such as the 'Emanation that was wont to play before thy face' who Blake refers to at the start of *Jerusalem*. Whereas the zoas represent eternal qualities, the emanations are those qualities acting in the world. The distinction is not quite strong enough that we can think of the zoas as nouns and the emanations as verbs, for there is some blurring of roles and zoas can also be active, most notably Urizen. But we can think of emanations as what comes from the qualities which the zoas represent, rather than those qualities themselves. An emanation is what that quality does.

The title character of *Jerusalem* is an emanation. As the poem's full title explains, she is *Jerusalem: The Emanation of the Giant Albion*.

Blake describes the relationship between Jerusalem and Albion as being 'As the Soul is to the Body', which gives an insight into the difference between an emanation and the character that produced them.

That Jerusalem is named after the earthly city currently claimed by both Israel and Palestine can mistakenly give the impression that she is intended to represent a city, and perhaps an idealised spiritual form of London. Blake gave most emanations made-up names such as Enitharmon, Ahania and Enion, and it may have been less confusing if he had done the same for Albion's emanation. Jerusalem should be thought of not as a physical city but as society, an accumulation of all the actions of the people of Britain. Or at least, what those accumulated actions would have been if Albion had not fallen into the sleep of death and the British people were still aware of the inspired divine imagination. With Albion gone, his emanation Jerusalem wanders the world, lost.

As well as generating emanations, the characters in Blake's mythology can also produce a shadowy being called a spectre. A spectre represents the dark qualities of a character, which grow and strengthen when they are cut off from the divine vision. In *Jerusalem*, Los's spectre is depicted as a dark, bat-winged dragon that emerges from his back as he works away at his creative labours:

> [...] and the Spectre stood over Los
> Howling in pain: a blackning Shadow, blackning dark & opake
> Cursing the terrible Los: bitterly cursing him for his friendship
> To Albion, suggesting murderous thoughts against Albion.

Los's spectre is his dark thoughts that criticise and doubt, the voice that declares that friends are false and that creative work is pointless. It is the black dog of depression that cannot see any light or hope. As it tells Los:

O that I could cease to be! Despair! I am Despair
Created to be the great example of horror & agony: also my
Prayer is vain I called for Compassion: compassion mockd
Mercy & pity threw the grave stone over me & with lead
And iron, bound it over me for ever

The birth of a spectre leads to conflict and struggle, but it is important not to attempt to destroy your spectre, because this would destroy part of you. The goal, instead, is to re-assimilate it. Los achieves this by putting his spectre to work and using it in his creative projects. Work and art were always Blake's response to depression.

Blake's spectre is a similar idea to the Jungian concept of the shadow, the name Jung used for the hidden, usually negative and unknowable aspects of our psyche. Blake's spectre, like Jung's shadow, is our blind spot. It knows things that are kept from our conscious minds. As Los's spectre tells Los:

O! thou seest not what I see! What is done in the Furnaces.
Listen, I will tell thee what is done in moments to thee
    unknown

The spectre is misguided, due to existing without light, but it is neither worthless nor an enemy. If light can be cast on it, then it can be reintegrated into a healthy psyche, and the knowledge it contains will be revealed.

Jerusalem, the emanation of Albion, also has a shadow, which is the lovely nature goddess Vala. She is also the daughter and the emanation of the emotional zoa Luvah and represents nature as the deists see it, in the single vision of Newton's sleep. Vala represents the physical world entirely devoid of imagination. In the myth, it is Vala who seduces Albion away from Jerusalem and sacrifices him

263

with a druid's knife. This results in his fall and all the subsequent struggles between the zoas and their emanations and spectres.

The conflict that makes up Blake's Albion myth, then, comes from the clashes between these central components. The giant Albion, who represents man, Britain, Blake, you and the cosmos, contains four zoas. Both Albion and the zoas produce emanations and spectres. Out of the first man comes the entire cast of this melodrama. This was the structure that Blake used to reframe the internal energies of his own mind into the epic battles of a new spiritual pantheon.

The characters of Blake's myth should not be thought of, as is often assumed, as a coherent system of psychological categorisation. Instead, they are a wonderful artistic record of the interplay of mental energies and a creative engagement with many contradictions present. For Blake, the spiritual realm was active, engaged and involved. The mind could be at peace at times, and it will be again after the zoas have returned to balance. But until then, the internal psychological soap opera needs to be brought into the light and understood.

The depth and importance of the works that explore Blake's myth were not immediately apparent. There were only four copies of *Milton* printed in Blake's lifetime, and five of *Jerusalem*. *The Four Zoas* was never finished.

Blake had always made little attempt to introduce his characters, or explain who they were or what they represented. He assumed that we would know and recognise them – they were part of us, after all. In his shorter books from the Bible of Hell series, such as *The Song of Los* or *The First Book of Urizen*, this was less of a problem because of their focus on a single central character. In the works he produced in the early nineteenth century, particularly *Milton*, the unfinished *Four Zoas* and his great masterpiece *Jerusalem*, the scale and number of characters referenced are considerably greater. As a result, they are frequently incomprehensible to a reader approaching them without prior knowledge of Blake's mythology. If we were to compare his writings to that of the later English mythmaker J. R. R. Tolkien, then *Songs of Innocence and of Experience* was Blake's *Hobbit*, the Bible of Hell was his *Lord of the Rings*, and his nineteenth-century works were his *Silmarillion*. For example, in *Milton* we find passages such as:

> And these the Labours of the Sons of Los in Allamanda:
> And in the City of Golgonooza: & in Luban: & around
> The Lake of Udan-Adan, in the Forests of Entuthon Benython
> Where Souls incessant wail,

Writing like this is not to everybody's taste. Or, to give an even more extreme and challenging example, consider the following passage from *Jerusalem*:

> Tho divided by the Cross & Nails & Thorn & Spear
> In cruelties of Rahab & Tirzah permanent endure
> A terrible indefinite Hermaphroditic form
> A Wine-press of Love & Wrath double Hermaph[r]oditic
> Twelvefold in Allegoric pomp in selfish holiness
> The Pharisaion, the Grammateis, the Presbuterion,
> The Archiereus, the Iereus, the Saddusaion, double
> Each withoutside of the other, covering eastern heaven

Blake's nineteenth-century writing in general had become denser, deeper and richly rewarding, but at times it was clearly off-putting for those new to his work. Instead of reacting to his lack of audience by retreating and attempting to produce something more commercial and superficially appealing, Blake was doubling down on his vision and amplifying all the things that alienated him from the public. It was as if he had given up on the idea of his illuminated books ever finding a readership. He was producing them just for himself and the spirits.

Gilchrist struggled to make sense of them. 'Few are the readers who will ever penetrate beyond the first page or two,' he says about *Milton*. After reading page after page of dense text, he simply couldn't work out what the poem was supposed to be about. We now understand the poem to be about Milton's selfless decision to return to the mortal world in order to redeem creation with imagination, fix his mistakes and, in the course of epic struggles with both Urizen and Satan, reconcile with his wives and daughters. None of this was comprehensible to Gilchrist. As far as he could tell, Milton didn't even seem to figure highly in the narrative. 'About Milton we hear very little,' he writes, 'but his name *is* occasionally mentioned.'

When we approach the poem now, it is with the insights of over a century of academic study. We may have a copy of S. Foster Damon's *A Blake Dictionary* to hand, which explains every character and what they represent. Failing this we have Wikipedia, or informative editor's notes in the back of the book. Gilchrist came to the text without any of these aids. It is not surprising he was lost.

When Gilchrist encountered a list of the names of the Sons of Albion, he responded that, 'Of these names, many never occur again throughout the book; and to the remainder we, to the last, fail to attach any idea whatever. Their owners cannot even be spoken of as shadows, for a shadow has a certain definiteness of form. But these continue *mere* names.' Given his reaction to reading *Milton*, it is perhaps fortunate that Gilchrist did not attempt to read *The Four Zoas*. This may be an incredibly valuable insight into Blake's mythology, but it is widely seen as the most daunting and incomprehensible thing he ever wrote.

Gilchrist has no more luck when he tries to make sense of *Jerusalem*. Twice as long as *Milton*, and arguably more dense and abstruse, he finds himself asking how it is that, 'in the midst of such a chaos of words, names and images, that, as the eye wanders, hopeless and dispirited, up and down the large closely-written pages, the mind cannot choose but busy itself with the question, how a man of Blake's high gifts ever came to produce such; nay, to consider this, as he really did, his greatest work'. That Gilchrist included the phrase 'as he really did', to clarify that Blake did indeed think *Jerusalem* his greatest achievement, shows how implausible that idea seemed at the time.

Pondering the problem, Gilchrist wondered if in 'casting away all idea of ordering and shaping his thoughts and imaginations in such wise that other minds could lay hold upon them, he followed the less laborious and more exciting pleasure of pouring his conceptions freely forth, all crude and inchoate, in words so vaguely and arbitrarily expressive of his meaning, that to him alone could they suggest it'. Blake, Gilchrist thought, may have been making no effort to be comprehensible, on the grounds that this made writing easier and more fun.

This was not what Blake thought he was doing. Having spent the best part of two decades labouring over *Jerusalem*, it was clearly something more than a lark to him. Near the start of the work, in July 1803, he announced that his intention was 'to speak to future generations by a Sublime Allegory, which is now perfectly completed into a Grand Poem'. That the work was intended for 'future generations' may indeed show he had given up on a contemporary readership, but not on an eventual one. He still expected the poem to be studied, when the time was right.

Blake clearly did, as Gilchrist stressed, consider the work to be his most important. As he wrote: 'I may praise it, since I dare not pretend to be any other than the Secretary the Authors are in Eternity I consider it as the Grandest Poem that the World Contains.' Being a myth that originated in Eternity, it follows that it must always have existed and so logically he can't take any credit for it. He simply did the work of writing it down in the earthly realm. The numerous autobiographical elements it contains, of course, suggest he deserves a little more credit than this.

Modesty aside, if he considered the poem to be his most important work and if it was intended to reach an audience at some later point in time, then the confusing style was intentional. As he described it, 'Allegory address'd to the Intellectual powers while it is altogether hidden from the Corporeal Understanding is My Definition of the Most Sublime Poetry.' The puzzle-like nature of the poem was a feature, not a bug.

Blake was aware that his meaning was then 'altogether hidden from Corporeal Understanding'. He did, however, expect 'future generations' to be able to understand it. We have made significant advances on this front and have found far more of worth in the text than Gilchrist did, but few would pretend that we are there yet. As the highly respected Blake scholar Harold Bloom admits in his notes on the poem, 'The structure of *Jerusalem* raises many problems, which the poem's critics (this one included) have not been able to solve. Yet the problem may be only that the poem has not had enough accurate and close readers yet.'

The main reason why the poem is so intriguing and baffling is that it appears to be the work of someone in a different state of consciousness. Its incomprehensibility comes from it being written from the fourfold perspective of Eternity, which suggests that Blake thought that we future generations would, eventually, develop an understanding of this higher perspective. This is, after all, the message of the poem. Albion, who is also the reader, will one day awaken.

Here the difficult nature of Blake's writing can be said to have

268

a distinct purpose. As all teachers will confirm, if you simply tell your pupil something, it is unlikely to make much of an impression. If you put them in a position where they realise it for themselves, however, then this becomes a lesson they are unlikely ever to forget. The dense, difficult nature of work such as *Jerusalem* forces you to study it, and those rare moments when you solve a mystery and understand an insight have a profound effect. Blake's myth is an attempt to show you the 'fourfold vision' that he has experienced throughout his life. When he makes you realise that you too are Albion, you may find yourself, if only for a moment, seeing the world through his eyes. At moments like this, the idea that it is 'the Grandest Poem that the World Contains' does not seem quite so crazy.

In a section of *Jerusalem* titled 'To The Jews', Blake argues that Albion predates the Hebrew religious tradition and that important Jewish patriarchs including Abraham and Noah were druids. Blake then proclaims that 'you O Jews are the true Christians [...] Take up the Cross O Israel & follow Jesus.' At first sight, these arguments can seem dubious and more than a little insulting. To make sense of them, it is necessary to understand how Blake interpreted our deep history.

The eighteenth-century understanding of history was very different to how we think of it now. Blake was writing long before Charles Darwin, and he had no knowledge of evolution, palaeontology, or the long millennia during which our ancestors were no different to the rest of the animal kingdom. If this knowledge had been available in his day, it would be in character that he would have refused to believe it anyway. Instead, Blake's sense of history began with the arrival of the giant Albion, his equivalent of the biblical Adam.

The giant Albion could perceive the divine light of the

imagination, which Blake also calls 'Poetic Genius', because the different parts of his mind were still in balance. It flowed through him in a pure and uncorrupted form, just as it would enter the world again at a later date in the form of Jesus Christ, who referred to himself as 'the light of the world'. Because the nature of Albion's and Jesus' light was identical, Blake saw Albion as a Christian, even though that religion would not arrive for countless centuries after Albion's fall.

The myth of Albion, Jerusalem and their spectres at the beginning of humanity also has strong echoes with the story of Adam, Eve and the serpent in the Garden of Eden. In this scenario, Albion is Adam, Jerusalem is Eve, and the spectre of Jerusalem – and indeed the spectre of anyone cut off from the divine light – is Satan. But while the biblical narrative presents Adam, Eve and the serpent as separate beings, Blake saw them as aspects of the same psyche. This is a profound change and one potentially far healthier. It avoids the patriarchal power divide between men and women that has dominated Church teachings for centuries. It also avoids the dualistic split between Satan and man, in which Satan is seen as a separate 'other' to be fought, instead of a dark part of ourselves we need to illuminate. The Fall occurs in both myths, but only Blake sees a reunification between male, female and Satan as the solution. It was Blake, after all, who called for *The Marriage of Heaven and Hell*.

Blake, therefore, associated Albion with both Adam, who represents mankind not yet cast out of Eden, and Jesus, who as we have noted was interchangeable with divine imagination. With our more modern understanding of prehistory, we might instead see Albion as a personification of the time after recognisably human consciousness appeared in our ancestors, and we moved from the world of animal consciousness into the worlds of gods, cave art and the tribal telling of stories around the camp fire. This was when imagination first arrived in the material world and the moment when the cosmos first gained the ability to intentionally shape itself. It is because this illumination arrived in a human form that many occult traditions speak of the spiritual universe as being the Universal Man.

This period did not last, however. A shift in human consciousness occurred in which the egocentric rational mind gained superiority over other ways of perceiving. Blake repeatedly dates this change to 6,000 years ago, which is roughly the time when the first Sumerian and Mesopotamian temple cities appeared, along with the wheel, calendar and complex writing and number systems. These were not the first large cities, as places like Çatalhöyük in modern-day Turkey were considerably older, but they were the first to show signs of social hierarchy, inequality and organised warfare. They represent a time when humanity moved from a cooperative, prelapsarian existence into the more pathological behaviours we know today.

An echo of this shift in human consciousness at this time is recorded in the origin myths and scriptures of the world, which tell of the arrival of bearded, patriarchal, controlling 'sky gods' such as Zeus, Jupiter, Odin and Jehovah. These sky gods typically viewed themselves as creators, even though their acts of creation were limited to imposing order on chaos by abstracting and dividing. In the Book of Genesis, for example, Jehovah creates the world by defining the contraries of light and dark, day and night, land and sea, good and evil, and so on. These sky gods brought law, judgement, reasoning and language. They were often said to have fought and overpowered immense giants or Titans, which were linked with the earth and judged to be brutal, irrational, disobedient or animalistic. In Blakean terms, this story is the rise of Urizen. The description of how he overpowered the creative, physical and

271

emotional zoas, and imposed strict law to police the delusion that he was the one true god, is identical.

In the old British myths, however, there remain hints of the time before the reign of Urizen. The concept of sky gods and the idea that the spiritual realm is in some way above us first appeared in the writings of Plato and was taken up and propagated by the Roman Church. The old myths of the British Isles, however, still recall a time before this suspect idea arrived on this island, when the spiritual realm was not above or distant, but within and present. They tell of a timeless otherworld known as *Tír na nÓg* by the Irish and *Annwfn* or *Annwn* by the Welsh. Remnants of this 'land of the ever-young' still linger in the later English concept of Avalon. To Blake, these myths told of a time before the Fall when the mind was in balance, and the rational Urizen still worked in harmony with creative Urthona, emotional Luvah and the physical sensations of Tharmas.

The rise of Urizen and the imbalance of the zoas caused what Blake calls 'the sleep of Albion'. At this point, direct divine inspiration was lost. All that remained were echoes of it in a corrupted form. This original inspiration became codified into ritual and tradition, and the rise of priestcraft began with the emergence of the druids. Our current historical knowledge of the druids comes mainly from Roman writers, who described a priestly caste of authority figures and magicians who studied the sky. We now know that druids existed centuries after the stone circles of Britain had been constructed, but at the time Blake was influenced by the antiquarian William Stukeley, who claimed that the druids had built Stonehenge and other temples. When he talks about druids, then, Blake is referring to the much earlier class of 'proto-druids' who measured the heavens and erected the countless stone temples on hills and moors. Blake believed that druids practised ritual human sacrifice which, as he saw it, re-enacted the fall of Albion and marked the corruption of inspired imagination into violent, controlling law. As much as Blake admired the bardic tradition, he saw druidism as a terrible wrong.

There were elements of the original inspired imagination which managed to survive in druidical teaching, however. As noted, Blake claimed that Noah and Abraham were descended from the druidical tradition, and that the Jewish people 'are the true Christians'. This was his explanation for how his beloved Old Testament contained such rich, visionary elements. Outside of this exception, though, he usually saw little of value in the knowledge that druids preserved. He claimed that deeply flawed Greek philosophy, for example, was 'a remnant of Druidism'.

Another difference between Blake's myth and the Adam and Eve story was that the Garden of Eden existed in some unknown, far-off location which we can never find or connect with. Because Albion was simultaneously the first man, the place where Blake lived and the psyche of Blake himself, Blake's myth connected the cosmic and universal to the local and personal. This prevented his story from being ancient and irrelevant, and made Eden local and accessible to the attentive reader. It was this cross-time link that situated Blake's origin myth in his familiar streets of London and southern England. It is also what made Albion the founder of not just Britain but all of humanity. Had Blake lived elsewhere, his myth would have taken on an equally local flavour.

This is why nationalists demonstrate how little they understand Blake when they attempt to co-opt him for patriotic support. It is not that Britain is innately special in itself, Blake tells us. It is that Britain becomes special when visionary imagination is projected upon it. And in order to experience that visionary perspective, it is necessary, if only for a moment, to lose all sense of self and know that there is no division between you and the seven billion kin with whom you share the planet.

That said, because Blake was English and experienced his visions here, his country became inseparable from his work and his imagination. The clearest example is the way that the hymn 'Jerusalem' has become the unofficial English national anthem, despite most not understanding what it is about or why they are drawn to it. As we saw earlier, there has been a long, scholarly debate about whose feet Blake is talking about when he wrote:

And did those feet in ancient time,
Walk upon Englands mountains green:
And was the holy Lamb of God,
On Englands pleasant pastures seen!

We've already noted that the common assumption that 'those feet' and the 'holy Lamb of God' refer to Jesus is suspect, because the tradition of Jesus visiting England probably did not exist when the lines were written. But as we have also noted, Blake saw Jesus and the divine imagination as being one and the same thing, and that divine imagination was first experienced by the giant at the heart of his mythology. That giant did indeed walk upon this green and pleasant land.

In the context of both Blake's myth and his interpretation of history, then, the most likely candidate for the character walking upon 'Englands mountains green' is the giant Albion, containing as he did the same light that illuminated Jesus. Blake's poem talks of the building of Jerusalem 'In Englands green & pleasant land' as something that has yet to happen. This strongly supports the idea that the poem is talking about the giant Albion, given that Jerusalem is his emanation and that she will be created from him.

The hymn is not officially the English national anthem, because there is no such thing. State occasions instead make do with the British national anthem 'God Save the Queen'. But it has become the English national anthem because the people recognise it as such, and not because the State insists on it. It is through the collective acts, opinions and preferences of the people who make up the country of Albion that the unique status of the hymn emerges. While there have been campaigns to have 'Jerusalem' officially recognised, this would downgrade it from the special position it is now in. Here, perhaps, we can see a glimpse of the emanation Jerusalem in modern-day Britain. If the British people collectively form Albion, then the hymn 'Jerusalem' is genuinely the emanation of the giant Albion.

When people from all walks of life across England raise their heads and sing 'Jerusalem', they are singing about the giant who first let light into the world. This giant is everything, and he is us. As a product of Blake's imagination, he links both him and us to the source of that imagination. They are singing about the once and future personification of the divine inspiration who sleeps now but who will, perhaps if we sing loud enough, awaken.

It doesn't matter that most people are unaware of this. Blake was open from the start about how the meaning of his myth was 'altogether hidden from the Corporeal Understanding'. He knew it was going to bypass our inner Urizen, and leave our rational sides confused and bewildered. But he also knew that this did not matter, because the rational Urizen is small and limited and there are things beyond it which it cannot measure.

This is not an ancient, long-dead myth that gathers dust in a museum. Every time people gather and those words are sung, the myth is a living thing. The current cross-society popularity of the song, then, proves that Blake was right. Despite the denials of many, the modern world is still connected to the source of imagination itself.

15.
IN LOVE WITH THE PRODUCTIONS OF TIME

Outside Blake's workshop, the late eighteenth century was not a time that concerned itself with myth or the source of imagination. It was much more interested in shopping. The Industrial Revolution had generated an outpouring of consumer goods never before widely available. For the homeowner, there was a dizzying supply of furniture, pottery, wallpapers, clothes, soft furnishings, jewellery and crockery, along with increasingly common luxuries such as spices, sugar, chocolate, tea and coffee. Thanks to the raw materials and markets of the emerging British Empire, there was also enough money with which to buy them. Middle-class households were now able to ape the habits of the aristocracy, in that they could display stylish furnishings as a demonstration of social standing and good taste. The late eighteenth century, as a result, became a time which delighted in fads, fashion and what we would now call conspicuous consumption. For an artist with no interest in changeable fashion and a desire to represent the eternal, Blake had been born at the wrong time.

Blake was never going to have his head turned by the new and contemporary. Eternity was profoundly important to him, and the concept runs through his work. The opening of 'Auguries of Innocence', for example, represents some of his best-known lines:

> To see a World in a Grain of Sand
> And a Heaven in a Wild Flower
> Hold Infinity in the palm of your hand
> And Eternity in an hour

Blake's concept of eternity sits at the heart of his Albion mythology and was central to his understanding of the universe. He often uses the word as you might expect a Christian to use the word heaven, as some blissful realm different to the material world. But while heaven is distant, Blake's eternity is always just within reach, simultaneously within and without and potentially available to all. In his copy of Swedenborg's *Divine Love and Divine Wisdom*, Blake had written that Swedenborg's argument was 'False' on the grounds that 'if a thing loves it is infinite'. After a moment's reflection, he then added, 'Perhaps we only differ in the meaning of the words Infinite & Eternal.' Eternity is a word that can be used in ways that are only loosely defined, and he recognised that his understanding of the word may be different to how others used it. So what, exactly, was Blake talking about when he used the word 'Eternity'?

One common definition of eternity is that it refers to an infinite period of time. Understood in this way, eternity is simply time without end. This definition does not fit well with modern cosmology, however. This claims that time did not exist before the creation of the universe in the Big Bang, and that time may also end at some far-off future moment if the universe does indeed cease to exist, as some models predict. Eternity cannot refer to infinite time, therefore, because according to our current understanding of the universe there will only be a finite amount of time.

Instead, eternity can be defined as all of time. Understood in this way, eternity is the period that contains everything that has ever happened and everything that will happen. Yet for this definition of eternity to be something more than an intellectual abstraction and to describe something real, it is necessary for all of time to actually exist. If Blake's eternity is a meaningful concept, in other words, then the future and the past need to be as real as the present. They need to be physical things, and not just a thought experiment.

During Blake's time, eternity was more of a religious or spiritual idea than a scientific one. As far as eighteenth-century science was concerned, the past no longer existed and the future was yet to happen. Eternity was little more than a metaphor. In the twenty-first century, however, this is no longer the case. This aspect of Blake's idiosyncratic cosmology is supported by the work of Albert Einstein.

In his special theory of relativity, Einstein showed that time passes at different rates in different circumstances. As hard to accept as this may be, the passing of time is changed by increases in speed and gravity. As a result, there are circumstances in which an event has not yet happened from the perspective of one observer, but which has already occurred from the perspective of someone else. This raises the question of how it is possible to say that something has happened, given that this may be true in some circumstances but false in others. According to Einstein, the answer is that we cannot. After relativity, the idea of 'now' became something that could not be satisfactorily defined.

This led to the cosmological theory known as the 'block universe'. In a block universe all of time, including that which appears to us to be the past and the future, exists together, as one large 'block' of four-dimensional spacetime. Events that occur within the block universe are defined by the four dimensions of breadth,

width, height and duration. The block universe solves the problems of defining 'now' by making the concept irrelevant. In a block universe, the passing of time is little more than an illusion. Every event exists always, regardless of whether it happened hundreds of years ago or hundreds of years in the future. Every first kiss and every last word is like an exhibit preserved in a museum that only beings with a godlike perspective can explore.

After the death of his lifelong friend the engineer Michele Besso, Einstein sent a letter of condolence to Besso's family. He wrote that, 'Now [Besso] has departed from this strange world a little ahead of me. That means nothing. For us believing physicists the distinction between past, present, and future only has the meaning of an illusion, though a persistent one.' Einstein himself died one month later. Or at least, that is how it appears to those of us trapped within the persistent illusion of linear time. From Einstein's perspective, he and Besso are still alive and joking around, and neither of them has been born yet, and they have been dead and gone for uncountable millennia. Blake displays a similar understanding about the illusion of passing time in *Jerusalem*, where he writes that, 'I see the Past, Present & Future, existing all at once.' He also writes:

And all that has existed in the space of six thousand years:
Permanent, & not lost not lost nor vanishd, & every little act,
Word, work, & wish, that has existed, all remaining still

These are descriptions of eternity that perfectly describe Einstein's block universe.

Belief in the literal existence of a block universe is called eternalism. The implications of eternalism are complex and, to most people, extremely disturbing. If the future already exists and cannot be changed, then there can be no free will. Your future actions were fixed before you are even born. This idea offends our sense of morality and justice, and reduces any feelings of pride and accomplishment we may have about our achievements into little more than vanity. How can we strive to prove ourselves if our life's work was going to happen regardless? And likewise, how can we condemn Adolf Hitler or Judas Iscariot if the Holocaust and the betrayal of Jesus were always going to occur, and indeed already existed long before Hitler and Judas were born? If it was physically impossible for Hitler or Judas to act differently, how can we judge and blame?

From the perspective of eternalism our legal system is absurd, because it assumes the existence of free will when it judges those accused of crimes. But in an eternalist universe there is no free will, so we are effectively condemning people for the crime of existing. In a similar way, victims of abuse were preordained to suffer. Their abuse was destined to occur even before life appeared on earth, or the solar system formed. You can debate at length whether this makes the universe immoral or amoral, but it's clear that such a universe is a hard one to love.

Supporters of eternalism respond to these issues in two ways. The first is to remind us that just because something is unappealing doesn't mean that it can't also be true. There is no guarantee that our universe will be something that we like. There is no reason why our own moral perspectives and sense of justice should coincide with the construction and behaviour of the entire universe.

The second response is to dismiss the problem on the grounds that, in terms of how we live our lives on a moment-to-moment basis, it doesn't really matter. Even if our sense of free will is nothing but an illusion, it is a consistent and convincing illusion and it is easy enough to go through life acting as if it was real.

The greatest literary exploration of the concept of eternalism is the epic, Blake-inspired novel *Jerusalem* by Alan Moore, which includes a conversation about the true nature of reality between the eighteenth-century nonconformist minister Philip Doddridge and an angel. 'Might I ask if, anywhere in this ingenious arrangement, any of us ever truly had Free Will?' Doddridge asks the angel. The angel somewhat apologetically tells him that nobody had. 'After a well-timed pause as if before the punch line of a joke', the angel replies with a further question: 'Did you miss it?'

This exchange is overheard by a character called Bill, who understands the reason for the laughter triggered by the angel's question: '[Bill] got the gag. In some ways, it was almost comforting, the notion that whatever you did or accomplished, you were in the end only an actor running through a masterfully scripted drama. You just didn't know it at the time, and thought you were extemporising. It was sort of comical, Bill saw that now, but he still found some solace in the thought that in a predetermined world, there was no point at all in fretting over anything, nor any purpose to regret.' Moore's exploration of eternalism has led to him offering the following advice: 'Never do anything that you can't live with for eternity.' Of course, it's not like you have any choice in the matter.

Despite these arguments, many people reject the idea of a block universe on principle and have attempted to find a different model of the universe, which, they hope, will work with relativity but also turn out to be more appealing. One such model is the 'growing block universe' theory of time. This claims that both the past and the present exist, in a similar way to the block universe proposed by eternalists, but that the future does not. The future remains ours to invent, and thus free will is back in the picture, along with morality and justice.

In this model, the block universe is said to be continually growing as time passes, like a tree trunk expanding and adding more rings as the years pass. The past is continually present, which accounts for the temporal anomalies reported by the theory of relativity, but the future has yet to appear and, as such, it is not determined. The idea was first proposed in 1923 by the English philosopher C. D. Broad, who wrote that: 'It will be observed that such a theory as this accepts the reality of the present and the past, but holds that the future is simply nothing at all. Nothing has happened to the present by becoming past except that fresh slices of existence have been added to the total history of the world. The past is thus as real as the present.'

Broad's growing block universe is intuitively closer to our common-sense understanding of the world than the eternalist approach, but it appeals more to philosophers than it does to scientists. It still leaves the knotty problem of being unable to say if the current moment is actually 'now', as the ever-preserved past will feel as much like 'now' as the actual present moment. This uncertainty around the concept of 'now' makes definitive statements about the non-existence of the future somewhat problematic. From a scientific perspective, the existence of the future is not any weirder than the existence of the past, and to have one but not the other requires explaining.

The growing block universe model has never shaken off the suspicion that, ultimately, it's a bit of a fudge based on wishful thinking. That said, it is a model that fits well with the Gothic sensibilities that Blake shared. In Gothic art, the past is never really gone. It remains as an eternal, permanent presence which weighs on the present moment, and its cold, ominous atmosphere teases the idea that what appears to be 'now' may also be an undead past, unaware that its time has gone.

It could be argued that if the future exists but can in no way affect the past or the present then it is ultimately irrelevant. Its existence or non-existence makes no difference. But if we find evidence that the future does influence the past, then we have to take seriously the idea that the future genuinely already exists. In the counterintuitive world of quantum mechanics, the idea that the future influences the past is still controversial, but it has its supporters.

One of the most bewildering aspects of quantum mechanics is what Einstein memorably called 'spooky action at a distance', a phrase he used to describe a situation in which two separate particles have properties that are linked and which are not independent of each other. Physicists call this process entanglement, and it is one of the wildest and most counterintuitive descriptions of reality that we have.

Imagine a pair of adult twins. Now imagine that they are heading out to a polling booth to vote in an election where there is a left-wing and a right-wing candidate. Both twins are undecided about who to vote for. On the way, however, one twin decides to vote for the left-wing candidate. Now imagine that, because he made this decision, at that exact same moment without there seeming to be any communication between them, the other twin is compelled to vote for the right-wing candidate. Alternatively, if the first twin had decided to vote for the right-wing candidate, then the other would have immediately chosen the left-wing one. This would be the case even if the twins lived in different parts of the country. It would even be the case if they lived on opposite sides of the universe.

For a rationally minded scientist, this situation is horrible. How can one decision suddenly create a separate decision that is made a great distance away, with seemingly no communication between the two? There seems to be no conceivable possible mechanism which could cause this to happen. Unfortunately for rationally minded scientists, experimental physicists have shown time and time again that this is exactly how two entangled particles behave.

Entanglement was a problem for Einstein, because it

contradicted his work which showed that the idea of events occurring simultaneously a great distance apart was meaningless. It also seemed to suggest that information was travelling between the two particles faster than the speed of light, by some currently unimaginable process. None of this seemed in any way likely, or indeed possible. Entanglement contradicted so many laws of physics that there were many scientists who, like Einstein, wanted to reject it outright. And yet, experiment after experiment on entangled particles kept showing that it exists. If you affect one of a pair of entangled particles by measuring it in some way that fixes its properties, then the properties of the particle's twin instantly become fixed also, even if the two particles had been separated by countless thousands of miles.

There are many ways to interpret results of experiments like this, but all of them seem fantastical, and none are universally liked. To give an example, one possible interpretation is that the particles aren't separated at all because space is an illusion – it doesn't physically exist. The two particles, therefore, are not really apart from each other. While this idea explains the observed phenomena, you can appreciate how hard it is for all but the most theoretical of scientists to get behind such notions.

This is where the idea that events in the future can affect things in the past comes in. If we base our interpretation of entanglement on this idea, we find that there is no 'spooky action at a distance' occurring. Under this interpretation, instead of instantaneous communication occurring across space as if by magic, measuring one particle causes the change in the other to occur in the past, at the moment they were entangled.

This 'retrocausality', as scientists call it, is as extreme as the other interpretations of entanglement, but it doesn't break quite as many laws. It fits well with the theory of relativity because it has no need for simultaneous separate events. It also gets rid of any suggestion of faster-than-light communication occurring through some process that is currently unimagined and seemingly unimaginable. The idea that the future already exists is shocking, of course, but this explanation for entanglement is otherwise eminently neat and sensible. Given how horrible other explanations are, you can understand why it had supporters.

The idea that the future exists and has the ability to affect the past is far from widely accepted among the scientific community, but it continues to linger, simultaneously absurd and implausible yet also temptingly neat and logical. If the Eternity that Blake spoke of is the simultaneous existence of all of time, then from a modern scientific perspective it can't be ruled out yet.

For all that we can find passages in Blake's work that support the idea of a block universe, there are other passages that contradict this model. He repeatedly argued against the idea that the future was already fixed. In his copy of Swedenborg's *Divine Providence*, for example, Blake marked multiple passages that showed signs of Swedenborg's acceptance of predetermination, to illustrate how he was in error. In the margins of chapter 14, Blake wrote: 'Predestination after this Life is more Abominable than Calvins [belief that those chosen as God's elect are predetermined] & Swedenborg is Such a Spiritual Predestinarian.' Blake's rejection of predeterminism seems to come from an understanding that the four-dimensional block universe it implies is a fixed, static thing, and that this is entirely at odds with his view of the cosmos as a place of energy and delight.

There is another definition of eternity, however, other than all of time. This eternity is a state of timelessness, somewhere beyond the time-based real world. In this definition, there is no past or future, so the idea of 'all of time' becomes meaningless. Instead, there is just the present moment which, being free from the passing of time, exists as an eternal now. This definition is more common in religious and mystical circles, such as the work of the German-born spiritual writer Eckhart Tolle. His multimillion-selling book *The Power of Now* argued that an individual's past and future, which are a source of pain and anxiety, are only illusions created by their minds. He argued that remaining focused on the present is the key to peace and happiness, a position which has led to the growth of the mindfulness movement.

Tolle came to this realisation about the nature of the present during an enlightenment-like epiphany he underwent at the age of twenty-nine, which followed a period of 'almost unbearable' depression. At his lowest point, Tolle's sense of self collapsed into nothing, and he found himself experiencing consciousness in a way that sounds like it was undisturbed by the narrative of his default mode network. 'For the next five months, I lived in a state of uninterrupted deep peace and bliss,' he wrote. 'I had no relationships, no job, no home, no socially defined identity. I spent almost two years sitting on park benches in a state of the most intense joy.'

A similar sense of timelessness was experienced by the American neuroanatomist Jill Bolte Taylor, after she suffered a serious stroke in December 1996. This was caused by a major haemorrhage in the left side of her brain, which left her initially unable to speak, read, write, walk or remember her past. With the loss of what she calls 'left brain' functions – our capacity for logical, egocentric, analytical, and linguistic thought – she experienced the world through her remaining 'right brain' functionality. This was more emotional, holistic, spontaneous and spatially aware. The right brain, she wrote after her recovery, 'thinks in pictures and learns kinaesthetically through the movement of our bodies. Information, in the form of energy, streams in simultaneously through all of our sensory systems and then explodes into this enormous collage of what the present moment looks like, what this present moment smells like and tastes like, what it feels like and what it sounds like [...] in this moment we are perfect, we are whole and we are beautiful.' This is a profoundly Blakean image.

The result of the loss of her left brain was an experience of profound joy and a different relationship with time. 'The present moment is a time when everything and everyone are connected together as one,' she wrote. This contrasts with the world as it is experienced by the left brain. 'By organizing details in a linear and methodical configuration, our left brain manifests the concept of time whereby our moments are divided into past, present and future,' she explained.

Bolte Taylor used a 'bicameral' model to describe the brain, in which the left and right hemispheres are said to work in fundamentally different ways. This model is less fashionable among neurologists now – the brain is far more complex than this neat, 'broad strokes' model suggests, and individual brains develop in different ways. If we are less concerned with how these functions map onto the physical brain, however, the model still proves to be a useful tool. The systematic and rational left hemisphere is what Blake called Urizen. The other three zoas are the domain of the right hemisphere, which is creative, emotional and in touch with the body. Bolte Taylor's account of losing her left hemisphere reveals the extent to which Urizen has become dominant and works to drown out the other aspects of our mind, or even attempts to convince us that they are not real. This Urizenic domination is what Blake sees as the Fall of man and the cause of the sleep of Albion. It is what cuts us off from Blake's divine spirit, which is the deep holistic 'right brain' bliss that Tolle and Bolte Taylor experienced after trauma to their left hemisphere or sense of ego. If they are to be believed, Blake may be right when he says this divine

288

spirit will return when Urizen is tamed and the zoas brought back into balance.

The experiences of Tolle and Bolte Taylor were extreme, but a more manageable version is familiar to practitioners of meditation, who often report entering a state of timelessness. Transcendental meditation, for example, is like microdosing Tolle's epiphany in small, manageable daily doses that leave you energised and productive, and less likely to spend years grinning on park benches. Other forms of meditation attempt to quiet the ever-chattering dialogue of the mind through different methods, but the aim is always for the meditator to quiet the chattering 'left brain' voice of Urizen and sink into a deep state of 'right brain' consciousness, which has the quality of timelessness. This type of awareness is always present, but the domineering left brain drowns it out and leaves us blind to it. It is like when we see words printed on a page of a book. We are drawn to those words in order to lose ourselves in what they are telling us. It is only if the words dissolve away to nothing that we become aware of the paper.

The idea of timelessness is not just a product of mystical thinking, however. The notion of a world without time has also been gaining in prominence scientifically. Its most vocal supporter is the Italian theoretical physicist Carlo Rovelli, known both for his poetically readable physics books and his work on quantum gravity.

As Rovelli notes, one of the strangest things about time is that, at a fundamental level, there doesn't seem to be any. In the equations that describe how the basic building blocks of the universe behave, a variable for time is absent. If it were somehow possible to film quantum events, the footage would make just as much sense played forwards as it would backwards, to the extent that it would not be possible to work out whether the film had been reversed. On a quantum level, events occur relative to each other, rather than relative to an external sense of the passing of time. As

Rovelli explains: 'The absence of time does not mean, therefore, that everything is frozen and unmoving. It means that the incessant happening that wearies the world is not ordered along a timeline, is not measured by a gigantic tick-tocking. It does not even form a four-dimensional geometry. It is a boundless and disorderly network of quantum events. The world is more like Naples than Singapore.'

There is only one fundamental physical process which requires the presence of time, Rovelli notes. That process is entropy, the tendency of complicated things to fall apart. Its role in physics is defined by the second law of thermodynamics which states that, in an enclosed system, entropy will increase over time. Importantly, this process is irreversible. If you filmed a snowman melting it would be easy to tell if that footage had been reversed, because puddles of water don't spontaneously form into snowmen. A snowman melting into a puddle requires the presence of time passing in one specific direction, in the way that a quantum event does not.

With entropy, unlikely combinations of particles give way, over time, to a more random, jumbled combination of particles. But, as Rovelli points out, there is a problem here. Who gets to say when a combination of particles is unlikely? Who gets to judge if the position of particles in a system forms an intricate pattern that will be prone to entropy? If you looked at a sealed container of a number of gas molecules and found that those molecules were positioned in such a way that they spelt out your name, you would see this as a highly unnatural and unlikely distribution pattern. In technical terms, you would say that it possessed a low level of entropy. And yet, mathematically, every unique pattern of particle distribution is equally unlikely. What is it, other than the opinion of the observer, that marks this particular distribution out as different?

As Rovelli sees it, defining whether a system is in a high entropy state is very often a subjective judgement call. It requires the presence of a conscious observer, who can declare that one pattern of particles is unlikely and another is not. Entropy, then, is the one physical process that brings the arrow of time into the world, and that process relies on conscious awareness. Or, in other words, time is created by the mind. As Rovelli writes, 'The initial low entropy of the universe, and hence the arrow of time, may be more down to us than to the universe itself.' Or, more poetically: 'Do we exist in time, or does time exist in us?'

Blake also describes time as being created by the conscious imagination. In *The Book of Los*, Blake describes how Los's descent from the Eternal realm creates time itself:

> Falling, falling! Los fell & fell
> Sunk precipitant heavy down down
> Time on times, night on night, day on day
> Truth has bounds. Error none: falling, falling:
> Years on years, and ages on ages
> Still he fell thro' the void, still a void
> Found for falling day & night without end.
> For tho' day or night was not; their spaces
> Were measured by his incessant whirls
> In the horrid vacuity bottomless.

In Blake's mythology it is Los, the personification of imagination, that creates time, just as it is his emanation Enitharmon who creates space. In this way, it is imagination, and not the deluded rational Urizen, who is the ultimate creator of what Blake called, in the title of an 1821 watercolour, *The Sea of Time and Space*, or the earthly world we inhabit.

Perhaps this subject only seems difficult because we have yet to adequately grasp what time is. As Rovelli notes, 'If by "time" we mean nothing more than happening, then everything is time.'

*

The word 'eternity', it seems, is a contrary. It contains two opposing definitions: all of time exists, and only the present moment is real. The past, present and future are a static, deterministic, unchanging universe or, alternatively, there is only the present moment, and it exists as an ever-changing process rather than as a solid thing.

As with the rest of Blake's contraries, he wasn't interested in choosing one and dismissing the other. He was interested in the tension and dynamics introduced by these opposing ideas, because those dynamics were the engines that powered the universe. What is produced by the interplay of two contrasting models of time is richer and more interesting than if only one of them was presented as valid and the other dismissed. Blake always allowed room for two seemingly contradictory positions to be revealed as different aspects of a larger truth.

In Blake's work, you can find evidence for both perspectives. As we've seen, in *Jerusalem* he wrote that 'I see the Past, Present & Future, existing all at once', and he describes the fall, sleep, and eventual awakening of Albion as fixed events in linear time. Yet he disagreed with Swedenborg about predestination, believing instead that the future was not fixed and that we had free will and responsibility for our choices and actions. The importance he places on energy and creation only makes sense in this context. Rovelli's idea that time is not an innate quality of physics, but emerges through the active engagement of human observation, fits Blake's work well, most obviously in the labour of Los, his personification of the imagination.

For Blake, the definition of eternity seems dependent on whether you are inside the human-scale universe looking out, or outside looking in. From outside the present moment, eternity is all of time, and it exists. From inside, in contrast, there is no time but a permanent moment of holistic peace, as Bolte Taylor discovered after her stroke. The reason we are rarely consciously aware of this timeless moment is because the Urizen-like default mode network in our minds has constructed a narrative called the self, a useful and practical illusion we have come to identify with. Being a story, this self needs to believe in the past and future, which fools us into experiencing Einstein's 'stubbornly persistent illusion' of the passing of time.

Our two contrary definitions of eternity, it's worth noting, closely match how the two hemispheres of the brain perceive the world. The brain functions associated with the left hemisphere are abstracting, systematic and rational, and give rise to language and the perception of time as linear. This is the controlling, egocentric domain of Urizen, which believes itself to be the creator god of the ordered, prison-like block universe. The right hemisphere, in contrast, only perceives the present moment, and is focused on sensation, emotion and creativity. This is the domain of Tharmas, Luvah and Urthona, the remaining three zoas who are usually drowned out by attention-seeking Urizen. Our two contrasting models of eternity, then, are an illustration of how differently the two hemispheres function. They are also the exact same models you would expect the two hemispheres to create, given that we perceive the external world in our own image. Once again, we are reminded that we live inside our models, and rely on them to make sense of the otherwise unknowable external world.

An intriguing remark Blake made in the margin of his copy of Swedenborg's *Divine Providence* reads: 'Devils & Angels are Predestinated.' This suggests that the perspective of spiritual creatures is like Einstein's block universe, in which all of time exists. For all that Blake criticised Swedenborg for believing in predestination, he also saw angels and devils as trapped in an unchanging Eternity devoid of free will. But Blake's phrase suggests that it is only these higher spiritual creatures that this applies to. For human beings, it is another story.

Angels and devils, as Blake saw them, were creations of the human mind. As hierarchical inhabitants of an ordered cosmos, they were the invention of Urizen. This makes sense, because the egocentric Urizen understands himself to be an isolated individual, separate from the rest of the cosmos, and the universe can only be perceived as constricting when you see yourself as separate from it. You cannot be a prisoner if you are also the prison.

From this perspective, to perceive the timeless present moment is to escape from the limiting horror of the block universe. It is here in the right hemisphere's model of time that we may find Bolte Taylor's and Tolle's conscious experience of pure bliss and joy. All we need to do to achieve this liberation, Blake tells us, is to balance the zoas so that Urizen no longer dominates. Human consciousness can experience liberty while the trapped, static eternal angels and demons of the block universe can only look on, amazed. Perhaps this is why, as Blake wrote in *The Marriage of Heaven and Hell*, 'Eternity is in love with the productions of time.' How the angels must envy us.

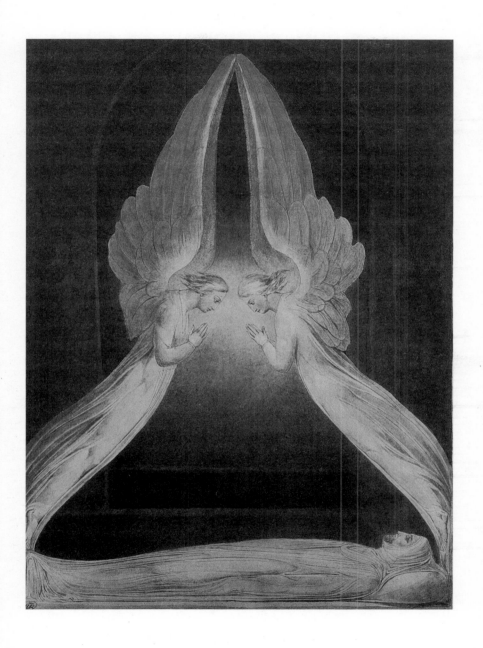

16.

THE WORK OF THE DEVIL

In 1798 the English poets William Wordsworth and Samuel Taylor Coleridge, friends in their late twenties, issued a joint collection called *Lyrical Ballads*. It contained four lengthy poems by Coleridge and nineteen shorter ones by Wordsworth. The collection did not initially generate much interest, but in time its reputation grew, and it is now celebrated as the beginning of the English Romantic movement in literature. This was the movement which would posthumously adopt Blake and provide a frame within which his work would be understood and studied. For all that Blake and the Romantics shared certain similar sensibilities, however, Blake's philosophy differed from them significantly.

The Romantic period, which peaked in the first half of the nineteenth century, was in part a response to the dehumanising effect of both the Industrial Revolution and the scientific era. Quantities had become more important than qualities, and the Romantics reacted against this. The Romantics had a great love of nature, which they contrasted with the inhuman and unnatural world of modern industry. It can be hard now to appreciate just how radical this stance was at the time. Before the late eighteenth century, there

WILLIAM BLAKE VS THE WORLD

was little sense that nature itself was beautiful, beyond individual flowers or animals.

The early Renaissance Italian poet Petrarch is the first person we know of who climbed a mountain for pleasure, rather than necessity. The mountain was Mount Ventoux in southern France, and he made the ascent simply so that he could see the view. This was considered an absurd idea at the time. He met an elderly shepherd on his way up, who thought that Petrarch was crazy when told of his intentions. The shepherd had gone to the summit fifty years earlier, he explained. There was nothing there and the shepherd could see no reason why anyone would ever go up there again.

Even by the early eighteenth century, people generally didn't travel to scenic locations such as the Alps. Mountain ranges were viewed as obstacles to travel between cities, rather than destinations in their own right. Before we could recognise that nature was beautiful, we had to first think of ourselves as separate to it. The word 'nature' came to mean everything in this world that is not us, and not built by us. We could only admire and appreciate it after we saw it as the other. This is still the way that nature is typically understood today.

A key factor in this new concept of the natural world was the binomial system, which was created in the late 1750s by the Swedish botanist Carl Linnaeus. Linnaeus was a rector at Uppsala University whose lectures on the natural world were hugely popular and, when his students travelled the world, they brought back botanical samples for him to study. When he died in 1778, his collection included 14,000 plants and over 3,000 insects – the first natural history collection of its kind in the world. Brought together like this, the specimens vividly showed the extraordinary diversity and endless variety that define the worlds of plants and animals.

Linnaeus dedicated decades to collating and recording samples and clippings from Mother Nature's ever-shifting chaos, because he believed he could make sense of them. His system of binomial nomenclature was a categorisation structure that reduced a plant or animal down to two Latin or Latinised words, which in turn defined the genus and the species, such as *Canis lupus* for a wolf or *Homo sapiens* for a human.

We take the system of binomial nomenclature for granted now, so it can be hard to recognise what a huge change it was in how we understand the world. The natural world was large and overwhelming, and we were inside it. It was never static, a constant dance of change and growth. The idea that we could create a mental system large enough and sophisticated enough to contain it all was incredibly bold. But thanks to Linnaeus's painstaking labour, that is exactly what happened, and the natural world is now defined by the system he imposed. It is labelled, categorised and understood, and as a result we now think of it as something comprehensible to man. By naming and defining, nature was mastered. This was a highly Urizenic left-brain endeavour.

Once we had become separated from the natural environment, we finally saw it, as if for the first time, as something that had beauty and value. The idea that we might now walk up a mountain to see the view no longer seemed crazy. This was the new perspective which the Romantic movement arose to express.

Romanticism valued emotion over rationality and individualism over a rigidly hierarchical society. It often favoured the medieval over the classical, and so it can be seen as northern Europe shaking off southern European ideas from Greece and Italy in favour of more localised culture. People began to feel intuitively that they had lost something of great value after large parts of the population moved to cities, began working in factories, and started to view the world as a type of machine. The Romantic movement expressed this sense of loss; it was the music and poetry of yearning.

The poems in *Lyrical Ballads* were described by Wordsworth and Coleridge as experimental, because they consciously used the language of the 'middle and lower classes of society' instead of the formal, histrionic and often faintly ludicrous language that was so popular with eighteenth-century poets. As the poets admitted in the advertisement for the collection, 'Readers of superior judgement may disapprove of the style in which many of these pieces are executed, it must be expected that many lines and phrases will not exactly suit their taste.'

It was not just the language of the common man or woman that set these poems apart. In many cases labouring or agricultural workers were the poem's subjects, which was revolutionary at the time. The audience for poetry and books in general was wealthy and refined, and many held the view that the poor were in the condition to which God called them. Poetry readers were often uninterested in those other parts of society, except as an example of what they themselves were not.

Although we credit the joint authorship of *Lyrical Ballads* with the start of the English Romantic movement, Wordsworth and Coleridge had very different styles and characters. Their working relationship, friendship and quarrels came to define their lives, and it is tempting to see them as the nineteenth century's version of John Lennon and Paul McCartney.

Wordsworth was the McCartney of this analogy. He was the most traditional of the two, despite his initial enthusiasm for the French Revolution. He gravitated to a comfortable role in the establishment, and eventually became the Poet Laureate of the United Kingdom. He was also the poet who focused on the importance of nature, and the effect it had on the mind.

For Wordsworth, observation of the natural world was sufficient to reach states of bliss and ecstasy, both in the moment and in memory. In this, he saw the world very differently to William

Blake. Wordsworth reacts to the sight of a host of daffodils in his most famous poem, 'I Wandered Lonely as a Cloud', in a very different way to how Blake reacts to the thistle he encountered while walking in Sussex.

For Wordsworth, observing nature aroused feelings of the sublime, and he recognised that those feelings were generated by a combination of both nature and the human soul. As he notes in 'Lines Written a Few Miles above Tintern Abbey', the final poem in the original edition of *Lyrical Ballads*:

> [...] Therefore am I still
> A lover of the meadows and the woods,
> And mountains; and of all that we behold
> From this green earth; of all the mighty world
> Of eye and Ear, both what they half-create,
> And what perceive;

This was not how Blake saw things. For him, the sublime and the spiritual were purely the product of the mind alone. Nature lacked the power of imagination, and therefore could not be an aspect of heaven or have an innate spiritual quality when it was not being perceived by man. This was why he told Henry Crabb Robinson that, 'I fear Wordsworth loves Nature and Nature is the work of the Devil.'

Blake admired Wordsworth and was happy to describe him as the greatest poet of the age, but this was despite Wordsworth's philosophy, not because of it. In Blake's eyes, Wordsworth was a Platonist, not a Christian. He had been particularly disturbed by the following passage in Wordsworth's long poem *The Excursion*:

> Jehovah, with his thunder, and the choir
> Of Shouting Angels, and the empyreal thrones –
> I pass them unalarmed

The phrase 'I pass them unalarmed' so upset Blake that he claimed it brought on a fit of illness. That Wordsworth thought he could pass Jehovah and his choir of angels unalarmed was, in Blake's eyes, utter madness and vanity. Wordsworth seemed blind to how small and feeble his mind was, compared to the mind of God. For this reason, Blake thought Wordsworth brilliant but mad.

This was also Wordsworth's view of Blake. After reading *Songs of Innocence and of Experience* he remarked, 'There is no doubt this poor man was mad, but there is something in the madness of this man which interests me more than the sanity of Lord Byron and Walter Scott!'

Coleridge, in contrast, was a very different poet to Wordsworth. When he read *Songs of Innocence and of Experience* in 1818, Coleridge was critical of the illustrations, but recognised Blake as a visionary. In a letter to a friend, he described reading this 'strange publication'. It was 'printed and painted by the Author, W. Blake. He is a man of Genius – and I apprehend, a Swedenborgian – certainly, a mystic emphatically. You perhaps smile at my calling another Poet, a Mystic; but verily I am in the mire of common-place common-sense compared with Mr Blake, apo- or rather ana-calyptic Poet, and Painter!'

While Wordsworth was inspired by nature, Coleridge was more interested in the imagination. As he saw it, 'A poet ought not to pick nature's pocket. Let him borrow, and so borrow as to repay by the very act of borrowing. Examine nature accurately, but write from recollection, and trust more to the imagination than the memory.' It seems likely that Blake briefly met Coleridge in later life, although he never met Wordsworth, despite Henry Crabb Robinson's intention to bring the pair together.

Lyrical Ballads originally opened with Coleridge's *The Rime of the Ancyent Marinere*, a long, dreamlike horror poem about a cursed mariner. For Coleridge, inspiration could be found in dreams and reveries, including those induced by opium and hashish. His poem *Kubla Khan*, he explained, came to him in an opium-induced dream. On wakening he immediately began writing down lines that were fully formed in his head:

In Xanadu did Kubla Khan
A stately pleasure-dome decree:
Where Alph, the sacred river, ran
Through caverns measureless to man
  Down to a sunless sea.

Famously, Coleridge was interrupted after only fifty-four lines by a visit from a gentleman from Porlock. After dealing with this interruption, he was unable to remember how the rest of the poem was supposed to go, and so it was lost.

The importance of the imagination to Coleridge becomes clear in his 1817 autobiographical work *Biographia Literaria*. Inspired by the earlier proto-Romantic German *Sturm und Drang* movement, he writes, 'The primary IMAGINATION I hold to be the living power and prime Agent of all human Perception, and as a repetition in the finite mind of the eternal act of creation in the infinite I AM.' Such an elevated belief in the primacy of imagination made sense to William Blake, as we have seen. In Blake's words, 'Imagination is the real and eternal World of which this Vegetable Universe is but a faint shadow', or, more bluntly, 'The Imagination is not a State: it is the Human Existence itself.'

For Coleridge, there was an important difference between imagination and simple fantasy. Most people in the twenty-first century assume that 'imagination' means just making stuff up. This is not what Coleridge meant when he talked of the imagination, although he would have thought this was a fair description of fantasy. For Coleridge, fantasy was essentially a form of mental

303

collage that took existing ideas and put them together, in a way that was unrelated to the real world of time and space. If you took the idea of a horse and the idea of a horn and stuck them together as a form of collage, then you had the idea of a unicorn in a world where no physical unicorns exist. This is fine, as far as it goes, and could even be entertaining in its own right. But it is unconnected to reality. It doesn't change things.

As Coleridge saw it, imagination was the arrival, from the depths of consciousness, of something new. True, it might contain things that already exist, but they had now become part of something larger and unprecedented. Coleridge invented the word 'esemplastic' to describe this process, in which separate elements were combined to create something original. Fantasy was just the same old stuff rearranged with a healthy disregard for the real world. Imagination, in contrast, was engaging with existing stuff to produce something never seen before, and it had the power to change the world in a way that fantasy did not. Something new now existed, and the world had to adapt around it. When the filmmaker George Lucas dreamt up the *Star Wars* universe – which became a mental playground for generations of children, spawned a multibillion-dollar empire and irreversibly changed the movie industry – that was an act of imagination. When committees of creatives are tasked by the current owners of the *Star Wars* intellectual property to produce more *Star Wars* content, that is no longer an act of imagination. Instead, it is playing around with existing ideas and falls into Coleridge's lesser category of fantasy.

This distinction would have made sense to the Enlightenment philosopher Immanuel Kant, who differentiated between what he called productive and reproductive imagination. For Kant, a reproductive imagination simply made associations between previous experiences and memories. Productive imagination, on the other hand, synthesised a number of existing concepts into a genuinely new organic whole. This was a distinction also made by the sixteenth-century alchemist Paracelsus, who contrasted what he called true imagination with mere fantasy. Paracelsus called fantasy 'the madman's cornerstone', which was an 'exercise of thought without foundation in nature'.

For Blake and the Romantics, imagination had a vivid quality that fantasy lacked. In fantasy, a thought was just a thought. In deep imagination, a thought was something that you encountered. It was participatory – a living, vital process that you were part of. You were not separate from what you imagined, and imagination was not separate from the world, because the world and imagination could not be understood without each other.

This linking of the imagination with the arrival of the genuinely new was important to Blake because he knew the rational, material world created by Urizen was fundamentally limited. It extended to the edges of the circle drawn by Urizen's golden compass and went no further. Being closed off in this way, it could not see or be influenced by the formless void or the light of the spiritual sun which lay over this horizon. As a result, this finite world was fated to decay and fall apart. As the second law of thermodynamics reminds us, entropy can only increase in a closed system.

If there was a way to introduce genuinely new things into this world, however, then that would mean our world was not a closed system, and entropy could be held back. For Blake, as we have seen, human imagination was the loophole that kept this closed, limited world from collapsing in on itself. As such, imagination generated by the labour of Los kept the world alive, and allowed the true light which Urizen had turned his back on to make itself felt in his handiwork.

It was Blake's Coleridge-like beliefs about the fundamental importance of imagination, then, which were the reason he was adopted by the Romantic movement. These were sufficiently important that all the ways he differed from the rest of the Romantics could be overlooked. As we have seen, his thoughts about nature were profoundly out of sync with Wordsworth. He was also of a different class to the majority of the Romantics. He did not have the aristocratic background or private income that allowed, for example, Percy and Mary Shelley and Lord Byron to spend years travelling around classical antiquity. Blake had to work and hustle in order to eat, so the aspect of Romanticism which rejected commerce and labour in favour of leisure, luxury and contemplation was alien to him.

Blake may not have been a perfect fit for the Romantic movement, but the fact that he had been claimed by it was nevertheless of profound importance. For the first time, there was a way of looking at Blake which people could grasp. A net had been cast over his work, and the ideals of Romanticism orientated an audience and helped them navigate through it.

So it was that, towards the end of his life, the world finally began the long slow process of understanding William Blake. From this perspective, it was possible to see that the story of the world versus William Blake had not been the full picture. Other motivations and different priorities had long been in play. Ignored or misunderstood for decades, the saga of William Blake versus the world was finally revealed.

17.
VERY WEAK & AN OLD MAN FEEBLE & TOTTERING

In 1813, when Blake was fifty-five years old, he was introduced to a young artist called John Linnell by their mutual friend George Cumberland. Despite Linnell being thirty-five years younger than Blake, the pair became friends. Blake gave Linnell help and training in engraving, and Linnell treated Blake like the respected master that the rest of the world refused to see. Linnell is remembered now as a rival to John Constable and one of the great landscape painters of his age. When he met Blake, however, landscape painting had yet to take off culturally. He made his money by painting portraits and miniatures, unaware that society would soon take an interest in the landscapes that he painted simply for his own pleasure.

In the 1820s, the Linnell family moved to an old five-room farmhouse in a hollow on Hampstead Heath, which was then countryside to the north of London. When his health allowed, Blake would walk from his home near the Thames to visit the Linnells in their cosy domesticity at Collins's Farm, with bucolic country vistas stretching into the distance soundtracked by the gentle sound of the lowing of cows. Blake was a great favourite of the Linnell children and, even in old age, their daughter would remember how she used to excitedly look out for him approaching when she was a girl of around five or six. The tiny figure of Blake would appear on the far horizon across the heather- and gorse-covered heath, and she would know it was him from a particular signal he then made. She remembers Blake as a kind old man who would sit her on his knee and tell her stories, and who taught her how to draw. Blake would sing ballads, although his voice was weaker now, and he used to be particularly moved by Mrs Linnell's rendition of traditional Scottish songs.

In the age of Romanticism, a new generation of poets emerged for whom Blake's values and attitudes struck a chord and proved to be highly influential. In 1824, a group of like-minded artists formed a loose society called the Ancients. John Linnell was a friend of many of these artists, who included the painters Samuel Palmer, George Richmond and Edward Calvert, and through him they got to know William Blake. In the eyes of the Ancients, Blake embodied everything an artist should be.

The Ancients called Blake's home the 'House of the Interpreter', in a reference to John Bunyan's *The Pilgrim's Progress*. They would regularly visit William and Catherine in order to learn from the one true visionary in their lives. The young men befriended him, helped take care of him as he became infirm, and were instrumental in preserving his work so that we can experience it today. Consequently, his last years were happier. After decades of independent struggle, an audience proved to be the one thing he genuinely needed.

Many of the Ancients left detailed reminiscences about the Blake they knew, and it is striking how much these differ from the angry, paranoid figure we saw fifteen years earlier. Samuel Palmer wrote a long letter to Alexander Gilchrist in 1855 to help him with his biography, for example, and at times it sounds like Palmer is describing a saint. Trying to explain how Blake affected him, he wrote that: 'In him you saw at once the Maker, the Inventor, one of the few in any age: a fitting companion for Dante. He was energy itself, and shed around him a kindling influence; an atmosphere of life, full of the ideal. To walk with him in the country was to perceive the soul of beauty through the forms of matter.' Palmer goes on to describe a quietly spoken yet fiercely independent man who loved to watch children play and seemed devoid of earthly ambition: 'He was a man without a mask; his aim single, his path straightforwards, and his wants few, so he was free.'

One of Palmer's recollections illustrates the respect this circle had for their older mentor. Palmer recalled visiting an exhibition at the Royal Academy in 1823 or 1824 and looking up at a picture by Thomas Griffiths Wainewright, an artist who would in later years become notorious as a suspected serial murderer. Palmer vividly remembered 'the image of Blake looking up at Wainewright's picture; Blake in his plain black suit and rather broad-brimmed, but not quakerish hat, standing so quietly among all the dressed-up, rustling, swelling people, and myself thinking "How little you know who is among you!"'

Palmer was clearly aware of Blake's earlier reputation as difficult, aggressive and mad, but he was insistent that it was unwarranted. 'Those who may have read some strange passages in his [exhibition] *Catalogue*, written in irritation, and probably in haste, will be surprised to hear, that in conversation he was anything but sectarian or exclusive, finding sources of delight throughout the whole range of art,' he wrote. Blake did not turn against this circle of artists or form grudges about them as he might have done in earlier years. In the words of Gilchrist: 'He was no longer angry with the world and its often unworthy favourites, or rebellious against its rewards.' After labouring for decades on a myth about the rebalancing of the mind, Blake had made peace with his own demons. It was as if he had written himself into harmony.

Blake attempted to rebuild his relationship with Stothard in this period. At a gathering of artists Blake approached him and offered him his hand. Stothard, who would have been aware of the way Blake talked about him to mutual friends, understandably refused. When Blake heard that Stothard was ill he called on him, but an audience was not granted. There is no indication that Blake apologised or recognised that he was the abuser, and such an occurrence would have been out of character. But Blake was no longer showing signs of paranoia and delusion, and he was no longer declaring others to be his enemy for reasons that only he understood. He did at least attempt to mend the bridges that he had burnt.

In 1821, John Linnell commissioned a set of watercolours from Blake based on the biblical Book of Job. Blake then created a set of engravings based on these designs, which are considered to be some of the finest examples of his engraving. They were some of his first works to achieve critical admiration after his death. In 1857, for example, the leading Victorian critic John Ruskin wrote that Blake's 'book of Job, engraved by himself, is of the highest rank in certain characters of imagination and expression; in the mode of obtaining certain effects of light it will also prove a very useful example to you. In expressing conditions of glaring and flickering light, Blake is greater than Rembrandt.'

Blake had a long history of exploring the story of Job, having first sketched designs on the subject in 1785. The Linnell designs were copies of a set he had made for Thomas Butts in 1806. The Book of Job was a story exploring how a good man who worshipped God might still suffer in an unjust and unfair way from the cruelties of fate. Blake clearly identified with the story and took comfort from it. It begins with Job wealthy and successful, with ten children, 7,000 sheep, 3,000 camels, 500 yoke of oxen, 500 'she asses' and countless servants. He was also extremely pious, performing all the required sacrifices and worshipping God without fail. Satan asks God if he may ruin Job's life, in order to see whether his piety is nothing more than a product of his comfortable lifestyle and something that would evaporate under the pressures of misfortune. God is intrigued and agrees. This incident has caused much debate among theologians over the centuries, because it suggests that God is not omnipotent. The idea that God would allow Satan to torture people has also taken some explaining.

Satan got to work. Soon the servants were slain, the camels were stolen, the sheep were on fire and Job's children were killed when a building collapsed on top of them. Job was distraught, and shaved his hair off, but he remained pious. 'Naked came I out of my mother's womb, and naked shall I return thither,' he said. 'The Lord gave, and the Lord hath taken away; blessed be the name of the Lord.' Satan had to up his game, so he gave Job boils. This did the trick, and before long Job was a broken man, shunned by his former friends and tormented by pain and grief, crying out about the injustice of a God who would punish his faithful servants in this way.

God then appears in a whirlwind. He doesn't answer Job's complaints or explain His actions, but He convinces Job that He is too great to be comprehended by the mind of men. Blake also grants Job a vision of Jesus Christ at this point in his version, a detail obviously not found in the Old Testament.

After Job has given up on fairness and justice, God takes over from Satan and ends the experiment. In order to make amends, God makes Job even richer than before. By the end of the story, Job has 14,000 sheep, 6,000 camels, 1,000 oxen, 1,000 'she asses' and another ten children to replace the ones he lost. Job lived to be 140 years old, and the story finishes by telling us that, 'Job died, being old and full of days.'

It is easy to see the appeal of the story to a man like Blake, who was unwaveringly loyal to his spiritual vision throughout his life, yet who was granted ridicule and poverty in return. Ultimately, the Book of Job answers the question of why bad things happen to good people by arguing that awareness of the nature of God is a far greater gift than health, family, social status or peace of mind. In the modern age there are many who find this unconvincing, but for Blake it was a powerful truth.

The other two major projects of Blake's later years grant us further insight into the nature of his mind during this period. Unlike his later epic illustrated poems, in these we see the spiritual struggles of a mind from a human perspective, rather than the perspective of Eternity. It is as if Blake has returned to us, after his sojourn among states of mind that few can grasp. He is still describing the complicated interplay of our mental energies, but he is doing so with narratives that we can more easily understand.

The first of these projects was a series of 102 watercolours and seven engravings of the *Divine Comedy*, the lengthy medieval narrative poem by the Italian Dante Alighieri. In the *Divine Comedy*, Dante is taken on a tour of heaven, purgatory and hell, each of which is divided into nine circles. The narrative has clear similarities with the visions reported by Swedenborg, and indeed the English language translation by Henry Francis Cary which Blake worked from was titled *The Vision*. Blake, always a master of languages, learnt Italian in order to compare this with Dante's original text.

In the poem, Dante's guide through Hell and Purgatory was not the expected Christian saint or mythological hero, but the Roman poet Virgil. Dante was not looking to philosophers or religious figures for guidance, but to a revered pagan master of the poetic imagination. It is easy to see how this would have appealed to Blake. The relationship between Dante and Virgil, which can be interpreted as the passing of the torch from a long-dead classical poet to a living, contemporary one, is a clear inspiration for Blake's *Milton*. The way Dante merged and blended biblical theology with classical, mythological and pagan ideas would also have appealed to Blake, even if he would have been less enamoured of the classical elements that Dante employed.

Dante's poem was structured with strict numerical rules. Each of the three sections, Hell, Purgatory and Paradise, consisted of thirty-three cantos, and the numbers three and nine featured heavily as a reference to the Trinity. For Dante, as for Swedenborg, earthly numbers were symbols of higher realities. Although the three sections were the same length in the poem, Blake heavily favoured Hell in the work he completed before his death. He produced seventy-two drawings for Hell, but only twenty for Purgatory and ten for Paradise. He may have intended to make a similar number of paintings for each section, but he was unable to finish the work before his death. It is also possible, however, that Hell simply inspired him the most.

Although these paintings are in various stages of completion, the images are held in high regard by Blake aficionados. There is wild imagination on display, a deep understanding of the spiritual meaning of the text and original use of colour. The palette differs between the three spiritual realms, with Hell being particularly striking. It is often painted as if lit from below, as if the ground of Hell itself was emitting a harsh, white-hot light. Although the Paradise drawings are mostly rough sketches that were never completed, and the abstract, ethereal air of heaven is harder to imagine and reproduce than the flames, serpents and caves of Hell, the surviving images suggest that Blake would have been uniquely capable of doing them justice.

Dante was a visual poet who concerned himself with architecture, textures and landscapes. There was a long tradition of artists illustrating his poem, inspired by the rich imagery it contained. For Blake, Dante displayed the highest embodiment of 'poetic genius', despite the poem's adherence to the Catholic worldview of sin and punishment that Blake was scornful of. Dante was on his shortlist of history's true greats, along with Homer, Shakespeare, Milton and the authors of the Old Testament.

Blake's other major project was a series of watercolours based on *The Pilgrim's Progress* by the seventeenth-century English nonconformist preacher John Bunyan. At the age of fifteen, Bunyan had enlisted as a soldier in the Parliamentarian army during the Civil War, where he would have been exposed to the radical ideas that circulated among the troops. When peace came, he underwent a religious conversion and began preaching in Bedford. He was arrested for not possessing a licence to preach, and, being committed to his beliefs and unwilling to conform, he remained in prison for twelve years. For Bunyan, being a true Christian was a difficult journey during which he was constantly tested. From this background comes his great work, the allegorical story *The Pilgrim's Progress*.

It is often argued that *The Pilgrim's Progress* is the first novel written in English. Because Chaucer's *Canterbury Tales* is also seen as the first major work in the English language, the importance of pilgrims and pilgrimages will forever be embedded in English literature. In his essay 'Overcoming Tourism', the anarchist writer Hakim Bey stresses the difference between tourism and pilgrimage. Tourists are consumers. When they flock to a location, they take away some of its magic and leave it less special than before. Pilgrims, in contrast, travel to places and in doing so add to them.

They leave sites of pilgrimage more special than they found them. The process of adding or subtracting meaning is, of course, a mental act. It is Blake's twofold vision in action.

Blake did not undertake pilgrimages himself – not even to relatively accessible sites of pilgrimage like Canterbury Cathedral. Partly this would have been cultural, for the Catholic associations of these journeys would have been frowned upon during Blake's time. But for Blake, the proper destination of a pilgrimage was inwards. The imaginative creation of works such as the *Divine Comedy* and *Pilgrim's Progress* were true journeys of pilgrimage. Bunyan had stated clearly that *Pilgrim's Progress* was a dream vision. Dante did not claim that his accounts of travels through heaven and hell were anything more than just poetic imagination, but for Blake this did not matter. He considered Dante's *Divine Comedy* to be every bit as visionary a journey as that recorded by Swedenborg, such was the power and vividness of Dante's writing.

The Pilgrim's Progress is the story of a man named Christian. Overcome with fear after having read the Bible, Christian leaves his wife and children to embark on a journey. Weighed down by the heavy sack he carries, Christian travels from the City of Destruction through the 'wilderness of the world' to the Celestial City. Along the way he must get past the Slough of Despond, the temptations of Vanity Fair and a giant named Despair, who locks him in the dungeons of Doubting Castle. During his journey he meets characters including Hopeful, Obstinate, Faithful, Mr. Worldly Wiseman and Lord Hate-Good.

For anyone who has read *Jerusalem* and struggled to remember which qualities characters such as Tharmas, Enitharmon, Ahania or Enion represent, Bunyan's straightforwardness can be something of a relief. Blake generally considered allegory to be a lesser form of communication than vision, yet he wrote that, 'Fable or Allgory is Seldom without some Vision Pilgrims Progress is full

317

of it.' Bunyan's use of allegory was intended to achieve a similar effect to Blake's work – a reminder that the material world is not the full story, that there is a different form of reality behind it, and that our world can be interpreted as a series of signs and symbols that refer to a higher immaterial reality.

The full title of Bunyan's work, according to the original title page, is *The Pilgrim's Progress from This World, To that which is to come: Delivered under the Similitude of a Dream Wherein is Discovered, The manner of his setting out, His Dangerous Journey; And safe Arrival at the Desired Countrey.* The title is something of a spoiler, for it is indeed the case that Christian successfully reaches the Celestial City of Heaven at the end of his trials. It is a positive book, offering hope to other Christians struggling with doubt or other difficulties. This is not to say that it was as simplistic a tale as this outline or some of the names might suggest. Bunyan's strength lay in his ability to express spiritual truths with the force of felt experience. He was particularly good when writing about fear, and how fear of other people pales in the face of fear of God himself. With Bunyan, the stakes were always high. He intended that reading his allegory of a pilgrimage would make readers aware that they too were pilgrims. As he writes in his apology, 'This Book will make a Traveller of thee.'

Blake's *Pilgrim's Progress* watercolours have historically received less attention than his *Divine Comedy* series, in part because they were known to be largely coloured by Catherine, probably after William died leaving them unfinished. They once belonged to the Frick Collection in New York, although they were removed from the museum's collection because it was felt that Catherine's involvement made them less important. It is probably fair to say that her colouring did not always have the subtlety of William's, especially when compared to his much-lauded work on the *Divine Comedy* series. Yet to contemporary eyes her involvement makes this sequence more precious, not less. Knowing the strength of their relationship in the later years of his life, and the importance of her unflagging belief in her husband and his work, the idea of them both working on the images makes them extremely special.

What is striking about Blake's choice of both *Pilgrim's Progress* and the *Divine Comedy* is the similarity of their themes. Both are concerned with the journey of the human soul through trials and misfortune, horrors and wonders. Both show how such trials can refine and lighten that soul, bringing them to redemption and union with God. That Blake was drawn to both depictions of this universal story shows how important the narrative must have been to him at that point, in the last years of his life. Both stories were ultimately positive, in that they depicted the higher elevated states of mind as attainable goals. Christian makes it to the Celestial City. Dante's story was the Divine Comedy, not the *Divine Tragedy*, and after his travels through Hell and Purgatory he receives a beatific vision of God. In the terms of Swedenborg's visionary philosophy, where people were free to choose their own place in the many different circles of heaven and hell, Blake was aiming high.

The development of the soul during a lifetime spent in an imperfect world could leave a person bitter and angry, or selfless and open. The deciding factor may come in a moment of revelation, but for most people it was the product of the gradual accumulation of a lifetime's worth of acts and thoughts. Blake's intense engagement with these subjects in his final years tells us that, despite everything, his difficult life had not broken him. Blake was not reduced to a state of pessimistic nihilism. Penniless, ignored and mocked, he ended his days a profoundly happy man.

By August 1827 the energy that had characterised Blake's life was all but gone. The days when he and Catherine would walk for miles were behind them. He was largely confined to the house, and for periods confined to his bed. He suffered from attacks of what was then called the 'ague', which was probably a series of fevers and bouts of shivering. This would come over him in repeated bursts, after which he would recover for a while before the next attack laid him low.

In April that year he believed that he had been very close to 'the Gates of Death', as he wrote to Cumberland, being 'very weak & an Old Man feeble & tottering, but not in Spirit & Life not in The Real Man The Imagination which Liveth for Ever'. His brother James died that March. The painter John Linnell had visited him in April and quickly sketched the frail older man in bed, propped up by pillows. He wrote in his diary that Blake was not expected to live. He was sixty-nine years old, and a lifetime of poverty had left its mark.

But even confined to bed, he could still work. On his last day he had been working on his *Divine Comedy* series, which he was determined to finish. The last shilling he spent was used to send out for another pencil.

His final paid commission was for a hand-painted print of the frontispiece to *Europe: A Prophecy*. Tatham paid him three guineas and a half, which was considerably more than Blake had been used to. This image was one of Blake's favourites and Tatham noted that 'he always bestowed more time and enjoyed greater pleasure when colouring the print, than any thing he ever produced'.

The image is called *The Ancient of Days,* and it is a portrait of Urizen in a dark formless void, his hair and beard blown sideways by fierce winds, leaning forward out of a golden orb with an enormous golden compass in his left hand, about to create the world of matter beneath him. Urizen, of course, is so focused on this work that he can no longer see the light of the orb behind him. It is an image inspired by Proverbs 8:27:

When he prepared the heavens, I was there: when he set a compass upon the face of the depth

Blake's beloved Milton also described the scene in *Paradise Lost*:

[...] and in His hand
He took the golden compasses, prepared
In God's eternal store, to circumscribe
This universe, and all created things:
One foot he centred, and the other turned
Round through the vast profundity obscure,
And said, Thus far extend, thus far thy bounds,
This be thy just circumference, O world.

But even allowing for these sources, it was a scene that Blake made his own. Only Blake understood the psychology behind this act of creation. Only Blake recognised and highlighted the creator's blind spot, and only Blake understood exactly where the wielder of those compasses resided.

Like most of Blake's work, it was a scene that had come to him in a vision. Urizen as depicted here had hovered above him at the top of his staircase in his Lambeth home, back in the revolutionary 1790s. Blake told friends that this sight had made 'a more powerful impression on his mind than all he had ever been visited by'. Simple, dramatic and deeply profound, it is for many people the quintessential William Blake artwork.

Blake finished this last version of *The Ancient of Days* just a few days before he died. After repeatedly colouring and tinting, then holding it at a distance, he threw it down and declared, 'There! That will do. I can not mend it.' William Blake had fulfilled his commission. As a reward, his eyes fell upon his wife Catherine and he was struck by the sight of her. 'Stay! Keep as you are!' he

321

told her. 'You have ever been an angel to me, I will draw you!' As Tatham records the story, after finishing this sketch, 'He then threw that down, after having drawn for an hour & began to sing Hallelujahs & songs of joy & Triumph which Mrs. Blake described as being truly sublime in music and in Verse.'

William Blake died peacefully around 6 p.m. on Sunday 12 August 1827. Gilchrist reports that a female neighbour was present for his death and later said that, 'I have been at the death, not of a man, but of a blessed angel.' The painter George Richmond, then only eighteen, arrived just after Blake departed. In a letter to Samuel Palmer, he wrote that Blake died 'in a most glorious manner. He said He was going to that Country he had all His life wished to see & expressed Himself Happy, hoping for Salvation through Jesus Christ – Just before he died His Countenance became fair. His eyes Brighten'd and he burst out Singing of the things he saw in Heaven.'

It was Richmond who closed Blake's eyes. In later life he said this was 'to keep the vision in'.

18.

AS A MAN IS, SO HE SEES

On 28 November 2019 – William Blake's 262nd birthday – and for four nights afterwards, the final painting of Urizen that bedridden Blake completed for Tatham was projected onto the dome of St Paul's Cathedral in London. This copy of *The Ancient of Days*, which Blake finished tinting only days before his death, had become the defining image of the retrospective exhibition then running at Tate Britain. It hung at the end of the show, presented as the inspired climax of Blake's life's work. It had been used for the exhibition poster and was an unavoidable image in London tube stations for many months that year. The idea of projecting it onto the dome of St Paul's was a scheme to further promote the exhibition.

For admirers of William Blake, this felt like a vindication. Blake had hoped that his designs would become large-scale public artworks, even though it never looked possible in his lifetime. There are not many 'unfortunate lunatics' who end their days in an unmarked pauper's grave yet go on to have their work used to crown the great temple of Britain two centuries later.

Organising the projection was, by all accounts, a logistical headache. Permission was needed from everyone from the air traffic authorities to the emergency services, but the result was worth all the bureaucracy. Urizen's long hair and white beard, which Blake drew blown dramatically to the side, were animated so that they rippled in the fierce winds of the formless unseen void beyond our world. Squatting, naked and muscular, he leant out of the spiritual sun of the imagination and reached down with an open golden compass in his hand to construct the limited rational world that we live in. From a viewing position on the London Millennium Footbridge across the Thames, the top of the compass merged with the pointed roof of the south transept of the cathedral. It looked as if Urizen was creating this great church, both the physical building and the religion that it represents.

With his long white patriarch's beard, it is easy to mistake Urizen for God, especially when he is pictured in the act of creating the world. Urizen, as we have seen, made this same mistake himself. But Urizen is not God, no matter how much he may look like Him in that image, and no matter how much he deludes himself into thinking he is. Urizen is, in Blake's words, 'the mistaken Demon of heaven' or, as he states simply in *Milton*, 'Satan is Urizen'. Blake insisted that Satan/Urizen was a necessary part of all of us, of course, something that we should understand and learn from rather than deny. It was Urizen who divided and abstracted chaos to build our models of the world, the past and the future and our sense of ourselves. Yet he was still Satanic or demonic, due to his deluded sense of self-importance, his belief in the soulless, material world he created, and his refusal to acknowledge the true spiritual sun that gave birth to him. He was not what you'd expect St Paul's Cathedral to celebrate.

For those familiar with the symbolism of Blake's mythology, it was difficult to believe this was actually happening. If anyone had approached the officials of St Paul's to ask if they could project an image of Satan onto the dome, they surely would have said no. Why they agreed in this instance is unclear. It is possible that they did not understand Blake's mythology, and that Blake's current reputation or the general godlike appearance of Urizen were enough to convince them. The alternative is that they fully understood the implications of branding a cathedral with Urizen and, in a moment of clarity, agreed that it made sense.

There is now a long tradition of Blake being celebrated by authorities in ways that were, to those who understand his work, fantastically inappropriate. When the Labour and Conservative parties sing 'Jerusalem' at their party political conferences, they are presumably unfamiliar with the context of those words in the preface to the poem *Milton*. As they heartily bellow the lyric, moved by the stirring music, they seem unaware that they are calling for the revolutionary overthrowing of the 'ignorant Hirelings' of 'the Camp, the Court, & the University'. The song is sung by schoolboys in places such as Eton College who seem not to know that they are the uninspired, insipid targets of Blake's words. Blake is trying to persuade them to take up mental weapons, such as 'Arrows of desire', as well as physical ones, such as the sword that shall not 'sleep in my hand', in order to burn their college down. They sing about doing this in the name of the inspired mythical giant Albion, whether they know this or not.

Then there is the 12-foot-tall metal statue of Newton, created by the sculptor Eduardo Paolozzi in 1995, which is based on Blake's painting of the same subject. Blake showed the great scientist as an avatar of Urizen, focused on a pair of compasses marking a circle on paper and oblivious to the immense wild world beyond his limited logic. That wild world is absent in Paolozzi's statue, yet it is still an impressive statue which is only funny because of where it is sited. It was placed on a high plinth in the courtyard outside that great establishment dedicated to book learning, the British Library. That the image is intended to mock the limitations of this form of knowledge is as clear an illustration of Urizen's blinkered nature as you can get. It is also another example of the establishment not just failing to understand Blake, but getting him so wrong that it is hard not to suspect a trickster spirit is somehow at play. To misunderstand something and place it in an unfortunately ironic context can easily happen once, but when it seems to happen every time, it does make you wonder.

These misunderstandings show a clear gulf between Blake's worldview and that of the powers that be. On one level, it should not be surprising. His work is deep and rich and no matter who looks into it, they will always find their own prejudices and interests reflected back. Perhaps he is too big a mind for us to ever properly grasp, and we are doomed to always fail. Perhaps the best we can do is find our own version of Blake, and take pleasure in knowing how incomplete it will appear to others. We owe it to Blake, though, to at least attempt to get the basics right. For example, how should we best describe his beliefs and philosophy? This is a question that academics have struggled with over the past century.

Blake himself would have no difficulty answering the question. He would simply insist that he was a Christian. Yet it is unlikely that modern Christians would be as sure about this as he was, given his dismissive attitudes to organised religion, his renaming of the Church's God as 'Nobodaddy', and his belief that the God of the Old Testament was a controlling, deluded aspect of our own minds. The idea that the original religion of the British Isles was Christian, long before Jesus Christ was born, is far from Christian doctrine, as is his idea that Jesus Christ was man transformed by imagination. As Blake explained, 'I know of no other Christianity and of no other Gospel than the liberty both of body & mind to exercise the Divine Arts of Imagination.' To be a Christian, as Blake understood it, was to be an artist. As he explained:

A Poet a Painter a Musician an Architect: the Man
Or Woman who is not one of these is not a Christian

This is clearly not Christianity as most modern adherents would recognise it. Blake was not a churchgoer, and by the time you get to his opinions on the roles of priests and 'priestcraft', it becomes very hard to agree with Blake's opinion of himself as a Christian.

But if Blake was not Christian, then what was he? As we noted earlier, the poem 'Auguries of Innocence' begins:

To see a World in a Grain of Sand
And a Heaven in a Wild Flower
Hold Infinity in the palm of your hand
And Eternity in an hour

This sounds like it comes from a religion like Buddhism, and Zen Buddhism in particular. Yet the passive nature of Zen Buddhism and the focus on watching the mind when it is clear and free of illusionary forms are entirely different to Blake's philosophy. Blake loved energy and work, and as far as he was concerned the illusionary forms of mind were hugely valuable. At times, his thoughts showed signs of Taoism, as we've noted, but the importance he placed on Christian concepts such as forgiveness and redemption means that he was far from a regular Taoist. His belief that the body was part of the soul has sometimes led to Blake being described as a pagan, but his unwillingness to extend a spiritual aspect to the rest of nature surely rules out that particular label. That same belief in the divine nature of the body also rules him out of being described as a Gnostic, because Gnostics saw the body, like the rest of the physical world, as a Satanic prison.

Some critics have gone so far as to suggest that Blake's beliefs made him an atheist – a suggestion based on his understanding that the spiritual world, with all its gods, demons and angels, is entirely internal. There is the basis of a logically convincing argument here, but you can imagine how Blake would have railed against it. Would an atheist insist that 'every thing that lives is Holy!' with as much passion and commitment? Blake recognised and stressed the importance of a divine quality in the world, which modern-day atheists deny. If Blake were to attend a modern atheist movement meeting, it seems likely that he would not be invited back. In a similar way, Blake was not an agnostic. He was almost entirely devoid of doubt and far too certain about his own beliefs to embrace that noble perspective.

Few people are as difficult to pigeonhole as Blake. Our inability to categorise his faith and belief system is a credit to his blazing originality, which may be a consequence of his lack of schooling. Blake was always critical of the 'Hirelings' from universities because, as he saw it, their formal education brainwashed them into a limited form of groupthink. The Greek idea that heaven was above rather than within, for example, became so internalised during formal education that it was never questioned. In these circumstances, it is not surprising that his peers were incapable of understanding his work or seeing the world through his eyes. As the late maverick theatre director Ken Campbell used to insist, 'I'm not mad, I've just read different books.'

Our lack of a label to describe Blake's beliefs is, perhaps, an important factor in the tradition of the establishment getting Blake astonishingly wrong. It would help, therefore, if we gave a name to his philosophy, even if he is the only adherent to that particular belief system. The most suitable name, I would suggest, would be to say that William Blake was a Divine Humanist.

Humanism, as the term is currently used, is a movement that gives primacy to the agency of human beings, both individually and collectively. It is, in its current form, a largely secular, non-religious movement, which looks to science rather than any form of supernatural revelation to understand the world. In doing so, it has a materialist view of the universe, rather than an idealist, dualist or dual-aspect monist one. The universe is a story of matter in motion, where atoms and particles and anti-particles collide, annihilating and creating each other in a constant dance of energy. In this materialist universe, there is no room for an immaterial or spiritual component. There is no meaning or purpose in a cosmos of matter.

Of course, materialists, humanists and atheists experience meaning, purpose and other, non-material experiences as much as everyone else. Indeed, they will often call upon such things to help promote their materialist worldview. Much is said about the 'wonder of science', for example, even though science cannot explain or account for the experience of wonder. The materialist universe is a place of measurable quantities rather than experienced qualities, yet those who believe in it frequently rely on immaterial qualities to celebrate it.

The reason for this centres on the thorny question of mind. We don't know how mind – or the illusion of mind – is generated from the damp matter of the brain but, materialists promise, one day we will work it out. Everything can theoretically be explained in a materialist framework, the argument goes, because ultimately there is only matter. Therefore, it is fine for a rational, materially minded person to talk of wonder, awe, love and other immaterial experiences, because these must ultimately arise from physical processes. This, clearly, is a circular argument which presupposes exactly what it is trying to prove. This is not to say that it won't ultimately turn out to be true, of course, and that a scientist might one day hold a test tube full of wonder. But there are no grounds for assuming it to be true now, with our current level of know-ledge. It remains a plausible theory or, perhaps, an act of faith.

The Divine Humanism of William Blake is focused on a specific type of consciousness – one that seems to us to be extremely rare. Consciousness can be found in the animal kingdom and even, perhaps, in forests, mycelium and other forms of plants. As a society we like to celebrate examples of animal intelligence, such as elephants able to recognise themselves in a mirror or rats who learn their way around mazes. We talk about their brains as being more or less like ours, only differing in a matter of degree. There is a tendency to highlight the similarities and play down the differences, for fear those differences will support the argument that people have the right to abuse animals and ecosystems. Viewing humans as qualitatively different, more advanced and in some way superior to the rest of the natural world, we increasingly recognise, can have terrible consequences. We are all part of the same ecosystem, and seeing ourselves as separate from it has had such a harmful effect on the natural world.

In certain ways, we are more like our animal relatives than we like to admit, particularly in physical and behavioural matters. But for all that evolution has explained where we as mammals sit in the tree of life, and how we have evolved over the millennia, the difference between the human minds we have now and those of our animal kin is, clearly, profoundly significant. Humanity is capable of language, art, comedy, technology and other forms of culture which the animal kingdom cannot begin to conceive of. However much we marvel at the sophistication of octopus consciousness, no one believes that any animal could create something like the works of Shakespeare, Einstein or the Beatles. Our ability to communicate, plan, tell stories and cooperate has allowed us to build complex societies and cultures that have no equivalence in the animal kingdom. All of these require the practice of imagination; none are possible without it.

Divine Humanism, then, sees humanity as central in the

conception of the universe, in the same way that secular humanism does. But it does not agree that this position leads to an atheistic, material universe. On the contrary, it sees that position as a failure to recognise that the minds of humanity are the vehicle in which the light of the spiritual sun finds its way into Newton's pointless, dead, material world. It declares that what exists in the mind is vital, and that ignoring or dismissing it is to fail to have a useful or truthful conception of reality.

To a Divine Humanist, we are the light. We are what we have been searching for, and what we have prayed to. As Blake wrote in *Jerusalem*, 'there is no other / God, than that God who is the intellectual fountain of Humanity'. Without imagination there is nothing. Such was the philosophy of William Blake.

Now we have a sense of William Blake's philosophy, in its general outline at least, the question is what should we, in the secular twenty-first century, make of it?

Blake lived during a time when Enlightenment values were in ascendance. Rationality and the single vision of Newton's sleep were proving to be too powerful for the old, faith-based philosophies. Blake set himself up in opposition to this, a lone voice proclaiming an entirely different truth. In his lifetime at least, this appeared a one-sided battle. Blake was outgunned and overpowered, but he had chosen the hill he was prepared to die on and neither the cruelties of fate nor the indifference of society were going to cause him to back down. The fundamentalist level of pig-headed stubbornness that he displayed has been reason enough for many to applaud him. From the perspective of a culture on the other side of the post-modern era, however, we now have a greater awareness of the dangers of fundamentalism.

Blake set himself up as a contrary. Helpfully, he also taught us about the nature of contraries. The goal isn't to choose one side and declare it to be the one correct truth. Instead, we must accept that both contraries are necessary, and that any philosophy that includes one at the expense of the other is incomplete. It is the tension between the two poles, and the dynamic conversation which they start, that matters. Having learnt this, we should no longer feel that we must choose between Blake and the deist Enlightenment philosophy of a dead, meaningless material world. We do not need to plant our flags on one hill and believe wholeheartedly in everything that dogma stands for. Instead, we can learn from the dissonance and questions generated by those two contrasting worldviews.

There are many aspects of Blake's thought which, from a twenty-first-century perspective, we can comfortably deny. The idea that the male is primary and that the female is an emanation of the male, for example, can be dropped without much controversy. It may still be staunchly defended by theologians, alchemists and traditionalists, but they are an increasingly small minority. We are all a product of our time, and many of our views will seem outrageous in a couple of centuries. Perhaps if we make allowance for this when we consider Blake, future historians will be kind enough to make a similar allowance when they look back at us.

Blake's denial of reason has also not aged well. Blake only believed in what his senses showed him, and, as a result, he insisted that the world was flat and that atoms did not exist. We can be charitable and recognise that for someone attempting to highlight the limitations of reason at a time when the glorification of it was forging a new world, a stance of outright denial rather than nuanced criticism would have seemed necessary. Now, however, we can recognise the value of reason and the gifts it has given us, while still seeing it as an incomplete description of the universe.

Blake's attitude to nature is another issue which we now might struggle with. His brand of Divine Humanism draws a clear line between mankind and the natural world. Blake declared that 'nature is the Devil', because it was devoid of the light of consciousness and the imagination. But he was living at a time before ecosystems were under the stresses they are now and before the interconnectedness of the biosphere was formally understood. There was not then the current understanding of systems theory, or an awareness of how reliant we are on the rest of nature from the level of microbes upwards. We now understand that humanity is a part of the biosphere and that we depend on it for our very survival.

Blake recognised the beauty in nature, of course, but he saw it only in terms of how it made him feel. We are only now coming to terms with the level of intelligence embodied in nature, such as how trees in a forest communicate with each other through the fungal mycelium under the ground, and how they rely on this network to help them react to threats and damage. The complex web of feedback loops across species and ecosystems which adapt to changing conditions across the entire biosphere is only now being glimpsed. In the twenty-first century, we need a deeper understanding of our relationship to the natural world than that found in Blake.

One aspect of Blake that has drawn admirers was his absolute faith in his own truth. This stubborn unwillingness to bend, doubt or waver has made him a role model for outsiders who feel mis-understood, ignored or derided. A common feature of mystical states is an absolute certainty about the vision revealed which, as we noted earlier, is possibly related to a weakening or loss of the experiencer's sense of self. There are profound similarities between the visions of saints and mystics, as William James recognised, but a quick glance at the history of theology will reveal a lot of troubling discrepancies too. Blake's absolute belief in his own vision became increasingly attractive as the nineteenth century gave way to the twentieth, and the philosophy of individualism grew from its *avant garde* roots in the Age of Enlightenment to its mass cultural acceptance in the mid to late twentieth century. In the current century, in contrast, we are learning to mistrust such absolutes.

Recognising that certain aspects of Blake's philosophy have dated badly makes it tricky to place him on a pedestal as a visionary oracle of absolute truth, no matter how much we admire other aspects of what he had to teach us. But when we look at Blake now, we don't need to take a fundamentalist stance and declare that he was right about everything and that all his enemies were wrong. We can recognise the flaws in his philosophy surrounding gender, reason and nature. We are lucky enough to be in a better position than he was when it comes to understanding these subjects, and it would be foolish to deny what we have learnt over the past two centuries in order to defend him. These subjects are peripheral to the one central pillar of the Blakean worldview, which is the idea that the imagination is divine. How, in the secular modern world, should we respond to this?

Two centuries of reason have not yet lifted the mystery that surrounds this subject, despite the occasional claim to the contrary by fundamentalist materialists. Science has been unable to explain what consciousness is or why it exists. Because science is a method of observation, theorising and testing based on objective measurement, it seems particularly unsuited to this task. Consciousness remains a blind spot for science, even though it is the arena in which scientific thought takes place. It is a great irony that fundamentalist materialists use consciousness and imagination to convince themselves that consciousness and imagination are unimportant.

The type of consciousness we experience is clearly related to that extraordinary biochemical marvel, the human brain. Our

understanding of the structure and complexity of this organ continues to expand, but we are no closer to an explanation as to how
it could produce the experience of awareness, let alone why. That
is assuming, of course, that this is what it is doing. The common
assumption is that the brain is like a theatre – it contains within it
everything needed to put on the show we experience. There is also
the possibility that it is like a radio or television, however, which
contains all the circuitry needed to interpret signals that originate
elsewhere. In this scenario, studying the brain to understand the
experience of consciousness is like studying the insides of a television in a sports bar in order to understand what is happening
in the cup final. You may be able to determine which circuits are
active when the screen glows green to show the pitch, but you
will not be able to find in those circuits the rules of the game, or
why they matter.

For all we can find neural correlates for consciousness, there just
aren't any convincing theories as to why the biochemical soup of a
human brain should know that it exists and experiences feelings,
emotions and qualities. Perhaps the materialists are right, and the
brain is entirely responsible for the experience of mind. Perhaps
the poets, saints and some quantum physicists are correct, and
consciousness itself is a fundamental aspect of our universe which
our brains filter or process for us. Neither of these scenarios can
currently be proved or disproved. There are arguments in favour
of both. We are free to believe in either, but we can only do so
from a position of faith.

Blake's central argument, then, that imagination is divine,
can't be ruled out or dismissed as easily as his views on nature,
reason and gender. His position is not argued in the language of
his opponent, with logical proofs and measurements of matter.
Instead, he presents his body of work and awaits our reaction. That
work is an illustration of the experience of imagination at a far

deeper and more overwhelming level than most of us are familiar with. Like early explorers returning from their ocean voyages with exotic plants and strange beasts, or Apollo astronauts returning to earth with a case full of moon rocks, he has travelled to inner places that we knew nothing about and returned with exhibits to convince the sceptical.

When we see his images or hear his words, what exactly attracts us to them? They are strange and powerful, and we can't claim to fully understand them. Yet they resonate with us, as if they wake up something inside. They are not from our world, as we do not see their like elsewhere. It is our reaction to them that convinces us that the world they are said to come from is real. After all, haven't we all dipped our toes into the sea of the imagination? Should it surprise us that others have dived deeper?

The human mind is the one thing that emits imagination into our closed, limited, finite universe. It is we and we alone who are the source of meaning, purpose, love and hate in this otherwise cold, dead cloud of matter. If our eyes had evolved to see the light of the imagination rather than sunlight, then we would see ourselves as part of the constellations of the heavens, down here on earth rather than up in the night sky. We are the source of what we perceive. We are that which we crave. You might argue about the semantics of a word like 'divine' to describe this. It is certainly true that many will reject such a word for deeply ingrained reasons. But as a rough approximation of what we are talking about, it is not entirely off the mark.

In the Divine Humanism that Blake practised and which his work represents, we have a responsibility to recognise the imaginative aspect of our lives and use it well. As Blake told us, how we see is as important as what we see, 'For the Eye altering alters all.' For Blake, there was a moral component to perception. As he wrote,

'The tree which moves some to tears of joy is in the Eyes of others only a Green thing that stands in the way [...] As a man is, So he Sees.' We paint the world around us in the colours of the world inside. Just as the driver who complains how bad the traffic was fails to recognise that they themselves were the traffic, so too do those who complain about being trapped in a terrible world fail to realise the extent to which their choice of focus has helped create that world. At stake is our experience of the precious, too-short span of years which we are lucky enough to have right here, right now, and which we can paint as either paradise or hell. This is one of our actions which we have to take responsibility for, and can't blame on others.

Blake's work was not just a description of the human mind and the world it built in its own image. It was also a diagnosis. He believed that he understood what had gone wrong, and he was telling us what we need to do about it.

As Blake saw it, the rise of Urizen into a position of dominance over the other three zoas created the 'mind forg'd manacles' which keep us from experiencing the paradise that is our birthright. As the stories of Eckhart Tolle and Jill Bolte Taylor show, the shutting down of Urizen or 'left brain' neural functions in favour of other areas of the brain can result in an experience of profound, timeless bliss. This is still something we are all capable of achieving – it was not lost when we left Eden, and neither do we need to wait until after death to be granted it as some form of reward. Blake was regularly in paradise, particularly towards the end of his life. He wanted us all to join him.

Our inner Urizens fight against this idea, of course, because it is a threat to their self-image. They usually begin by denying that any such experience is real. When confronted with examples to the contrary, our rational minds become manipulative. They may argue that some people may be able to experience a blissful state like that. But to do so is indulgent and elitist, and we ourselves have no right to spend time in paradise. We are too busy and have too many responsibilities, and we probably couldn't do it if we tried. Of all Urizen's lies, this is possibly his most malicious. As those who have experience of paradise will confirm, this couldn't be more wrong. The state is there for everyone, and the only harm involved comes from a refusal to enter.

Blake did not view Urizen as an enemy to be defeated, however. He could at times be sympathetic or even pitying towards him. He knew he did not mean to cause the harm he did, and that he only did so out of ignorance rather than intention. Blake did not want to see Urizen vanquished. Instead, he wanted the four zoas to return to balance. Urizen does much that is good and valuable and if he could only understand his limited nature, he would no longer deny or drown out the heavenly parts of our minds represented by Tharmas, Urthona and Luvah.

There are two responses to this, and the first is focused on how we deal with Urizen. It is not necessary to try to weaken or even destroy our rational side – if Urizen can come to realise his own nature, then he will be a powerful tool in the rebalancing of the mind. It is Urizen, after all, who reads and thinks and can study books like Blake's *Jerusalem*. Urizen's innate rationality is a tool which can be used to realise his own nature, even if this requires a little humility. Urizen needs to accept the limitations of his awareness, to no longer feel compelled to control and dominate, and to be prepared to step back and listen. He needs to recognise his desire to be seen as right for the psychological failing it is. If Urizen can grasp the scale of the potential reward this offers, however, then he will come on board gladly.

The other response is to strengthen the parts of our selves represented by the other three zoas, in order that they can better balance our rationalising ego. Blake himself focused particularly on Urthona,

the creative zoa, who was active in the form of Los. With his particular artistic talents, strengthening Urthona was an ideal way for
Blake to counterbalance the rational world through the burning fire
of real creativity. This is a far more potent weapon than we might
first realise. True imagination, Blake knew, has no limits. It is an
active process fundamental to the workings of the universe, and to
dismiss it is to voluntarily live a poorer life. Given the strength of
Blake's Urthona, what chance did his Urizen really have?

Those of a less creative nature may instead focus on strengthening Luvah, the emotional zoa. It was Luvah that Blake evoked
when he stressed the importance of forgiveness, empathy, and
compassion as a route to heaven. As he wrote, 'Where Mercy,
Love & Pity dwell / There God is dwelling too.' Such emotions
dissolve the Urizenic hard ego, revealing ourselves to be connected
rather than isolated, and revealing the category of 'others' to be
nothing more than Urizen's invention. Opening our heart, then,
is another route to rebalancing our minds. As Blake explained,
'Mutual forgiveness of each Vice / Such are the Gates of Paradise.'

Then there is Tharmas, the zoa of physical sensation. Blake's
embrace of his sexual nature was his method of strengthening
Tharmas, which explains why he viewed sex as holy. This was
a scandalous position to take at the time, but he was far from
alone in realising it. The French term for orgasm, for example, is
la petite mort or the little death. This refers not to actual death, but
instead to the temporary dissolving of the Urizenic ego that allows
a moment of transcendence.

It is not just sex that strengthens Tharmas, as dancers and
athletes in many fields will confirm. The experience of a 'flow
state' during intense focus on a physical activity is another blissful
way to shut down Urizen. In Kathryn Bigelow's 1991 action movie
Point Break, Patrick Swayze's surfer dude describes the spiritual
nature of surfing as 'a state of mind. It's that place where you lose

yourself and you find yourself.' Insecure Urizen will bristle at this threat and try to dismiss the line as cheesy or meaningless. Blake, in contrast, would have seen the truth of it.

Here, then, is Blake's map to the gates of paradise. As his grave marker promised us,

> I give you the end of a golden string
> Only wind it into a ball
> It will lead you in at Heaven's gate
> Built in Jerusalem's wall.

To follow that string we need to strengthen our emotional, physical and creative aspects – the 'right hemisphere' part of our minds. At the same time, our rational side needs to step down and understand and accept the limitations of its mental models. When these two things are achieved, our mind will finally be in balance and we, like the giant Albion, can awaken into a perfect timeless moment. We will step outside of the everyday modern world of noise, anxiety and fear, and experience the world as a Blakean paradise. This does not have to be a life-changing trauma of the kind experienced by Swedenborg, Tolle, Rousseau or Bolte Taylor. A gradual readjustment will take you to the same location. Even if we spend the majority of our time in the world as Urizen sees it, knowing that we are not trapped there makes all the difference. Just a few transcendent moments every day are enough. Once Blake's 'Heaven's gate / Built in Jerusalem's wall' has been found, we know that at any point we can step from a hell of our own making into the paradise where we truly feel at home.

This is not a religion to control us. It is not a struggle or a burden in which we have to deny our own instincts and desires, and it's not a creed that will divide us or generate a delusional elite. It's simply a testable model of how things are.

*

In Westminster Abbey, near the remains of Geoffrey Chaucer, there is now a bronze bust of an aged William Blake attached to a pillar. The bust was sculpted by Sir Jacob Epstein, and it was placed in position in 1957, to mark the 200th anniversary of Blake's birth. Surrounded by centuries-old engravings and tombs, it looks uncomfortably modern.

Blake is shown with strong, bare shoulders, his thinning hair swept back, and his eyes looking up like an ageing superhero. He looks up not with an expression of revelation, as in the famous oil painting by Thomas Phillips, but in a stern and determined manner. His eyes are fixed on a sculpture of the eighteenth-century political essayist Joseph Addison, which stands on the west wall of the south transept. Thanks to the position of these sculptures, Blake has been forced to stare at Addison for decades. Perhaps this explains his unhappy expression.

When he was a boy, still apprenticed to James Basire, Blake spent long hours exploring this Abbey, sketching and climbing over the royal tombs. Now, his presence has become as unmoving as the medieval effigies he used to record. It is good to see this mocked and ignored man celebrated and remembered in this way, but it is also strange seeing him still. Blake was a man for whom energy was 'eternal delight'. When you bring him to mind his face should be animated and his eyes should dart around, always in the process of actively projecting his imagination onto the world. Blake was always working. He was always trying to explain that his visions were the product of the imagination; that the imagination could be exercised and increased; that sexual energy was an important part of this process; that time itself was created by thought; that the laws of religious authorities were irrelevant and damaging; that all gods and spirits were products of the human imagination; that we have the power to turn our world into heaven if we so choose; that forgiveness, creativity and relationships were the keys to paradise; that the material and immaterial worlds depend on each other, and that we can all join him in the experience of Eternity. From Blake's perspective, the human universe was a process of continual becoming, whose most vital and fundamental aspect was imagination.

Fixed to a pillar like this, the bust serves as a constant reminder of this contrary position which Blake embodied throughout his entire life. By its very existence, the dynamic tension between that contrary position and its opposing, materialist argument also remains. That tension poses questions that would not otherwise be asked. It generates an energy we can engage with. His fight continues. It is still too early to call a winner.

In the great conflict that was William Blake versus the world, I would not rule out Blake just yet.

NOTES AND SOURCES

BR = *Blake Records: Second Edition* by G. E. Bentley, Jr. (Yale University Press, 2004).

CPP = *The Complete Poetry & Prose of William Blake*, ed. David V. Erdman (Anchor, 1988), newly revised edition.

1. THE END OF A GOLDEN STRING

p.1 'an expression of great sweetness...' – Henry Crabb Robinson's diary entry for 10 December 1825, BR, p.420.

p.2 'One remembers even in age...' – statement by Maria Denman recorded by Alexander Gilchrist, BR, p.419 (footnote).

p.2 'spoke of his paintings as being...' – Henry Crabb Robinson's diary entry for 10 December 1825, BR, p.421.

p.2 'There is a natural sweetness...' – ibid., p.425.

p.2 'Shall I call him Artist or Genius...' – ibid., p.420.

p.3 'It is strange that I...' – Henry Crabb Robinson's diary entry for 13 May 1848, Symons, *William Blake*, p.276.

p.3 'I found him in a small room...' – Henry Crabb Robinson's diary entry for 17 December 1825, BR, p.426.

p.4 'There was a strange expansion...' – Gilchrist, *Life of William Blake*, p.328.

p.4 'quite unembarrassed when he begged me...' – Henry Crabb Robinson, 25 February 1852, BR, pp.698–9.

p.4 'I live in a hole here...' – Gilchrist, *Life of William Blake*, p.330.

p.4 'I possess my visions and peace...' – ibid., p.330.

p.4 'I should be sorry if I had any earthly fame...' – Henry Crabb Robinson, 23 February 1852, BR, p.697.

p.4 'Though he spoke of his happiness...' – Henry Crabb Robinson's diary entry for 10 December 1825, BR, p.424.

p.5 'I thought I should have gone first...' – Henry Crabb Robinson's diary entry for 7 December 1826, BR, p.453.

p.5 'in a most glorious manner...' – letter from George Richmond to Samuel Palmer, 15 August 1827, BR, p.464.

p.7 'Caught in the crush: are our galleries now hopelessly overcrowded?' by Sirin Kale, published in the *Guardian* on 2 December 2019.

p.7 The *Evening Standard* review of the exhibition was 'William Blake review: Be drawn into a weird and wonderful fantasy universe' by Matthew Collings, 9 September 2019.

p.7 The *Sunday Times* review was 'William Blake at Tate Britain review – viewing it is like being drunk' by Waldemar Januszczak, 15 September 2019.

p.7 The *Guardian* review was 'William Blake review – blazing heresies from the artist who blows Constable and Turner away' by Jonathan Jones, 9 September 2019.

p.7 The *Daily Mail* review was entitled 'Naked genius! He was a nudist obsessed by sex who talked to angels for inspiration, but for all his madness, William Blake was one of our greatest artists – as a new exhibition reveals' by Melanie McDonagh, 19 September 2019.

p.7 The BBC review 'William Blake: Will Gompertz reviews "imperfect" Tate Britain blockbuster' was published on 14 September 2019.

p.10 'I give you the end of a golden string...' – Blake, *Jerusalem*, CPP, p.231.

2. TWOFOLD ALWAYS

p.14 'Sauntering along, the boy looks up...' – Gilchrist, *Life of William Blake*, p.9.

p.18 'no adequate report of its contents...' – James, *The Varieties of Religious Experience*, p.380.

p.18 'a world of consciousness...' – quoted in Kripal, *The Flip*, p.65.

p.18 'rather like being a chimpanzee...' – ibid., p.69.

p.18 'Although so similar to states of feeling...' – James, *The Varieties of Religious Experience*, pp.380–1.

p.19 'the mystic feels as if...' – ibid., p.381.

p.19 Philip Pullman's 2002 talk at the Oxford University Department for Continuing Education is transcribed in his book *Daemon Voices*, in the chapter 'God and Dust: Notes for a Study Day with the Bishop of Oxford'.

p.20 'I'm believing more and more...' – *The Adam Buxton Podcast*, episode 102.

p.21 'With happiness stretchd across the hills...' – Blake, poem included with letter to Thomas Butts, 22 November 1802, CPP, pp.720–2.

p.25 'A fool sees not the same tree...' – Blake, 'The Proverbs of Hell', *The Marriage of Heaven and Hell*, CPP, p.35.

p.26 'O how can I with my gross tongue...' – Blake, *Milton*, CPP, p.114.

p.27 'I came to a meadow...' – Gilchrist, *Life of William Blake*, pp.341–2.

3. I COME TO SELF ANNIHILATION

p.30 'O Saviour pour upon me...' – Blake, *Jerusalem*, CPP, p.147.

p.30 'know thou: I come to Self Annihilation...' – Blake, *Milton*, CPP, p.139.

p.30 'O that Death & Annihilation were the same!' – Blake, *Jerusalem*, CPP, p.167.

p.37 'Who can paint an angel?'– anecdote recounted by Thomas Phillips, recorded in *The Cabinet of Pictures* (1833) by Allan Cunningham, BR, pp.233–4.

p.38 'If the Sun & Moon should doubt...' – Blake, 'Auguries of Innocence', CPP, p.492.

p.38 'while [European] people appear to have been...' – Letcher, *Shroom*, p.49.

p.40 'Soon my Angel came again...' – Blake, 'The Angel', *Songs of Innocence and of Experience*, CPP, p.24.

p.40 'a man without a mask' – Blake described by Samuel Palmer in Gilchrist, *Life of William Blake*, p.321.

p.41 'Father, I do not like the man's face...' – ibid., p.16.

p.42 'He was an engraver well grounded in drawing...' – ibid., p.17.

p.43 'the legendary history of Britain revealed...' – Ackroyd, *Blake*, p.46.

p.44 'in the Impetuosity of his anger...' – BR, p.667.

p.45 'How sweet I roam'd from field to field...' – Blake, *Poetical Sketches*, CPP, pp.412–13.

p.48 'And did those feet in ancient time...' – Blake, *Milton*, CPP, p.95.

4. WITHOUT CONTRARIES IS NO PROGRESSION

p.52 'Little Lamb who made thee...' – Blake, 'The Lamb', *Songs of Innocence*, CPP, pp.8–9.

p.54 'Tyger Tyger, burning bright...' – Blake, 'The Tyger', *Songs of Innocence and of Experience*, CPP, pp.24–5.

p.55 'And the Angel told Tom if he'd be a good boy...' – Blake, 'The Chimney Sweeper', *Songs of Innocence*, CPP, p.10.

p.56 'A little black thing among the snow...' – Blake, 'The Chimney Sweeper', *Songs of Innocence and of Experience*, CPP, pp.22–3.

p.56 'Love seeketh not Itself to please...' – Blake, 'The Clod & the Pebble', ibid., p.19.

p.57 'Without Contraries is no progression...' – Blake, *The Marriage of Heaven and Hell*, CPP, p.34.

p.57 'Opposition is true Friendship...' – ibid., p.42.

p.58 'Energy is Eternal Delight...' – ibid., p.34.

p.58 'When people see some things as beautiful...' – Lao Tzu, *Tao Te Ching*, p.2.

p.60 'There is a place where Contrarieties are equally True...' – Blake, *Jerusalem*, CPP, p.196, and *Milton*, CPP, p.129.

p.60 'a pleasant lovely Shadow...' – Blake, *Milton*, CPP, p.129.

p.62 'Inwards, into a deep world within...' – Blake, *The Book of Urizen*, CPP, p.72.

p.62 'Spread a Tent, with strong curtains around them...' – ibid., p.78.

p.63 'One command, one joy, one desire...' – ibid., p.72.

p.65 'Creator of men, mistaken Demon of heaven' – Blake, 'Visions of the Daughters of Albion', CPP, p.48.

p.65 'Urizen is Satan' – Blake, *Milton*, CPP, p.104.

p.65 'And every Space smaller than a Globule of Mans blood...' – ibid., p.127.

p.66 'Thou percievest the Flowers...' – ibid., p.131.

p.66 'The Tao can't be perceived...' – Lao Tzu, *Tao Te Ching*, p.32.

p.69 'The brain is an illusion factory' – Buonomano, *Your Brain is a Time Machine*, p.172.

p.69 'we are much more the artist than we realise' – Nietzsche, *Beyond Good and Evil*, p.192.

p.69 'In your Bosom you bear your Heaven and Earth...' – Blake, *Jerusalem*, CPP, p.225.

p.69 'Everything possible to be believ'd is an image of truth' – Blake, 'The Proverbs of Hell', *The Marriage of Heaven and Hell*, CPP, p.37.

p.70 'The Sky is an immortal Tent...' – Blake, *Milton*, CPP, p.127.

p.72 'men forgot that All Deities reside in the Human breast' – Blake, *The Marriage of Heaven and Hell*, CPP, p.38.

p.73 'Wise, he was also wilful...' – Holland, *Dominion*, pp.42–3.

p.73 'Then old Nobodaddy aloft...' – Blake, Notebook verses, CPP, p.499.

p.74 'The Hebrew Nation did not write it...' – ibid., p.516.

p.74 'To God...' – ibid.

5. THE TYGERS OF WRATH

p.77 'Suddenly I feel my spirit dazzled by a thousand brilliant insights...' – Rousseau, Letter to Monsieur De Malesherbes, 12 January 1762.

p.79 'boys, pickpockets and "roughs"...' – Gilchrist, *Life of William Blake*, p.39.

p.80 'Showers of sparks and pieces of red-hot metal...' – Hibbert, *King Mob*, p.87.

p.80 'got to such a height that the sky was like blood...' Erskine, quoted in Hibbert, p.90.

p.80 'They were, and are, all mad' – Walpole, quoted in Hibbert, p.9.

p.81 'a damned nuisance wholly unsuitable for promotion' – Hibbert, p.13.

p.82 'every thing that lives is Holy' – Blake, *The Marriage of Heaven and Hell*, CPP, p.45.

p.83 'hurl'd the new born wonder thro' the stary night...' – ibid., pp.44–5.

p.85 'The tygers of wrath are wiser than the horses of instruction' – ibid., p.37.

p.86–7 'there was a greater background of class hostility...' – Hill, *The World Turned Upside Down*, p.19.

p.88 'The present hatred of the citizens...' – ibid., p.22.

p.89 'the people say it is the Word of God, and it is not' – ibid., p.226.

p.90 'To be called a libertine is the most glorious title under heaven...' – ibid., p.186.

p.90 'The Spirit of Jesus is continual forgiveness...' – Blake, *Jerusalem*, CPP, p.145.

p.90 'There is no such act as drunkenness, adultery and theft in God...' – Hill, *The World Turned Upside Down*, p.215.

p.91 'They are the merriest of devils for extempore lascivious songs...' – ibid., p.201.

p.91 'there's no heaven but women, nor no hell save marriage' – ibid., p.227.

p.93 'There is no man or woman who needs to go to Rome...' – ibid., p.145.

p.94 'Have you also a right to all the women in the world...' – ibid., pp.380–1.

p.95 'in consequence of his unbending deportment...' – Smith, quoted in BR, p.606.

p.96 'When I tell the truth, it is not for the sake...' – Blake, Public
   Address, CPP, p.578.
p.97 'he alone excels in that art' – Damrosch, *Eternity's Sunrise*, p.25.
p.98 'by printing in the infernal method...' – Blake, *The Marriage of
   Heaven and Hell*, CPP, p.39.
p.98 'I saw a mighty Devil...' – ibid., p.35.
p.99 'Trembling I sit day and night...' – Blake, *Jerusalem*, CPP, p.147.
p.100 'Tho in the Brain of Man we live...' – Blake, *The Four Zoas*, CPP,
   p.306.

6. CONVERSED NOT WITH DEVILS

p.104 'the truths contained in the Theological Writings' – Lachman,
   Swedenborg, p.21.
p.104 'Swedenborg had a Divine Revelation...' – BR, pp.51–2.
p.106 'I, in spiritual things, am a stinking corpse' – Lachman,
   Swedenborg, p.2.
p.106 'the experiences Swedenborg went through...' – ibid., p.3.
p.106 'the emergence of the unconscious opposite...' – Jung,
   Psychological Types, p.426.
p.107 'he would never find the soul in the manner...' – Lachman,
   Swedenborg, p.79.
p.107 'the sight during sleep...' – ibid., p.95.
p.107 'with closed eye, which is as vivid...' – ibid., p.95.
p.107 'Another vision is that between the time of sleep...' – ibid., p.94.
p.108 'when the eyes are open, and the things in heaven...' – ibid., p.95.
p.108 'enjoys all his senses, as that of touch...' – ibid., p.97.
p.110 'When we enter the spiritual world...' – Swedenborg, *A
   Swedenborg Sampler*, pp.31–2.
p.110 'We see the way we used to...' – ibid., p.32.
p.110 'can talk to anyone when we want to...' – ibid., p.10.
p.111 'after death we can no longer be reformed' – ibid., p.55.
p.111 'Just as we find delight in our own evil...' – ibid., p.11.
pp.112–13 'Such a life would not be active...' – Lachman, *Swedenborg*,
   p.117.

353

p.114 'Angels can say more in a minute...' – ibid., p.127.

p.115 'No one but God knows this secret' – ibid., p.107.

p.116 'As truly as you see me...' – Sigstedt, *The Swedenborg Epic*, p.754.

p.117 'This was known to me & thousands' – Blake, CPP, p.602.

p.117 'I must Create a System, or be enslav'd by another Mans...' – Blake, *Jerusalem*, CPP, p.153.

p.118 'Heaven & Hell are born together' – Blake, CPP, p.609.

p.118 'Rintrah roars & shakes his fires in the burdend air' – Blake, *The Marriage of Heaven and Hell*, CPP, p.33.

p.118 'Now the sneaking serpent walks...' – ibid.

p.119 'As a new heaven is begun, and it is now thirty-three years...' – Blake, ibid., p.34.

p.120 'Now hear a plain fact: Swedenborg has not written one new truth...' – ibid., p.43.

p.120 'walking among the fires of hell...' – ibid., p.35.

p.121 'I have always found that Angels have the vanity...' – ibid., p.42.

p.122 'These two classes of men are always upon earth...' – ibid., p.40.

p.123 'Good is Heaven. Evil is Hell' – ibid., p.34.

7. ONCE, ONLY IMAGIN'D

p.125 'Imagination created the world' – Baudelaire, quoted in Casey, *Imagining*, p.1.

p.125 'The imagination is the true fire, stolen from heaven...' – Wollstonecraft, letter to Gilbert Imlay, quoted in Gordon, *Romantic Outlaws*, p.286.

p.126 'Imagination is more important than knowledge...' Einstein, *Cosmic Religion*, p.97.

p.126 'imaginings are for the most part false' – Aristotle, *De Anima*.

p.126 'anti-world' – Casey, *Imagining*, pp.2–3.

p.127 'after I took mescaline, I started seeing crabs...' – Sartre, quoted in 'When Sartre Talked to Crabs (It Was Mescaline)', *New York Times*, 14 November 2009.

p.128 'A recognition of the multiplicity of the mental...' – Casey, *Imagining*, p.178.

p.134 'I must Create a System, or be enslav'd by another Mans' – Blake, CPP, p.153.

p.137 'always saw in fancy every form he drew' – CPP, p.233.

p.137 'I can't go on, it is gone! I must wait till it returns' – Gilchrist, *Life of William Blake*, p.271.

p.138 'A Robin Red breast in a Cage...' – Blake, 'Auguries of Innocence', CPP, p.490.

p.139 'When people describe things, especially gory things...' – Dudeney, quoted in Daniel Cossins, 'Inside the Mind's Eye', *New Scientist*, 8 June 2019, p.38.

p.139 'My practice considers how...'– www.claredudeney.com/biography.

p.140 'Recently, I've been thinking that maybe not being able to see...' – Bakes quoted by Matthew MacKisak in the 17 April 2019 blog post Artists With Aphantasia: Extended Imagining?, at junkyardofthemind.com.

p.141 'I must physically work on a drawing...' – Chance quoted by Matthew MacKisak in the 17 April 2019 blog post Artists With Aphantasia: Extended Imagining?, at junkyardofthemind.com.

p.141 'From my perspective, a writer without a mind's eye...' – Grinnell, How to Write With Aphantasia, a 12 May 2019 post on aphantasia.com.

p.141 'I've known many people with photographic memories...' – Venter quoted in Dustin Grinnell, 'Blind in the Mind', *New Scientist*, 23 April 2016.

8. SEEK LOVE THERE

p.147 'pitied him from the heart...' – Gilchrist, *Life of William Blake*, p.42.

p.147 'the Two Contraries of Humanity' – Blake, *Jerusalem*, CPP, p.216.

p.148 'an excellent Wife (a true Helpmate!)' – Catherine Blake described by William Hayley in 1802, BR, p.131.

p.148 'She seemed to have been created on purpose for Blake...' – Cunningham, writing in 1830, BR, p.632.

p.148 'They have been married more than seventeen years...' – Hayley, letter to Lady Hesketh, 15 July 1802, BR, p.140.

p.148 'You have ever been an angel to me' – Gilchrist, *Life of William Blake*, p.385.

p.148 'madder of the two' – Cumberland, writing to his son in 1815, BR, p.321.

p.148 'she was sure [his poems] had a meaning, and a fine one' – Cunningham, writing in 1830, BR, p.638.

p.149 'Those who restrain desire, do so because theirs is weak enough to be restrained' – Blake, *The Marriage of Heaven and Hell*, CPP, p.34.

p.149 'Prisons are built with stones of Law...' – Blake, 'The Proverbs of Hell', *The Marriage of Heaven and Hell*, CPP, p.36.

p.149 'Priests in black gowns, were walking their rounds...' – Blake, 'The Garden of Love', *Songs of Innocence and of Experience*, CPP, p.26.

p.149 'We are told to abstain from fleshly desires...' Blake, *Jerusalem*, CPP, p.231.

p.150 'a little to the scandal of wondering neighbours' – Gilchrist, *Life of William Blake*, p.125.

p.150 'Mr. Butts' visit to "Adam and Eve" had grown in the memory...' – Palmer writing in 1864, BR, p.xxvii.

pp.150–1 'He who desires but acts not, breeds pestilence' – Blake, 'The Proverbs of Hell', *The Marriage of Heaven and Hell*, CPP, p.35.

p.151 'Sooner murder an infant in its cradle...' – ibid., p.38.

p.151 'had committed many murders' – Robinson, BR, p.705.

p.151 'The road of excess leads to the palace of wisdom' – Blake, 'The Proverbs of Hell', *The Marriage of Heaven and Hell*, CPP, p.35.

p.151 'You never know what is enough unless you know what is more than enough' – ibid., p.37.

p.151 'The most sublime act is to set another before you' – ibid., p.36.

p.152 'jealousy on her side, not wholly unprovoked' – Gilchrist, *Life of William Blake*, p.337.

p.152 'O William if thou dost another Love...' – Blake, 'William Bond', CPP, pp.497–8.

p.153 'a strange mystical allegory, full of tender beauty...' – Gilchrist, *Life of William Blake*, p.84.

p.154 'Like a reflection in a glass. like shadows in the water...' – Blake, 'The Book of Thel', CPP, pp.3–6.

p.156 'clapping its hands for joy' – Gilchrist, *Life of William Blake*, p.66.

p.158 'The fact is – so I have been informed...' – Rossetti, *The Poetical Works of William Blake*, p.vii.

p.159 'to teach sexual procedures and practices...' – Schuchard, Chapter 3, *Why Mrs Blake Cried*, ebook Loc489.

p.159 'The instructions emphasised the importance...' – Fogleman, quoted in Schuchard, Chapter 3, *Why Mrs Blake Cried*, ebook Loc505.

p.160 'must become sinners in order to be saved' – Schuchard, Chapter 4, *Why Mrs Blake Cried*, ebook Loc749.

p.160 'My Dear Bretheren & Sistors, I have very littell to say...' – Schuchard, Appendix, *Why Mrs Blake Cried*, ebook Loc4880.

p.160 'by turns a searching critic of patriarchy...' – Bruder, quoted in Damrosch, *Eternity's Sunrise*, p.217.

p.161 'Kneel down and beg Robert's pardon directly...' – Gilchrist, *Life of William Blake*, p.65.

p.161 'let the men do their duty...' – Blake, CPP, p.596.

p.162 'One dread morn of gory blood...' – Blake, *The Four Zoas*, CPP, p.359.

p.163 'I loved Theotormon...' – Blake, 'Visions of the Daughters of Albion', CPP, p.45.

p.164 'sex under law' – Damon, *A Blake Dictionary*, p.238.

p.164 'Art thou a flower! art thou a nymph...' – Blake, 'Visions of the Daughters of Albion', CPP, p.46.

p.165 'she who burns with youth. and knows no fixed lot...' – ibid., p.49.

p.165 'beneath him sound like waves on the desart shore...' – ibid., p.46.

p.165 'Should I Marry a Harlot & an Adulteress...' – Blake, *Jerusalem*, CPP, p.211.

p.166 'There is none that liveth & Sinneth not...' – ibid., p.212.

p.166 'Such is self-love that envies all...' – Blake, 'Visions of the Daughters of Albion', CPP, p.50.

p.166 'The moment of desire! the moment of desire...' – ibid.

p.167 'catch for thee girls of mild silver, or of furious gold...' – ibid.

p.168 'Arise and drink your bliss, for every thing that lives is holy!...'
– ibid., p.51.

p.168 'Mutual forgiveness of each Vice...' – Blake, 'The Gates of Paradise', CPP, p.259.

p.169 'I thought Love lived in the hot sun Shine...' – Blake, 'William Bond', pp.497–8.

9. THEIR FORMS ETERNAL EXIST

p.175 'has written a book to prove that there is no such thing as matter...' – Lord Chesterfield, quoted in Porter, *Flesh in the Age of Reason*, p.25.

p.179 'every Natural Effect has a Spiritual Cause' – Blake, *Milton*, CPP, p.124.

p.179 'We who dwell on Earth can do nothing of ourselves...' – Blake, *Jerusalem*, CPP, p.145.

p.179 'The Oak is cut down by the Ax...' – Blake, *Milton*, CPP, p.132.

p.181 'sexual religion is dangerous' – Henry Crabb Robinson's diary entry for 10 December 1825, BR, p.424.

p.183 'God only Acts & Is, in existing beings or Men' – Blake, *The Marriage of Heaven and Hell*, CPP, p.40.

p.183 'All deities reside in the human breast' – ibid., p.38.

10. APPEARD AS ONE MAN

p.187 'I have also; The Bible of Hell...' – Blake, *The Marriage of Heaven and Hell*, CPP, p.44.

p.188 'The Labours of the Artist, the Poet, the Musician...' – Blake, prospectus, CPP, p.692.

p.190 'Deep pit of Melancholy...' – Blake, letter to George Cumberland, 2 July 1800, CPP, p.706.

p.191 'I know that our deceased friends are more really with us...' – Blake, letter to William Hayley, 6 May 1800, BR, p.89.

p.191 'I have now better prospects than ever...' – Blake, letter to George Cumberland, 1 September 1800, BR, pp.95–7.

p.192 'Sussex is certainly a happy place...' – Blake, letter to Thomas Butts, 10 May 1801, CPP, p.715.

p.192–3 'The Villagers of Felpham are not mere Rustics...' – Blake, letter to Thomas Butts, 23 September 1800, CPP, p.711.

p.193 'Felpham is a sweet place for Study...' – Blake, letter to John Flaxman, 21 September 1800, CPP, p.710.

p.193 'My Eyes more & more...' – Blake, letter to Thomas Butts, 2 October 1800, CPP, p.713.

p.195 'The Whole Heaven, Grasped as a single Entity...' – Swedenborg, *A Swedenborg Sampler*, p.25.

p.196 'in your own Bosom you bear your Heaven...' Blake, *Jerusalem*, CPP, p.225.

p.197 'Neither shall they say, Lo here! or, lo there!' – Luke 17:20–21, King James Bible.

p.197 'God only Acts & Is, in existing beings or Men' – Blake, *The Marriage of Heaven and Hell*, CPP, p.40.

p.197 'All deities reside in the human breast' – ibid., p.38.

p.197 'Man has no Body distinct from his Soul...' – ibid., p.34.

p.197 'The notion that man has a body distinct from his soul...' – ibid., p.39.

p.198 'the spirit is willing, but the flesh is weak' – Matthew 26:41, King James Bible.

p.199 'The philosophy of the east taught the first principles of human perception' – Blake, *The Marriage of Heaven and Hell*, CPP, p.39.

11. GREEN & PLEASANT LAND

p.203 'And did those feet in ancient time...' – Blake, *Milton*, CPP, p.95.

p.204 'The Stolen and Perverted Writings of Homer & Ovid...' – ibid.

p.205 'the Daughters of Memory shall become the Daughters of Inspiration' – ibid.

p.209 'the Human Imagination / which is the Divine Body of the Lord Jesus. blessed for ever' – ibid., p.96.

p.209 'Christianity is Art [...] Jesus & his Apostles & Disciples were all Artists' – Blake, 'The Laocoön', CPP, pp.273–4.

p.210 'Everyone is a potential Jesus Christ, really...' – George Harrison interviewed in *Melody Maker*, 2 September 1967.

p.210 'And all must love the human form, In heathen, turk or jew...' Blake, 'The Divine Image', *Songs of Innocence and of Experience*, CPP, p.13.

p.211 'LORD, I ascribe it to thy Grace...' – Watts, 'Song VI: Praise for the Gospel' in *Divine songs: attempted in easy language for the use of children*, 1777.

p.211 'To Generalize is to be an Idiot' – Blake, Annotations to the works of Sir Joshua Reynolds, CPP, p.641.

p.211 'General Forms have their vitality in Particulars' – Blake, *Jerusalem*, CPP, p.251.

p.211 'All things begin & end in Albions ancient Druid rocky shore' – Blake, *Milton*, CPP, p.100.

p.212 'We cannot be calm until Europe, all Europe, is in flames' – Jay, *The Influencing Machine*, ebook Loc 1336.

p.212 'an impertinent answer. I insisted on his leaving...' – Blake, letter to Thomas Butts, 16 August 1803, CPP, p.732.

p.213 'The English know within themselves...' – Schofield, statement to the Michaelmas Quarter Sessions, October 1803, BR, p.171.

p.213 'for Bonaparte as long as I am able' – Catherine Blake, quoted in Ackroyd, *Blake*, p.258.

p.214 '*William Blake* late of the said Parish of Felpham...' – Michaelmas Quarter Sessions, October 1803, BR, p.168.

p.214 'if this Country does go to War our King ought to lose his head' – Catherine Blake, quoted in Ackroyd, *Blake*, p.259.

p.215 'fog of amiability' – Gilchrist, *Life of William Blake*, p.168.

p.216 'To H —— Thy Friendship oft has made my heart to ache...' – Blake, CPP, p.506.

p.216 'To H You think Fuseli is not a Great Painter Im Glad...' – ibid., p.505.

p.217 'Burn what I have peevishly written about any friend...' – Blake, letter to Thomas Butts, 16 August 1803, CPP, p.733.

12. WHEN I SPEAK I OFFEND

p.221 'dangerous maniacs, most of them being chained and terrible to behold...' – *de Saussure,* A foreign view of England in the reigns of George I and George II: The letters of Monsieur César de Saussure to his family, 1902.

p.222 'stinking human breath' and 'gaz from the anus of the horse' – Jay, *The Influencing Machine,* ebook Loc 2362.

p.227 'O why was I born with a different face...' – Blake, letter to Thomas Butts, 16 August 1803, CPP, p.733.

p.227 'I mock thee not tho I by thee am mocked...' – Blake, CPP, p.507.

p.228 'Blake used to declare the Government, or some high person...' – Gilchrist, *Life of William Blake,* p.192.

p.228 'Money flies from me; Profit never ventures upon my threshold...' – Blake, letter to William Hayley, 7 August 1804, CPP, p.754.

p.229 'It is very true what you have said...' – Blake, Public Address, CPP, p.573.

p.230 'When H——y finds out what you cannot do...' – Blake, CPP, p.506.

p.230 'Corporeal friends are Spiritual enemies' – Blake, *Milton,* CPP, p.98.

p.231 'Come into my hand By your mild power...' ibid., p.96.

p.231 'the Elect cannot be Redeemed' – ibid., p.98.

p.231 'they cannot Believe in Eternal Life Except by Miracle & a New Birth' – ibid., p.122.

p.232 'Satans extreme mildness' – ibid., p.100.

p.232 'the Plow & Harrow to pass over the Nations' – ibid., p.99.

p.233 'Would to God that all the Lords people were Prophets' – Blake quoting Numbers 11:29, *Milton,* CPP, p.96.

p.233 'He smiles with condescension; he talks of Benevolence & Virtue...' – Blake, *Milton,* CPP, p.142.

13. MY WRATH DID GROW

p.237 'The execution of my Designs, being all in Water-colours...' –
Blake, Exhibition advertisement, 1809, CPP, pp.527–8.

p.238 'This Man was Hired to Depress Art...' – Blake, annotations to
The Works of Sir Joshua Reynolds, CPP, pp.635–6.

p.239 'Empire follows art & Not Vice Versa as Englishmen suppose' –
ibid., p.636.

p.239 'If Italy is enriched and made great by RAPHAEL...' – Blake,
Exhibition advertisement, 1809, CPP, p.528.

p.239 'If beside the stupid and mad-brained political project of their
rulers...' – Hunt, *The Examiner*, 17 September 1809, BR, pp.282–3.

p.240 'Hirelings in the Camp, the Court, & the University' – Blake,
Milton, CPP, p.95.

p.241 'Shall I call him Artist or Genius – or Mystic – or Madman?' –
Henry Crabb Robinson's diary entry, 10 December 1825, BR, p.420.

p.241 'Can you draw out Leviathan with a fishhook...' – Job 41:1–34,
English Standard Version Bible.

p.242 'In the last Battle of King Arthur only Three Britons escaped...' –
Blake, *A Descriptive Catalogue*, 1809, CPP, p.542.

p.243 'The dead and the dying, Britons naked, mingled with armed
Romans...' – ibid., p.545.

p.243 'the finest work of the painter' – Swinburne, *William Blake*, p.81,
footnote.

p.243 'a complete caricature: one of the bards is singing to his harp...'
– Hunt, *The Examiner*, 17 September 1809, BR, p.284.

p.243 'The antiquities of every Nation under Heaven, is no less sacred
than that of the Jews' – Blake, *A Descriptive Catalogue*, 1809, CPP, p.543.

p.245 'Adam was a Druid, and Noah; also Abraham...' – ibid.,
pp.542–3.

p.245 'of Abraham's religion' – Aldhouse-Green, *Exploring the World of
the Druids*, p.143.

p.245 'Tell me the Acts, O historian, and leave me...' – Blake, *A
Descriptive Catalogue*, 1809, CPP, p.544.

p.246 'One of the pictures represents *Chaucer's Pilgrims*...' – Hunt, *The
Examiner*, 17 September 1809, BR, p.283.

p.246 'You must know that I give myself great Credit...' – Cromek, quoted in Ackroyd, *Blake*, p.285.

p.247 'Blake was at no pains, throughout this business or afterwards...' Gilchrist, *Life of William Blake*, p.250.

p.247 'The only period in his life when Blake does not seem to have...' – Bentley, BR, p.229.

p.248 'Loneliness does not come from having no people about one...' Jung, *Memories, Dreams, Reflections*, p.356.

p.248 'A Hell of our own making' – Blake, *Milton*, CPP, p.106.

p.248 'Mutual forgiveness of each Vice...' – Blake, 'The Gates of Paradise', CPP, p.259.

p.248 '...having receiv'd the highest reward possible: the love and friendship...' – Blake, *Jerusalem*, CPP, p.145.

p.249 'I have Mental Joy & Mental Health...' – Blake, 'I rose up at the dawn of day', CPP, p.481.

p.252 'I was angry with my friend...' – Blake, 'A Poison Tree', *Songs of Innocence and of Experience*, CPP, p.28.

14. ALTOGETHER HIDDEN FROM THE CORPOREAL UNDERSTANDING

p.255 'He is Albion, our Ancestor, patriarch of the Atlantic Continent...' – Blake, 'A Vision of the Last Judgement', CPP, p.558.

p.257 'The Ancient Man upon the Rock of Albion Awakes' – Blake, *Milton*, CPP, p.122.

p.257 'All things begin & end in Albions ancient Druid rocky shore' – ibid., p.100.

p.257 'Albion covered the whole Earth' – Blake, *Jerusalem*, CPP, p.170.

p.257 'O Skofield why art thou cruel?' – ibid., p.221.

p.257 'Go thou to Skofield...' ibid., p.162.

p.260 'Also out of the midst thereof *came* the likeness of four living creatures...' – Ezekiel 1:5–11, King James Bible.

p.261 'the Vehicular Form of Strong Urthona' – Blake, *Jerusalem*, CPP, p.202.

p.261 'Emanation that was wont to play before thy face' – ibid., p.146.

p.262 'As the Soul is to the Body' – ibid., p.224.

p.262 'and the Spectre stood over Los...' – ibid., p.149.

p.263 'O that I could cease to be! Despair!...' – ibid., pp.153–4.

p.263 'O! thou seest not what I see! What is done in the Furnaces...' – ibid., p.149.

p.265 'And these the Labours of the Sons of Los in Allamanda...' – Blake, *Milton*, CPP, p.123.

p.265 'Tho divided by the Cross & Nails & Thorn & Spear...' – Blake, *Jerusalem*, CPP, p.248.

p.266 'Few are the readers who will ever penetrate beyond the first page or two...' – Gilchrist, *Life of William Blake*, p.211.

p.266 'About Milton we hear very little...' – ibid., p.212.

p.266 'Of these names, many never occur again...' – ibid., pp.200–1.

p.267 'in the midst of such a chaos of words, names and images...' – ibid., p.208.

p.267 'casting away all idea of ordering and shaping his thoughts...' – ibid., p.208.

p.267 'to speak to future generations by a Sublime Allegory...' – Blake, letter to Thomas Butts, 6 July 1803, CPP, p.730.

p.268 'Allegory address'd to the Intellectual powers...' – ibid.

p.268 'The structure of *Jerusalem* raises many problems...' – Bloom, Commentary on *Jerusalem*, CPP, p.928.

p.269 'you O Jews are the true Christians...' – Blake, *Jerusalem*, CPP, p.174.

p.273 'a remnant of Druidism' – ibid., p.200.

p.274 'And did those feet in ancient time...' – Blake, *Milton*, CPP, p.95.

15. IN LOVE WITH THE PRODUCTIONS OF TIME

p.278 'To see a World in a Grain of Sand...' – Blake, 'Auguries of Innocence', CPP, p.490.

p.278 'if a thing loves it is infinite' – Blake, Annotations to Swedenborg, CPP, p.604.

p.280 'Now [Besso] has departed from this strange world a little ahead of me...' – Einstein, letter to the Besso family, March 1955, sold at auction at Christie's, December 2017.

p.280 'I see the Past, Present & Future, existing all at once' – Blake, *Jerusalem*, CPP, p.159.

p.280 'And all that has existed in the space of six thousand years...' – ibid., pp.157–8.

p.282 'Might I ask if, anywhere in this ingenious arrangement...' – Moore, *Jerusalem*, p.636.

p.283 'It will be observed that such a theory as this accepts...' – Broad, *Scientific Thought*, pp.66–7.

p.286 'Predestination after this Life is more Abominable than Calvins...' – Blake, Annotations to Swedenborg, CPP, p.610.

p.287 'For the next five months, I lived in a state of uninterrupted deep peace and bliss...' – Tolle, *The Power of Now*, pp.2–3.

p.287 'thinks in pictures and learns kinaesthetically through the movement of our bodies' – Bolte Taylor, TED podcast, quoted in Tweedy, *The God of the Left Hemisphere*, pp.6–7.

p.288 'The present moment is a time when everything and everyone are connected...' – Bolte Taylor, quoted in Tweedy, ibid., pp.22–3.

p.290 'The absence of time does not mean, therefore, that everything is frozen...' – Rovelli, *The Order of Time*, p.92.

p.291 'The initial low entropy of the universe...' – ibid., p.128.

p.291 'Do we exist in time, or does time exist in us?' – ibid., p.2.

p.291 'Falling, falling! Los fell & fell...' – Blake, *The Book of Los*, CPP, p.92.

p.291 'If by "time" we mean nothing more than happening, then everything is time' – Rovelli, *The Order of Time*, p.92.

p.292 'I see the Past, Present & Future, existing all at once' – Blake, *Jerusalem*, CPP, p.159.

p.293 'Devils & Angels are Predestinated' – Blake, Annotations to Swedenborg, CPP, p.610.

p.294 'Eternity is in love with the productions of time' – Blake, *The Marriage of Heaven and Hell*, CPP, p.36.

16. THE WORK OF THE DEVIL

p.300 'Readers of superior judgement may disapprove of the style...' – Wordsworth and Coleridge, *Lyrical Ballads*, p.3.

p.301 'Therefore am I still / A lover of the meadows and the woods...' Wordsworth, 'Lines Written a Few Miles above Tintern Abbey', ibid., pp.89–90.

p.301 'I fear Wordsworth loves Nature and Nature is the work of the Devil' – Blake, BR, p.429.

p.301 'Jehovah, with his thunder, and the choir...' – Wordsworth, *The Excursion*, quoted in Gilchrist, *Life of William Blake*, p.368.

p.302 'There is no doubt this poor man was mad...' – Wordsworth, quoted in Damon, *A Blake Dictionary*, p.451.

p.302 'printed and painted by the Author, W. Blake...' – Coleridge, letter to H. F. Cary, 6 February 1818, BR, p.336.

p.302 'A poet ought not to pick nature's pocket...' – Coleridge, *Specimens of the Table Talk of S.T. Coleridge*, p.107.

p.303 'The primary IMAGINATION I hold to be the living power...' Coleridge, quoted in Casey, *Imagining*, p.5.

p.303 'Imagination is the real and eternal World...' – Blake, *Jerusalem*, CPP, p.231.

p.303 'The Imagination is not a State: it is the Human Existence itself' – Blake, *Milton*, CPP, p.132.

p.305 'the madman's cornerstone,' 'exercise of thought without foundation in nature' – Paracelsus quoted in Lachman, *Lost Knowledge of the Imagination*, pp.85–6.

17. VERY WEAK & AN OLD MAN FEEBLE & TOTTERING

p.311 'In him you saw at once the Maker, the Inventor...' – Palmer, letter to Gilchrist, 23 August 1855, in Gilchrist, *Life of William Blake*, p.321.

p.311 'He was a man without a mask...' – ibid.

p.311 'the image of Blake looking up at Wainewright's picture...' – Palmer, quoted in Gilchrist, *Life of William Blake*, p.295.

p.311 'Those who may have read some strange passages in his [exhibition] *Catalogue*' – Palmer, letter to Gilchrist, 23 August 1855, ibid., p.322.

p.311 'He was no longer angry with the world' – ibid., p.330.

p.312 'book of Job, engraved by himself, is of the highest rank...' – ibid., p.309.

p.313 'Naked came I out of my mother's womb, and naked shall I return thither...' – Job 1:21, King James Bible.

p.317 'Fable or Allgory is Seldom without some Vision Pilgrims Progress is full of it' – Blake, 'A Vision of the Last Judgement', CPP, p.554.

p.318 'This Book will make a Traveller of thee' – Bunyan, *The Pilgrim's Progress*, p.8.

p.320 'very weak & an Old Man feeble & tottering, but not in Spirit...' – Blake, letter to Cumberland, 12 April 1827, CPP, p.783.

p.321 'When he prepared the heavens, I was there...' – Proverbs 8:27, King James Bible.

p.321 'and in His hand / He took the golden compasses, prepared...' – Milton, *Paradise Lost*, p.156.

p.321 'a more powerful impression on his mind than all he had ever been visited by' – Smith, BR, p.620.

pp.321–2 'Stay! Keep as you are! You have ever been an angel to me, I will draw you!' – Smith, BR, p.621.

p.322 'He then threw that down, after having drawn for an hour...' – Tatham, BR, p.682.

p.322 'I have been at the death, not of a man, but of a blessed angel' – Gilchrist, *Life of William Blake*, p.387.

p.322 'in a most glorious manner. He said He was going to that Country...' Richmond, quoted in Gilchrist, ibid.

18. AS A MAN IS, SO HE SEES

p.326 'the mistaken Demon of heaven' – Blake, 'Visions of the Daughters of Albion', CPP, p.48.

p.326 'Satan is Urizen' – Blake, *Milton*, CPP, p.104.

p.328 'I know of no other / Christianity and of no other Gospel' – Blake, *Jerusalem*, CPP, p.231.

p.329 'A Poet a Painter a Musician an Architect...' – Blake, 'The Laocoön', CPP, p.274.

p.329 'To see a World in a Grain of Sand...' – Blake, 'Auguries of Innocence', CPP, p.490.

p.333 'there is no other God / than that God who is the intellectual fountain of Humanity' – Blake, *Jerusalem*, CPP, p.251.

p.338 'For the Eye altering alters all' – Blake, 'The Mental Traveller', CPP, p.485.

p.339 'The tree which moves some to tears of joy...' – Blake, letter to Rev. Trusler, 23 August 1799, CPP, p.702.

p.341 'Where Mercy, Love & Pity dwell / There God is dwelling too' Blake, 'The Divine Image', *Songs of Innocence and of Experience*, CPP, p.13.

p.341 'Mutual forgiveness of each Vice...' – Blake, 'The Gates of Paradise', CPP, p.259.

p.342 'I give you the end of a golden string...' – Blake, *Jerusalem*, CPP, p.231.

BIBLIOGRAPHY

Ackroyd, Peter, *Blake* (Sinclair Stevenson, 1995).

Aldhouse-Green, Miranda, *Exploring the World of the Druids* (Thames & Hudson, 2005).

Bentley, Jr., G. E., *Blake Records: Second Edition* (Yale University Press, 2004).

Blake, William, *Dante's Divine Comedy: The Complete Drawings* (Taschen, 2017).

— *The Complete Illuminated Books* (Thames & Hudson, 2000).

— *The Complete Poetry & Prose of William Blake* (ed. David V. Erdman, newly revised edition, Anchor, 1988).

Boehme, Jakob, *Genius of the Transcendent: Mystical Writings of Jakob Boehme*, tr. Michael L. Birkel and Jeff Back (Shambhala Publications, 2010).

Broad, C. D., *Scientific Thought* (Routledge, 2002).

Bunyan, John, *The Pilgrim's Progress* (Penguin Classics, 2008).

Buonomano, Dean, *Your Brain is a Time Machine: The Neuroscience and Physics of Time* (W. W. Norton & Company, 2017).

Byatt, A. S., *Unruly Times: Wordsworth and Coleridge in Their Time* (Vintage, 1997).

Casey, Edward S., *Imagining: A Phenomenological Study, Second Edition* (Indiana University Press, 1976).

Coleridge, Samuel Taylor, *Specimens of the Table Talk of S. T. Coleridge* (John Murray, 1836).

Damon, S. Foster, *A Blake Dictionary: The Ideas and Symbols of William Blake: Updated Edition* (Dartmouth, 2013).

Damrosch, Leo, *Eternity's Sunrise: The Imaginative World of William Blake* (Yale University Press, 2015).

Einstein, Albert, *Cosmic Religion and Other Opinions and Aphorisms* (Covici-Friede, 1931).

Eisenman, Stephen F. (ed.), *William Blake and the Age of Aquarius* (Princeton University Press, 2017).

Erdman, David V., *Blake: Prophet Against Empire* (Dover, 1991).

Gilchrist, Alexander, *Life of William Blake* (Macmillan & Co, 1863, republished by Harper Perennial as *Gilchrist on Blake*, 2005).

Gordon, Charlotte, *Romantic Outlaws: The Extraordinary Lives of Mary Wollstonecraft and Mary Shelley* (Windmill Books, 2015).

Hibbert, Christopher, *King Mob* (Longmans, Green & Co, 1958).

Higgs, John, *I Have America Surrounded: The Life of Timothy Leary* (Friday Project, 2006).

— *William Blake Now: Why He Matters More Than Ever* (Weidenfeld & Nicolson, 2019).

Hill, Christopher, *The World Turned Upside Down: Radical Ideas During the English Revolution* (Maurice Temple Smith, 1972).

Holland, Tom, *Dominion: The Making of the Western Mind* (Little, Brown, 2019).

James, William, *The Varieties of Religious Experience: A Study in Human Nature* (Longmans, Green & Co, 1902).

Jay, Mike, *The Influencing Machine: James Tilly Matthews and the Air Loom* (Strange Attractor Press, 2012).

Jennings, Humphrey, *Pandemonium: The Coming of the Machines as Seen by Contemporary Observers 1660–1885* (The Free Press, 1986).

Jung, Carl, *Psychological Types* (Rascher Verlag, 1921).

— *Memories, Dreams, Reflections* (Fontana Press, 1963).

Kripal, Jeffrey J., *The Flip: Epiphanies of Mind and the Future of Knowledge* (Bellevue Literary Press, 2019).

Lachman, Gary, *Swedenborg: An Introduction to His Life and Ideas* (Jeremy P. Tarcher/Penguin, 2012).

— *Lost Knowledge of the Imagination* (Floris Books, 2017).

Lao Tzu, *Tao Te Ching*, tr. Stephen Mitchell (Macmillan, 1989).

Lent, Jeremy, *The Patterning Instinct: A Cultural History of Man's Search for Meaning* (Prometheus Books, 2017).

Letcher, Andy, *Shroom: A Cultural History of the Magic Mushroom* (Faber & Faber, 2006).

Loukes, Andrew (ed.), *William Blake in Sussex: Visions of Albion* (Paul Hoberton Publishing, 2018).

Milton, John, *Paradise Lost* (Penguin Classics, 2000).

Moore, Alan, *Jerusalem* (Knockabout, 2016).

Myrone, Martin, and Concannon, Amy, *William Blake* (Tate, 2019).

Nietzsche, Friedrich, *Beyond Good and Evil* (Verlag, 1886).

Pollan, Michael, *How to Change Your Mind: The New Science of Psychedelics* (Penguin, 2018).

Porter, Roy, *Flesh in the Age of Reason: How the Enlightenment Transformed the Way We See Our Bodies and Souls* (Allen Lane, 2003).

Pullman, Philip, *Daemon Voices: Essays on Storytelling* (David Fickling Books, 2017).

Rossetti, William Michael, *The Poetical Works of William Blake* (G. Bell, 1874).

Rovelli, Carlo, *The Order of Time* (Allen Lane, 2018).

Schuchard, Marsha Keith, *Why Mrs Blake Cried: William Blake and the Erotic Imagination* (Pimlico, 2006).

Sigstedt, Cyriel Sigrid (Ljungberg Odhner), *The Swedenborg Epic* (Swedenborg Society, 1952).

Sinclair, Iain, *Blake's London: The Topographic Sublime* (Swedenborg Society, 2018).

Swedenborg, Emanuel, *A Swedenborg Sampler* (Swedenborg Foundation, 2016).

Swinburne, Algernon Charles, *William Blake: A Critical Essay* (John Camden Hotten, 1868).

Symons, Arthur, *William Blake* (E. P. Dutton & Company, 1907).

Thompson, E. P., *Witness Against the Beast: William Blake and the Moral Law* (The New Press, 1993).

Tolle, Eckhart, *The Power of Now: A Guide to Spiritual Enlightenment* (Hodder and Stoughton, 2005).

Tweedy, Roderick, *The God of the Left Hemisphere: Blake, Bolte Taylor and the Myth of Creation* (Routledge, 2013).

Wordsworth, William, and Coleridge, Samuel Taylor, *Lyrical Ballads 1798 and 1802* (Oxford University Press, 2013).

ACKNOWLEDGEMENTS

The first spark that led to this book came in 2001 on my thirtieth birthday, when Brian Barritt, Vikki Stephenson and Flinton Chalk gave me a copy of Blake's poems and prophecies as a present. This has since become a much-treasured possession – it was the spark that led me here.

The second key influence was C. J. Stone, from whom I first learnt about the political side of Blake and his place in the English dissenting tradition – I hope to always be learning from Chris. Thanks also to Professor Adam Zeman for helping me understand aphantasia, and to Clare Dudeney and Geraldine van Heemstra for their insights into hyperphantasia from an artist's perspective.

Thanks to my agent, Sarah Ballard, for nursing the proposal and wisely telling me I needed a less boring title. Thanks to Eli Keren, all at United Agents, and Paul Murphy at Weidenfeld & Nicolson who took it on and had the idea of turning a few modern-day chapters into the separate essay *William Blake Now*. Thanks also to the wonderful Jenny Lord who brought it in to land and nursed it into what you now hold, to Sue Lascelles for the polish Blake deserves, to Jo Whitford for making it manifest and to Ellie

Freedman, Ellen Turner, Brittany Sankey and everyone at W&N for all your support over the years.

I am insanely indebted to my four beta readers who ploughed through the mud and confusion of early drafts so that you don't have to. A medal for bravery goes to top wife Joanne Mallon for battling the brainmash that was the very first draft – much love always. Next came Jason Arnopp, lord of plot and prose, with his extensive first-hand knowledge of the infernal realms. Invaluable and profoundly lovely Alistair Fruish knows things that other people don't – who else could have told me about the sea critters that Sartre hallucinated? Finally, David Bramwell managed to critique it not only from his point of view, but from the perspective of the late Alan Watts as well. Huge gratitude to all four of these heroes.

Much of this book was written during pandemic lockdown, and the people I was unable to see were sorely missed. Much love to Paul and Sue and their families, Brice and Patricia, Helen, Maura and Eric. Love also to Tim, Laura, Anwen and the wider Sheffield crew for looking after me on my last travels before lockdown. Thanks also for the inspiration of the Liverpool Arts Lab, the Hove Space Programme, Michelle and Richard at Journey to Nutopia, Matt, Neil and Chris of the Old Man Gig Club (beach drinking department), Helen and Juliet at SALON London, the Cerne to CERN pilgrims, the Quietus and Heavenly/Social folk, Robin Scarlett for making me the Albionist riot shield that kept me safe this year and Ru Callender for the sapling grown from the seed of the tree whose roots mingle with Blake's bones.

Extra love, thanks and/or merry waves to Anna Richardson 007, Dominique Webb, Dr Nikki Queen of the Wirral, Lisa and family, grumpy Andrew, mighty Andrew O'Neill out there on the heath, Youth, malt loaf sculptor Steve Lowe, Jo Simmons, Victor Adebowale, Deborah Turnbull, whoever wins in a quiff-off between Scott Mcpherson and Cara Courage, Robin Ince, Mark 'no-choice' Sampson, Oliver Senton, Tocky Tom, Moksha, Nick Helweg-Lawsen, CyberAlan Edwards, Jamie Mathieson (no funnel), Daisy Campbell and magickal orphan, Kate and Tim and all they dream, Peter Addington, Pierre Hollins, national treasure Salena Godden, Rob Manuel, the eternally inspiring Alan Moore, DJ and tour guide Greg Wilson, Andy Starke, Lisa Lovebucket, Jo Neary, what's left of Mr Adam, Cat Vincent, Clare Callender, Jon Harris Money Burning Guy, Lovebucket, Clare Almond (too long!), Al Scott (also too long!), Richard Selby, Graham Silcock, Professor Seal, Kermit!!!, Emmy-clutching Stef Wagstaffe, (all Hail dis)Claudia, John Constable aka Crow, James Burt, Stefano Bollani, those individuals I feel terrible for leaving out but who I will make amends to in the paperback, and last but never least the ever-glowing Susannah Lafond.

Extra love always to my children, Lia and Isaac.

And finally, huge thanks to the wider Blake community – from the Blake Bloc to the Blake Society and all Blakean authors – for their welcoming openness, understanding, and for keeping the light of the spiritual sun burning. This book is for you all.

John Higgs
Brighton, 2021

PICTURE CREDITS

Chapter 1, p.12: *For the Sexes: The Gates of Paradise*, plate 8, 'At length for hatching ripe he breaks the shell', William Blake, 1826. Artokoloro / Alamy Stock Photo.

Chapter 2, p.28: *Songs of Experience*, frontispiece, William Blake, *c.* 1825. incamerastock / Alamy Stock Photo.

Chapter 3, p.49: *For Children: The Gates of Paradise*, plate 6, 'Air', William Blake, 1793. Etching and line engraving on cream-coloured paper. Album / Alamy Stock Photo.

Chapter 4, p.76: *Newton*, William Blake, 1795. Colour print, ink and watercolour on paper. Art Collection 2 / Alamy Stock Photo.

Chapter 5, p.102: 'The Red Dragon and the Woman Clothed in Sun', William Blake, *c.* 1802–1805. Heritage Image Partnership Ltd / Alamy Stock Photo.

Chapter 6, p.124: William Blake America e page 12 100, *America a Prophecy*. Art Collection 2 / Alamy Stock Photo.

Chapter 7, p.145: *The Angels appearing to the Shepherds*, William Blake, 1809. Pen, pencil, ink and watercolour on paper. Asar Studios / Alamy Stock Photo.

Chapter 8, p.170: *Pity*, William Blake, *c.* 1795. Colour print, ink and watercolour on paper. Heritage Image Partnership Ltd / Alamy Stock Photo.

PICTURE CREDITS

Chapter 9, p.185: *Enitharmon slept*, from *Europe a Prophecy*, William Blake, 1794. Relief etched plate in colours. agefotostock / Alamy Stock Photo.

Chapter 10, p.201: *The Marriage of Heaven and Hell*, William Blake, 1827. Fitzwilliam Museum object 21. The Picture Art Collection / Alamy Stock Photo.

Chapter 11, p.218: *Children Guiding a Serpent*, page 11, *America a Prophecy*, William Blake, 1793. Lebrecht Music & Arts / Alamy Stock Photo.

Chapter 12, p.235: *Europe A Prophecy*, plate 15, 'The red limb'd Angel', William Blake. Art Collection 4 / Alamy Stock Photo

Chapter 13, p.254: *The Stygian Lake, with the Ireful Sinners fighting*, William Blake, 1824–1827. Illustration for *Divine Comedy* by Dante Alighieri (*Inferno* VII). Pen, ink and watercolour over pencil and traces of black chalk with sponging. National Gallery of Victoria, Melbourne Felton Bequest, 1920. This digital record has been made available on NGV Collection Online through the generous support of the Joe White Bequest.

Chapter 14, p.276: *Albion Rose*, from *A Large Book of Designs*, Copy A, 1793–1796, William Blake, June 1793. The Picture Art Collection / Alamy Stock Photo.

Chapter 15, p.295: *Christ in the Sepulchre, Guarded by Angels*, William Blake, c. 1805. The Picture Art Collection / Alamy Stock Photo.

Chapter 16, p.307: *The Circle of Corrupt Officials: The Devils Mauling Each Other*, William Blake Illustration for *Divine Comedy* by Dante Alighieri (*Inferno* XXII). agefotostock / Alamy Stock Photo.

Chapter 17, p.323: *The Ancient of Days setting a Compass to the Earth*, William Blake. Watercolour drawing. British Museum. The Picture Art Collection / Alamy Stock Photo.

Chapter 18, p.345: *Children Guiding a Serpent*, page 11, *America a Prophecy*, William Blake, 1793. Lebrecht Music & Arts / Alamy Stock Photo.

INDEX

379

INDEX

384